NARRATIVE CONSCIOUSNESS

THIS BOOK IS PUBLISHED WITH THE ASSISTANCE OF THE
Dan Danciger Publication Fund

Narrative
Consciousness

Structure and Perception in the Fiction of
KAFKA, BECKETT, and ROBBE-GRILLET

by GEORGE H. SZANTO, 1940 -

UNIVERSITY OF TEXAS PRESS, AUSTIN & LONDON

Library of Congress Cataloging in Publication Data

Szanto, George H.   1940–
    Narrative consciousness.

    Bibliography: p.
    1. Kafka, Franz, 1883–1924.   2. Beckett, Samuel,
1906–   3. Robbe-Grillet, Alain, 1922–   I. Title.
PN3503.S9   809.3'3   78–37648
ISBN 0–292–75500–7

Composition and printing by The University of Texas Printing Division, Austin
Binding by Universal Bookbindery, Inc., San Antonio

For my parents

CONTENTS

Introduction: Narrative Consciousness 3

PART I: KAFKA

1. The Inevitability of Ritual: Life Cycle of a
Kafka Character 17
2. A Derivation of Meaning from Point of View . . . 41

PART II: BECKETT

3. The Form of Consciousness: Modified Patterns . . . 71
4. The Dominance of Point of View 104

PART III: ROBBE-GRILLET

5. Toward a New Novel: A Theory for Fiction 123
6. Internalized Reality: The Subjective Point of View . . 134
7. Structure as Process: The Temporal Point of View . . 149

CONCLUSION

Conclusion: A Third Way in Modern Fiction 159

APPENDIXES

1. Kafka in France 167
2. Kafka Criticism 173
3. Beckett Criticism 181

Bibliography 189
Index 213

ACKNOWLEDGMENTS

I am very grateful to a number of scholars whose teaching and encouragement over the years have helped me complete this work. Discussions with E. A. McCormick germinated some of these ideas, and Harry Levin sharpened my critical approach to them. Fredric Jameson aided me in the formulation of the analysis with a series of valuable suggestions. Most of all, Henry Hatfield supported both me and the idea of this book through difficult periods with friendship and wise counsel. In addition, Sandra Dijkstra, Janet Zittel, and Barbara Swearingen provided me with some much needed editorial assistance. Thanks also to Valerie Peacock for preparing the index.

Grateful acknowledgment is also made to the publishers of the works of Kafka, Beckett and Robbe-Grillet. All quotations from *The Trial* and *The Castle* are reprinted by permission of Alfred A. Knopf, Inc., from *The Trial*, by Franz Kafka, copyright 1937, 1956 by Alfred A. Knopf, Inc., and *The Castle*, by Franz Kafka, copyright 1930, 1941, 1954 by Alfred A. Knopf, Inc. Quotations from *The Penal Colony* are reprinted by permission of Schocken Books Inc. from *The Penal Colony* by Franz Kafka, copyright © 1948 by Schocken Books Inc.; quotations from *Parables and Paradoxes*, reprinted by permission of Schocken Books Inc. from *Parables and Paradoxes* by Franz Kafka, copyright © 1946, 1958 by Schocken Books Inc. Acknowledgment is also due Martin Secker and Warburg, Ltd., London, who hold the copyright for these works by Kafka in the British Commonwealth excluding Canada. Quotations from Beckett and Robbe-Grillet are reprinted by permission of Grove Press, Inc., from: *Watt*, by Samuel Beckett, all rights reserved, originally published by the Olympia

Press, Paris, 1953, first American edition published 1959; *Murphy*, by Samuel Beckett, first published 1938, first Grove Press edition, 1957; *Molloy*, by Samuel Beckett, translated from the French by Patrick Bowles in collaboration with the author, all rights reserved by the Olympia Press, Paris, and Grove Press, Inc., New York; *Malone Dies*, by Samuel Beckett, translated from the French by the author, copyright © 1956 by Grove Press, Inc.; *The Erasers*, by Alain Robbe-Grillet, translated by Richard Howard, copyright © 1964 by Grove Press, Inc.; *Two Novels*, by Alain Robbe-Grillet, translated by Richard Howard, copyright © 1965 by Grove Press, Inc., including *Jealousy*, copyright © 1959 by Grove Press, Inc., and *In the Labyrinth*, copyright © 1960, by Grove Press, Inc.; *The Voyeur*, by Alain Robbe-Grillet, translated by Richard Howard, copyright © 1958 by Grove Press, Inc. Acknowledgment is also extended to Calder and Boyars, Ltd., London, who hold the copyright for the preceding works by Beckett and Robbe-Grillet in the British Commonwealth excluding Canada, and who permitted me to use passages from *Towards a New Novel*, by Alain Robbe-Grillet, translated by Barbara Wright. The American edition of this work has been published by Grove Press, Inc., under the title *For a New Novel: Essays on Fiction*, by Alain Robbe-Grillet, translated by Richard Howard, copyright © 1965 by Grove Press, Inc. Particular thanks is due Alain Robbe-Grillet and Marthe Robert, who graciously allowed me to quote from personal correspondence.

NARRATIVE CONSCIOUSNESS

Introduction: Narrative Consciousness

Much of literature since the middle of the nineteenth century has involved the attempt of writers to cope with an environment they felt was growing away from them. The earlier complete identification of environment with other men, a concept established in the various renaissances and enlightenments and identified with the romantics' sympathetic natural world, seemed to be losing its validity. Previously, the content of the world could be understood: other men were like oneself, and nature, properly anthropomorphized, was identifiable with oneself. But in an increasingly industrialized society other men became no more than a part of an environment shared with machines and buildings; a purely social context for literature was insufficient. Industrialization established a totally new and nonhuman element on man's horizon—action by the machine. A sensitive individual could no longer integrate himself with the content of the world; indeed, he began to deal with his environment as an antagonist. Tension grew to doubt and fear of doubt (Angst in existential terms), which, if one was unable personally to perceive how the institutions of the social system worked, in turn became only a symptom of a much greater distrust of the system itself.

Without being fully aware of his situation the writer attempted to cope with it. Heretofore any separation between man and his environment had been easily bridged by the mind of the perceiving individual; now industrialization with its non-animal power source was a constant reminder of the increasing separation between man and the world about him and of the possibility that this separation had existed earlier but had been rationalized out of relevant existence. A new kind of writing was needed, and several were found.

Symbolism began by withdrawing into the aesthetic, stressing the way of writing rather than the importance of what was said; the leap from external reality to the immediacy of the poem had to be made by the reader if he was to relate this new kind of poetry to his own life. The realism of Zola broke out into the other direction, experimenting with the environment to show by discovery the result of attempted communication with the surrounding world. Much of expressionism, especially the *Maschinenstürmer* in Germany, attempted to destroy both the machines in the environment and men when they became machines, hoping for a return to Arcadia instead of moving forward in the direction of a possible Elysium.

But Flaubert's experiments were most relevant for upcoming literary generations.

Flaubert . . . sought to destroy the omniscient narrator who knew everything about everyone in his book, who, in his god-like way, described both the exterior and interior of all scenes and characters. In creating what he called "third observer" or "universal witness" Flaubert limited his presentation to the point of view of *one* observer at a given moment. He discovered also the third person pronoun, he or she, need not remain impersonal, but could (through "free and indirect discourse" and other devices), convey the interior perceptions and feelings of the characters. It was his effort to remove *himself* from the narrative that led Flaubert to the discovery that if the omniscient *author* is eliminated, the only remaining basis for the "point of view" that justifies the text has to be the *consciousness* of someone: a character of the novel or a plausible observer placed at the realistic level of the action within the novel. So preoccupied did Flaubert become with the application of this principle and with effecting scene linkages or modulations from one point of view to another that he even suggested that a novel could be written whose value would lie not in its subject at all but in its relationships and articulations: *un livre sur rien,* a book about nothing.[1]

From Flaubert, Henry James learned the importance of limiting the point of view. Like Proust, another of Flaubert's disciples, James experimented beyond the possibilities of the interior monologue shown him by Flaubert. To the beginnings of psychological analysis attempted by James, Proust added his experiments with time, allowing time to be governed by the psychological state of the narrator. The further experiments of Joyce and Faulkner attempted to find artistic unity for a work of fiction by basing it in a unified psychology. For them a novel becomes an existence in itself—it is not about something, it is something; within the novel the closest attention is paid to what happens in the life of the mind. Beyond these experiments Nathalie Sarraute has discovered and worked with *sous-conversations,* conversations in the mind. Outer conversation is merely the occasional surfacing, the extension, of *sous-conversations.*

In the other direction also Flaubert's discoveries were exploited and deepened. Maupassant understood the importance of objective description (exteriority rather than necessary narrative impartiality) arising from a unified point of view. His followers, especially Hemingway and more recently James Purdy, have suggested the presence of subsurface stresses and interaction while keeping their fiction entirely on the surface.

Between the inner monologues of James and Proust and the experiments in exteriority of Maupassant stands a third structuring technique—that of Franz Kafka. Kafka combined exterior description, without suggesting that something was going on under the described surface, with interior monologue, which did not attempt to analyze the subsurface nature of the mind with which it dealt. Just as there was no possibility of understanding what lay behind the surface of the things, the situations and events he perceived, so too was it impossible to detail with any certainty the life of the mind. For

---

[1] Bruce Morrissette, "The New Novel in France," *Chicago Review* 15, no. 3 (Winter–Spring, 1961–1962): 4. All quotation by permission of *Chicago Review.*

Kafka there was only one possibility—the conscious relationship between a man and his perceived world. His life brought him to a point
at which he realized that any bridge between man and his world
was a creation of man, yet an exploration of the chance for building
a more honest bridge must have seemed to him the only valid under-
taking.

Hence his narrative point of view: only the conscious mind of man
can narrate the story, and it alone can decide what is to be described.
Because literature was still, for Kafka as it has been for all great
literary inventors, "the impossible task of getting the sloppy richness
of life into the satisfying neatness of artistic shape,"[2] the world perceived from a specific point of view had to be limited to those parts
of it relevant not to the world, but to the man whose tale was being
told. The point of view edited the created picture according to the
needs of the narrator.

The narrator in each of Kafka's stories is not Kafka himself, but a
character created by Kafka. Whether a story is told in the first person
—the country doctor's tale or the ape's report to the academy—or in
the third person—Josef K.'s story, Georg Bendemann's, Gregor Samsa's—the narrative never goes beyond what the main character sees
in his immediate situation as he looks out at the world. If the narrative is in the third person, each name or pronoun referring to the
main character can be replaced by "I" without loss of meaning. In
the first person narratives, when the story is told in the past, it is as
if the character has transported himself back to the past and is once
more seeing the situation of the past at that moment. In neither first
nor third person narratives is there much reflection upon events or
situations; all is limited to description of externals. But it is a description limited both by the needs of a narrator and also by the manner
in which he sees the objects or events he describes; the narrator cannot always be relied upon to report what is, for the filter of his personality can distort his described picture. Yet he is not being dis-
honest, for he reports what he sees in the way he sees it. This process
is description by narrative consciousness: an inner, conscious mono-

---

[2] Robert Scholes, "George is My Name," *New York Times Book Review*, August 7, 1966, p. 1.

logue combines with a careful limitation of exterior reality to establish a point of view. Kafka was the first to succeed with the possibilities of narrative consciousness.

Kafka's immediate follower was Samuel Beckett. This is not to say that Beckett copied Kafka or that he was Kafka's disciple—merely that Beckett read Kafka, could not avoid a partial influence, and brought a great deal of his own to his writing. Their common ground is narrative consciousness. Starting with the *Trilogy*—*Molloy, Malone Dies, The Unnamable*—Beckett's narrators report only what they perceive. But for Beckett the problems of memory and projection become much more important than they were for Kafka; here Beckett is the student of Proust and Joyce. Although his narratives are presented in the past tense, the senses of perception are constantly at work, as if the narrative were being lived at the moment. For Beckett doubt becomes a living force: he will describe one situation from several sides, shifting his point of view as the narrator's eye (or his mind's eye) shifts, to demonstrate for the reader that there is no one simple "reality" that can be described sufficiently when viewed at any one arbitrary moment.

Robbe-Grillet's bearings are also defined by the narrative consciousness of his narrator. He returns to Kafka and Maupassant for his sense of the external and to Proust and Joyce for his experiments with psychological time, but the link he establishes between the point of view with the narrating consciousness and the external world viewed by his protagonists descends to him directly from Kafka and Beckett. His great ability is to combine the forward movement of nonchronological time with closely edited, realistic description (not the reproduction of a pre-existent reality, but the creation of a reality functional to the perceiving mind).

Having transcended those authors who are still attempting to come to terms with an environment growing away from man so quickly he can no longer cope with the whole of it no matter how great his intelligence and sensibilities, Kafka, Beckett, and Robbe-Grillet conclude by the example of their fictions that the writer's province is no longer the impossible environment, but is instead the only knowledge any one man can have, the knowledge he attains through his perceptions. The proper study for man as storyteller is a search for unique details that make him human—not details unprovable by hypotheses brought from the unconscious, but the describable perceptions a man chooses from the outside world and brings into his mind. In the end these perceptions define his nature.

The narrative device that best produces such knowledge is the immediate and sustained point of view, which allows the reader to take his place in the shoes of the narrator and to see as he sees, to experience as he experiences. And for a reader accustomed to explanations of the details an author uses, there are side effects:

> We remain walled up in the narrator's consciousness, never permitted to consult with the author or to depart even momentarily to get an outsider's look at the situation. No one tells us what actually happened or is going to happen. The hero is never sure whether a certain speech was actually spoken, whether his sense lied or his interpretation was erroneous. All he can do from his limited point of view is to conjecture. "Perhaps," "probably," "doubtless," stud his sentences to show the reader he does not know the truth himself. As we follow his unsure steps, we feel we are losing our foothold on the real, that we are in a dream or that we are victims of hallucination. The world that the hero constructs laboriously out of personal experience or hearsay can only be tentative . . .[3]

The reader's dream sensation not only explains much of the early reaction to Kafka, but also clarifies much of the present misunderstanding of these three writers.

In the works of Kafka, Beckett, and Robbe-Grillet the environment becomes known to the reader only according to the narrating consciousness, becomes known as a world of surfaces behind which nothing can be known. The narrator's unconscious has ascribed values to environment, to images both of the external world and of psychological pictures (memories and possibilities); the result is not a description of the world, but a Rorschach test of the perceiving individual. Each conscious narrator is a universe insofar as he has been able to internalize his environment, to systematize it for himself, and to see each new moment in it as part of the system he has constructed for himself. Everything fits somewhere; if it does not, some might call it "absurd," so the mind must struggle to find its proper place. Kafka,

[3] Laurent LeSage, *The French New Novel*, p. 27.

demonstrating the limitation of human consciousness as a factor separating man from the universe, is not unique in his attempt to describe the separation, but he is the first writer capable of structuring the separation into his fiction. The realization horrifies him—he is alone not only as a man, but also as a writer, understanding that aloneness is ineffable. Beckett is no longer horrified, he is merely displeased; he pushes his displeasure to a tangential extreme, where narrative is no longer necessary. Robbe-Grillet recognizes that such separateness is a fact of life, and his strength arises from his total acceptance of and his ability to work within what had previously seemed a great limitation for man and for fiction. For Robbe-Grillet, the limitation possesses many possibilities, each capable of exploration and exploitation.

Since shifting consciousness narrates the stories and controls their point of view, each novel is essentially concerned with process rather than with established fact. The novel becomes not a product but a medium, not the writing about something but the process of something being transmitted; the process becomes the created object. It is probably not accidental that Kafka called one of his major struggles with a novel-length work *Der Prozess (The Trial)*. The written word has become the end in itself in the experiments of Kafka, Beckett, and Robbe-Grillet. It leads backward to the narrating consciousness instead of forward to environment described. It is the written word itself with which the reader becomes involved, he need no longer look to the formulated message it transmits. To borrow the phrase from Marshall McLuhan, the written word, as medium, *is* the message.

Just as the sustained point of view dominates the style born of narrative consciousness, so it dominates the structures of the works of Kafka, Beckett, and Robbe-Grillet. For the first two authors the dominating structure is integral to the story being told: both Kafka and Beckett tell stories of unsuccessful, incompleted quests. The pattern of dissolution of the main character establishes the novel's form. The abstracted outline of events in Kafka's several works correspond to each other; the same may be said of Beckett's novels. But each work of Robbe-Grillet, dominated by the integral consciousness of a specific narrator who is no longer controlled by a fear of or displeasure at his separation from the universe, defines a structure unique to the created character's consciousness. Robbe-Grillet need no longer explore the possibilities of reuniting man with his environment; he is content to examine the existing relationship between man and the world about him. The quest, though still present in his works, has been reduced to a motif; the internal form is lacking. Instead, Robbe-Grillet allows each of his narrators their peculiar story: he creates for them structures highly relevant to their needs. Whereas form was inherent in the works of Kafka and Beckett because they themselves sensed such a form in the universe, Robbe-Grillet claims that form is imposed by each man onto the universe—the artistic imposition of shape—and he writes his novels accordingly. It is impossible to abstract a generalized outline from his works, since each character creates that pattern most important for himself; as the characters differ, their needs are dissimilar.

In a very real sense, Kafka, Beckett, and Robbe-Grillet were driven to their fictions by the prevailing environment. John Cruickshank, speaking of the first half of the twentieth century, remarks, "The ambiguity of experience, and the alien nature of the world in its resistance to rational systemization, were ideas which forced themselves with growing insistence on the attention of writers who thought about the raw material of their novels."[4] This mood characterizes not only the needs of writers but also the demands of philosophers. The approach to fiction that combined close description of external reality with the filter of narrative consciousness parallels to a considerable degree the school of continental philosophy called phenomenology. Husserl, Sartre, and Merleau-Ponty are its major proponents who come close to the concerns of the kinds of perception to be considered here. Although I do not wish to suggest exact correspondences in the process of attaining knowledge of the world between Kafka, Beckett, and Robbe-Grillet and the phenomenologists, it is important that similar problems of coping with the external

---

[4] John Cruickshank, ed., *The Novelist as Philosopher: Studies in French Fiction, 1935–1960*, p. 9. Similarly, see Lucien Goldmann, "The Theatre of Genet: A Sociological Study," *The Drama Review* 38 (Winter, 1968): 51–52.

universe through limited human perception were plaguing both fabu-
lators and philosophers.

Most simply, phenomenology attempts to attain truth by differen-
tiating between that which exists and the manner by which existence
comes to be known. "Known" means known to man—information
available to him through his senses and particularly through his sight.
Thus knowledge is necessarily subjective, for it must be filtered
through the mind; objectivity as conceived by the empiricists is by
definition unobtainable. Although the mind is asked to grasp what
the eye sees, the mind must avoid the interpretation of things, situations, events; it must refrain from the point of view of any previously
established philosophy. The mind, in short, must refrain from judging
what its senses experience. As basic as this tenet appears, achieving
its demands is difficult. Man is too intellectual, too critical to accept
willingly so naïve a position in relation to things; an attitude of unadorned assent would seem to renounce thousands of years of diffi-
cultly acquired abstrations and civilizations. Phenomenology would
seem to view the world as if no philosophy had been dreamed of by
man. (Merleau-Ponty responds, however, that phenomenology would
not be possible without the thousands of years of preceding thought,
since critical intelligence must grow from philosophy before man
can turn philosophy against itself. If, instead of positing realities, men
had always been phenomenologists, no philosophy would have been
possible.)[5] Yet in a world discovered to be more complex than it had
seemed to earlier perpetrators of thought systems, a new and clearer
understanding of things demands one of two alternatives: either a
philosophy yet more complex, to account for the changing vision man
has of his universe, or an unorganized review of the universe itself, a
new attempt to see more clearly all its properties, which must be
understood, and the interrelations of these properties. Philosophy,
even the tenets by which the uninitiated live, has left the universe
behind. Merleau-Ponty notes:

We never cease living in the world of perception, but we bypass it in critical thought—almost to the point of forgetting the contributions of per-

[5] Maurice Merleau-Ponty, *The Primacy of Perception*, ed. James M. Edie,
trans. Arleen B. Dallery, p. 29.

ception to our idea of truth. For critical thought encounters only bare propositions which it discusses, accepts or rejects. Critical thought has broken with the naive evidence of things, and when it affirms, it is because it no longer finds any means of denial. However necessary this activity of of verification may be, specifying criteria and demanding from our experience its credentials of validity, it is not unaware of our contact with the perceived world which is simply there before us, beneath the level of the verified true or false.[6]

The mind perceives; we grasp external space through our bodily situation. Everything about a person helps him attain a perception of the world; what he perceives, he interiorizes, he takes into himself. In his mind, each person integrates what he perceives into a previously formed body of information so that he may establish its proper place in relation to himself. In this way, before being aware of the information itself, a person interprets what he has perceived in order to fit it comfortably into the structure of his beliefs. "Living in the world, we make this world have meaning for us, we appropriate it, as it were, as a field of meaning. Sartre calls every individual a 'totalization' of the world."[7]

The world consists of what is and the manner in which it is known. A man is defined by those aspects of the world and of his memory which he chooses to know and by the manner in which he sees them; his descriptions rarely begin to clarify the nature of the world. This conception of the relation between man and the world is relevant to each man—to the ordinary man and to the man highly sensitive to the world about him, to the characters created by Kafka, Beckett, and Robbe-Grillet, and to Kafka, Beckett, and Robbe-Grillet themselves. In the fictions of these three authors the narrators are made to view their worlds so as to define themselves; in this respect one can even speak of a phenomenological novel. But these novels are phenomenological in another sense also. Since the author does not analyze for the reader, since there is no omniscient external reflection, the reader must himself engage in the analytic process—he "becomes" the protagonist in that he learns about the situation simultaneously with the narrator. The fiction therefore is the "thing itself," the world

[6] *Ibid.*, p. 5.
[7] Remy C. Kwant, *Phenomenology of Language*, p. 2.

itself to which Husserl demands that one return. Further, if the author's art is read as written, then the turn to a fiction unencumbered by the artist's analysis will result in immediate communication. Fiction cannot, of course, be used to achieve a "pure" view of the universe, but a specific fabulation alone, without the intercession of critical insight—either the author's or the critic's—can produce a view of the fiction in agreement with its artistic intention.

Part I: KAFKA

1. The Inevitability of Ritual:
Life Cycle of a Kafka Character

CLUES TO THE STYLE of a conventional narrative were once discernible through examination of the immediate passage, but when dealing with Kafka one must first grasp the whole, whereafter the particular segment will illuminate itself. Looking at a paragraph of Kafka's prose, the reader recognizes each moment in the narrative to be so closely integrated into the entirety of the work that he is at a loss without the guide of some context. In works of other writers, orientation is usually established by a verbalized point of view, but in Kafka, no statement, no directing voice guides one into the new fiction. The only context is the whole work—the whole story, the whole novel. There is no philosophy upon which the reader can rely, no previously secured understanding between the author and the reader. It is therefore to the whole work that one must turn, to the largest element of an author's style, his unifying structure.

Perhaps the most general correct comprehension of Kafka's structure was expressed metaphorically by Clemens Heselhaus.[1] Work-

[1] Clemens Heselhaus, "Kafkas Erzählformen," *Deutsche Vierteljahrschrift* 26 (1952): 376.

ing from the pattern of the fairy tale wherein the hero, confronted
with a problem, solves its successfully, Heselhaus notes the lack of
success displayed by Kafka's protagonists and categorizes Kafka's
tales as anti-fairy-tales, *Antimärchen.* The pleasant fairy tale is turned
about, and its hero, in Kafka's stories, comes to an unpleasant end.
Kurt Weinberg too notes the presence of mythic patterns and their
inversion in the tales but he relies heavily and almost consistently on
Kafka's apparent use and modification of classical archetypes.[2] Kafka,
however, deals only cursorily with the trappings of the Western heritage. He finds archetypes of little interest, since these imply spatial
relationships (as Weinberg would have it, the stories are attempted
dialogues between man and God's silence), whereas the importance
of Kafka's ritualized life cycle is its temporal nature: ritual is movement in time. Friedrich Beissner explains: "The unity of the themes—
or more correctly, of the theme, is in pure correlationship with the
unity of meaning in the portrayal. It is often said that great writers
have in fact only one theme, a 'permanent note' running through all
the manifold realizations and variations of the theme. Kafka's recurrent theme [is] *the unsuccessful arrival or the failure to reach the
goal...*"[3]

One of the clearest statements of the pattern cut by Kafka's life
cycle—the ritual prescribed for each segment of humanity that allows
itself even a moment of consciousness in an otherwise apparently
placid world—is made by Eliseo Vivas, who calls it "Kafka's conception of existence":

Kafka's discovery involves an ordered process which we can more or less
adequately capture in the following formula: a crisis leads either to a
sense of guilt or to a condition of alienation. In either case the crisis gen-

[2] Kurt Weinberg, *Kafkas Dichtungen: Die Travestien des Mythos.* See especially chapter 2, "Kafkas Archetypen," pp. 32–87, and chapter 3, "Zeit und Ewig-
keit," pp. 88–159. Weinberg is quite right in noting that Old and New Testament
and classical archtypes abound; but they are only the leftovers of another civilization, one about which Kafka is not writing. And when Weinberg notes (p. 32)
that "Kafka novels and stories move about in timelessness," he is right only so
far as noting that Kafka's characters do not belong, necessarily, to any one epoch,
but wrong in analyzing the movement of each character as existing out of time.
The temporal process of ritual structures all Kafka's stories.

[3] Friedrich Beissner, "Kafka the Artist," in *Kafka: A Collection of Critical
Essays,* ed. Ronald Gray, p. 19.

erates a struggle which expresses itself, among other ways, in the arrogant demands made by the hero. As he begins to feel the effects of the crisis the hero gradually trims his demands but he never altogether ceases to press them. The reduction of demands results from the hero's gradual discovery of a transcending organization which seems beyond his power either to look into, control, or understand. His discovery is based not upon unwarranted assumptions or gratuitous hypotheses but on more or less direct empirical evidence, and although what is discovered seems unintelligible to him, the evidence is ambivalent and points not only to the irrationality of the organization but to its rationality as well.[4]

Hermann Uyttersprot charges that much of the structural difficulty of *The Trial* and *The Castle* is involuntary on the part of Kafka; Uyttersprot lays the blame on Max Brod, asserting it was only Brod's clumsy ordering of Kafka's posthumous papers that led subsequent scholars to puzzle over a possible mistake. R. M. Albéres and Pierre de Boisdeffre offer the obvious response to Uyttersprot: incompletion and a nonlogical order of chapters as the cause for a sense of absurdity is a clever analysis of possible Brodian mischief, but it has little import, since so-called absurdity exists apparently throughout Kafka's works. Ronald Gray, in a direct response to Uyttersprot, sounds much the same note. Nevertheless, within the broader context Uyttersprot cannot be disregarded; he too notes the repeated pattern traced by all Kafka's works—in the beginning suddenness of the narrative, in the consistent turning point, and in the decline of the hero, often his death.[5]

There are five specific and discernible phases to a Kafka character's life cycle (or if, with the Symbolist poets, one wishes to acknowledge silences, possibly six); all can be found in Kafka's longer works and in his complete short works. Certain of the fragments illustrate each

---

[4] Eliseo Vivas, "Kafka's Distorted Mask," in *Creation and Discovery*, pp. 40–41.

[5] Hermann Uyttersprot, *"Zur Struktur von Kafkas "Der Prozess": Versuch einer Neuordnung*, in the *Collection Langues Vivantes*; "Zur Struktur von Kafkas Romanen," *Revue des Langues Vivantes* 20 (1954): 5; and *Eine neue Ordnung der Werke Kafkas? Zur Struktur von "Der Prozess" und "Amerika"*; R. M. Albéres and Pierre de Boisdeffre, *Franz Kafka*, p. 86; Ronald Gray, untitled review of Uyttersprot's book, *Eine neue Ordnung* . . . 1957, *German Life and Letters* 13 (1959): 234–235, and "The Structure of Kafka's Works: A Reply to Professor Uyttersprot," *German Life and Letters* 13 (1959): 1–17.

of the five points separately, as though to emphasize the impossibility of comprehending fragments removed from the context of any whole. Only by seeing such fragments within a structure (which the reader may need to build for them) can they be grasped within the too loosely bantered term, *Kafkaesque*.[6]

The ritual of life, according to Kafka, begins with the sudden awakening, with a complete realization that everything is different from what it was in the previous instant. Kafka often identifies waking in the morning with coming to consciousness, as in the case of Gregor Samsa or Josef K. Once the prime moment has passed, the hero usually takes a step backward in order to examine his surroundings. He finds all the expected landmarks; sometimes they are newly arranged, but this never seems to bother him. When he places himself back within these surroundings and finds (again without it bothering him) that he cannot make contact with other people, he causes *the reader* to feel a sense of despair. ". . . Kafka's narrative points to a new phase in the development of the European novel, for it allows the narrator to identify himself with the hero, *but also with the reader, and even makes of the reader a part of the story.* Kafka's appeal . . . depends to a large extent on this view" (italics mine).[7] Nothing appears unusual; everything functions as always. The reader retains his personal objectivity while at the same time, within the novel, seeing from the hero's point of view. It is also the reader, never the protagonist himself, who discovers that the protagonist is not furthering his own cause in the strange new situation, that he is disconnected from the rest of the world. This disconnection, felt but not understood by the protagonist, is the second part of Kafka's life cycle. All around the hero people seem to be talking and reacting as usual, but they have become hostile toward him.

---

[6] The term *Kafkaesque* covers a great many ambiguities. Simply because a process or a situation is difficult to understand is no excuse for it to be labeled "Kafkaesque." Yet this most commentators have done. If it is to be used properly, a distinction must be made: either the word refers to elements within the world itself; or it refers to Kafka's mode of perception. If it refers to the former, the term becomes dissipated, since Kafka saw the same world as all his contemporaries.

[7] H. S. Reiss, "Recent Kafka Criticism (1944–1955)—A Survey," in *Kafka*, ed. Gray, p. 173.

The third aspect of Kafka's ritualized structure is the impact of a still recognizable but estranged world on the hero's consciousness. The world is a totality, he is outside it, and he cannot penetrate its surface. The institutions within which he had previously functioned are still present, but it is as if he has no way of making physical or psychic contact with them. They impose themselves onto his life, they weigh on all his actions, but their functionaries do not respond when he reacts to their presence. He has become incapable of maneuvering himself within what he had previously known as and called "realities."

If the intrusion of external totality into the patterns of daily life can be withstood long enough for the hero to make an attempt at action before death takes place, then his act is expressed as a need to justify himself, to prove to the representatives of those institutions which have always mediated his values that he is capable of asserting himself properly before the world. The protagonist feels this need to demonstrate that he is still in control without ever understanding its implications—the resultant action is never more than a flailing, unsuccessful attempt at living up to a self-image that never existed beyond his own unexamined illusion. The impossibility of self-assertion is the fourth part of Kafka's life cycle.

In the parable in *The Trial*, the last words the man before the Law hears are those of the doorkeeper, who tells him that he was the only person who could ever have been able to enter the Law through those gates. This leads to the last part of Kafka's ritual: the hero's realization that at a given point it is too late to commit the only act by which he might have saved himself in order not to die as he has lived, passively, like a dog. Yet such action is never possible in life; in Kafka's world one cannot conceive of its being too late until it is too late in actuality. If such knowledge came simultaneously with physical birth, then there would be no need to remember or to forget the past, for there would be no past. But each of Kafka's protagonists does have a past, he is responsible for his past, and it is the essence of a Kafka story to show his characters that they are responsible, even though they do not understand the reason for this responsibility. By the time they become aware of it, it is too late. The man before the Law realizes only just before he dies that there had been at least a chance for him to gain admittance to the Law. Since he is about to die, it is too late. The life cycle is then complete.

The overall effect of the process described is separation. Every man bears a responsibility not so much for acts committed as for acts omitted. It is the responsibility of having wasted a life; the paradox results from an inability to do anything else. At the beginning of *The Trial*, Josef K. accepts the fact that he is charged. The function of the story is to explain to him the nature of the charge, of his relation to the novel's world, its landscape. But he will never discover the reason for the charge. There are no alternatives to living through the process of discovery, not for Josef K., not for any of Kafka's protagonists.

When we examine the life cycle more closely, it becomes apparent that, by necessity, the vision of Kafka's protagonists is partial: each hero's conscious mind does not perceive, and cannot report, everything before it. Still, if the reader places himself in the footsteps of the narrator/hero in any of the stories or novels, incomplete images fit into their context and illuminate that which is not mentioned. Although the stress remains on what is verbalized, silences and omissions are underscored in the reader's mind if he does not find objects or actions he expects to find. In a sense, Kafka is allowing the reader to complete from his own knowledge the areas between fragmentary descriptions, but such freedom for the reader has too often resulted in interpretation rather than in completion, since too many readers have based their views in some form of external, often philosophic, sophistication. The reader's world must not crowd Kafka's from the page. Rather, he must bring to bear his knowledge of Kafka's other stories. With them as point of departure the stories fall slowly into position in the life-cycle epic that Kafka sometimes linearly, sometimes disjointedly, relates. The stories fit into the life cycle as units and as such demonstrate their own completeness. Some of the fragments fall rather into categories, into points of the life cycle.

The beginning of reality for a Kafka protagonist, the first instant in which such a person catches sight of daylight, the figurative moment of birth, is the essential prerequisite for subsequent action. In this way all Kafka characters resemble each other. Somewhere, at some moment prior to the beginning of the narrative, a wedge of uncertainty crept into the mind of a protagonist-to-be. Somewhere he stepped, however momentarily, out of the prescribed universe of daily activity, and it became possible for him to reach, however briefly, a consciousness of his separation from his environment. The first moment of a story, the figurative birth of the protagonist, is the narrative's prime requisite. The moments of birth have striking similarities. Perhaps the most obvious is the character's unawareness before the moment arrives that something is about to happen, that he is about to be born. He is not on his guard, and so, like K. in the fragment "A Dream," (PC, 170), he is thrown off balance for just a moment, just long enough to alter the balance of his existence. Gregor Samsa and Josef K. are sleeping when the instant passes that changes their lives forever. Georg Bendemann walks into his father's room, a room in which he has not been for months; he finds it unusually dark, and it throws him off his guard. K. arrives in the town for the first time late in the evening when he is tired and willing to settle for any kind of quarters. All of them are unprepared for what they later recognize, or in some instances fail to recognize, as the most important moment of their existence.

Although the best way to describe this prime requisite is to liken it to actual birth, the concept of awakening, real or figurative, may also be applied. Josef K. does not believe he can be responsible for any wrongdoing. The country doctor alone reacts and, as we shall see, is consequently destroyed. Bendemann, on the other hand, does nothing. Although he has barely reached the moment of birth, he has also arrived at the time to die; his whole life cycle must be telescoped into a few instants.

The ape wakes up, too. Kafka says so in so many words: the ape awakens after the shots had been fired. It makes no difference that the bullets in the final analysis brought the ape to consciousness. When he does awaken, he immediately realizes the dimensions of the cage, but in relative, human terms—too short to lie down in and not high enough to stand up in. The moment one attains consciousness, one is trapped: in a cage, or in the shell of a dung beetle, or in a village to which one has been assigned and which refuses to recognize one officially, or in a caravansery somewhere in the desert. Anything that is conscious is trapped, trapped by its own consciousness, just as the conscious reader must be within the narrator/hero. Acceptance is the only possible reaction. By accepting, each of Kafka's characters sets the pattern of all that is to follow. The resolution of the narrative, visible already to the partially objective reader, who himself is in the process of accepting the terms of Kafka's story, remains invisible to the protagonist. The paradox of consciousness lies in the ability of the reader as separate consciousness to see what must result, and the inability of the reader trapped within the narrator/hero's consciousness to see beyond an awareness of the momentary phenomena.

At this point in Kafka's stories the protagonist feels the time has come to establish a course, to try to see something of this new world into which he has been born. So far the protagonist knows only that the change that has taken place has separated him from the life he had been leading. By attempting to look at the world from his new vantage point, he admits and accepts the change, possibly without liking it. He will wage the battle in the new context.

The passive avenue of examination lies open to the newly reborn protagonist. At last he has a chance to act, but he is able to muster up no more than a feeble question or two. In vain he attempts to scrutinize a new world that is to him at best erratic, at worst useless and even harmful both to himself and to the people he uses in the attempt. "And don't make such an outcry about your feeling innocent, it spoils the not unfavorable impression you make in other respects" (T 17), says the arresting officer to Josef K. Georg Bendemann says to his father: "A thousand friends wouldn't make up to me for my father. Do you know what I think? You're not taking enough care of yourself. But old age must be taken care of" (PC 56). A few moments later he tries to cover up his father completely, as if the old man were dead.

Of the greatest importance to the newborn hero, then, is what he perceives. The questions he asks deal directly with the new world and therefore only indirectly with his own fate, for although the protagonist is in the new world, he is not a part of it in the sense that he can manipulate it as he could his previous context. After he examines his immediate surroundings, his inquiries take him in several directions; a given protagonist may follow any or all of them. Most often he tries to compare his present situation with the life he has known. Or he may try to review the facts of his actual moment of birth, but such an attempt usually proves unrewarding. Or he begins what he believes to be the only correct approach—to look for a way out by demanding to know what will happen next. But by asking that question, he admits the situation has eluded his grasp; he must let the forces work as they will, and he will follow their drives, will allow himself to be acted upon. For the protagonist the new situation remains very unreal. It has no context, because the landscape is unfamiliar. The protagonist does not know what to do, let alone how to do it.

A clear link between birth and actualized disconnection may be found in "In the Caravansery." Here most of the elements of the new world are present. An unpleasantness dominates the atmosphere (to designate exactly from where it came is unimportant). People move about among the camels and the stench, but the "I" cannot make contact with them, even to ask where he is and how he can get out. The people are transients, members of passing caravans; if he were to ask them where to go or how to find his way, they would of course be unable to tell him. He knows only that he has wandered into the maze and now is a part of the oasis without being able to make contact with it. The "I" of "The Cell," caught within the walls of the room, is in much the same situation and realizes his captivity. There are doors, to be sure, but the doors, when tried, when questioned to see if they are real doors to the outside, reveal only blank rock-face. The adjoining room is at best neutral; it puts the narrator off no less than the blank walls. It is not even the "I" who tries opening the doors to see if a way out can be found; one realizes the nature of the world behind them only indirectly: "*If one* opened them" (PP 117; my italics). The passivity of the main character continues, even in so short a fragment. He can do no more than think about his situation. Gregor Samsa, even after his terrifying metamorphosis, cannot conceive of the possibility of being trapped in his shell, and so his

desperate thrashing about is reminiscent of the actions of a man trying to get out of bed, get dressed, and go to work. Because of glaring
incongruities, in the context of a beetle on a bed, the result is at once
hilarious and tragic. One laughs but realizes at the same instant that
Gregor Samsa is now literally as well as figuratively trapped. In his
new, real context, he is passive. He cannot even pass his time in
thinking; to the reader, the disconnection has been completed.

As there are almost no external changes in the actions of Samsa, so
are there few changes in the daily life of Joseph K. He is told by the
Inspector that he may continue his life just as he was planning to do
before his arrest. "You are under arrest, certainly, but that need not
hinder you from going about your business. Nor will you be pre-
vented from leading your ordinary life" (T 20). When the police are
gone, he does go to work as usual, to the bank where he need not
think; when he leaves the bank, he too has his period of pondering.
He thinks out loud when alone, and he thinks with others (or at least
he wants to), with those two people nearest to him. Since no one is
really close to him in his personal life, closeness can be measured
only by physical proximity. So he chooses to speak to his landlady,
Frau Grubach, and his neighbor, Fräulein Bürstner. He probably
would also have gone to speak with Elsa, the waitress and prostitute
who was more intimate with him than any other person, but this was
not his night to see her; to go would have ruined his well-defined
schedule. He thinks out loud to Frau Grubach, who only pities him;
his reaction, the easiest way to close the conversation, is to insult her
by telling her to throw him out of the boarding house. Next he goes
to Fräulein Bürstner, but she is not at home. As he waits for her until
late in the evening, he thinks about his case. By staying up so late, he
has broken his routine, but his late evening also defines his passivity.
He has started to do something, and the thrust of his brief action
pushes him forward. He will not turn from his trivial goal until it is
reached, for turning from it requires greater energy than does the
passive waiting outside her door.

The fragment "The Question of Our Laws" deals in its entirety
with the problem of pondering. It contains passivity, reflection, and
the knowledge of being caught within the Law, of being separated

from the outside world by laws. This is already evident in the opening words: "Our laws are not generally known: they are kept secret by the small group of nobles who rule us. We are convinced that these ancient laws are scrupulously administered; nevertheless it is an extremely painful thing to be ruled by laws that one does not know" (PP 155). Here total reality has not yet intruded. The inhabitants simply know that there is such a group of laws; the meaning or purpose of these they do not understand. The passage concludes with the realization that the act of reflecting in these circumstances is itself a paradox. The final words present the essence of Kafkaesque pondering: "Actually one can express the problem only in a sort of paradox: Any party which can repudiate, not only all belief in the laws, but nobility as well, would have the whole people behind it; yet no such party can come into existence, for nobody would dare to repudiate the nobility. We live on this razor edge. A writer once summed up the matter in this way: The sole visible and indubitable law that is imposed upon us is the nobility, and must we ourselves deprive ourselves of that one law?" (PP 159). The question cannot be answered, the paradox cannot be resolved. At best, a writer once (evidently long ago, for now such things are no longer possible) was able to phrase the problem, and it had to be phrased in the form of a question.

Georg Bendemann's pondering takes place after he has assured his father that a thousand friends could not replace him. He thinks out loud to the old man, speaking of his friend in Petersburg. The pondering takes the form of a seemingly irrelevant argument over the actual existence of the friend. Georg is challenged by his father, probably for the first time, to prove the reality of his friend; Georg finds that he can give no more solid proof than his father's remembrance that the friend actually spent some time in the Bendemann home.

In the more traditional sense of pondering over one's birth and the subsequent feeling of disconnection, the ape in "A Report to an Academy" phrases the words succinctly: "For the first time in my life I could see no way out. . . . Until then I had had so many ways out of everything, and now I had none. I was pinned down. Had I been nailed down, my right to free movement would not have been lessened" (PC 176). This is the ape's realization: he is disconnected from the world of men by his cage, and the cage must serve as his prison. Yet the cage is not a prison by dint of keeping the ape from freedom, for, as he himself asserts, he is free, by his very disconnection. But he does not want this sort of freedom. The ape wants to be united with something, and in his naïveté he settles his wish on man. Through rebirth into the world of man, the ape demonstrates the completeness of disconnection. He has, literally and figuratively, shifted worlds. In his little cage, he does not demand to be *let* out in the sense of wanting freedom; he demands a *way* out: "Only not to stay motionless with raised arms, crushed against a wooden wall" (PC 178).

But then, for each protagonist, something complete, external, and therefore awful, intrudes. Consider K., for example:

"I am the old assistant. I came today after the Land-Surveyor." "No," was shouted back. "Then who am I?" asked K. as blandly as before. And after a pause the same voice with the same defect answered him, yet with a deeper and more authoritative tone: "You are the old assistant." K. was listening to the old note and almost missed the question: "What is it you want?" He felt like laying down the receiver. He had ceased to expect anything from this conversation. But being pressed, he replied quickly: "When can my Master come to the Castle?" "Never," was the answer. "Very well," said K., and hung up the receiver. (C 28)

At the beginning of the passage, K. is still in his period of pondering; he is experiencing his disconnection. But when the voice on the telephone shouts at him that he will never be able to come to the castle— that he never again will be connected to the world he had known, the world of land-surveyors, a world where he does as he is told— from that moment on, the world as a unified, impenetrable, and external power has intruded into his own small life; its authority has locked him out, in much the way as the ape has been locked in. K. is thereafter one step further in his life cycle because his separation has been proclaimed by some higher authority, beyond himself, which agrees with his realization that he is apart. The new world reveals itself more completely to K. as the passage continues into the next chapters.

Before the intrusion, the protagonist's little world had been a well-defined subdivision of the much larger one, and he himself, in many instances, a part of some huge hierarchy. K. is a government official, a land-surveyor; Josef K. is a clerk in a huge bank; Gregor Samsa was a traveling salesman for a large concern; the Hunger Artist was part of a circus; the Officer in the penal colony was subservient to the Commandant, and so on. Now his little division loses connection with the greater world, although that other world does not cease to exist, somewhere. He can feel its force, but he cannot reach out to it. And then, with all the force it can muster, with old memories and new inferences, the greater world thrusts down upon the protagonist's tiny world and forces it, as it were, to burst at the seams, leaving nothing of the protagonist's old world. The sensation that everything outside him is connected with everything else outside him is omnipresent. He is subjected to the authority of a conspiracy with which he has no contact. But the authority precludes the usual sense of control. Life has not been fated in the sense that the protagonist will be forced to act; instead he is fated to be unable to do anything. The source of control keeps him *from* acting, rather than forcing him *to* act in a certain way. The authority separates, reveals, and condemns the protagonist. The authority itself assumes a variety of forms, all of which demonstrate its link in the outside world and its separation from the protagonist.

Perhaps the most complete instance of totality's intrusion is the story "Josephine the Singer, or the Mouse Folk." It begins with absolute statement: "Our singer is called Josephine. Anyone who has not heard her does not know the power of song. There is no one but is carried away by her singing, a tribute all the greater as we are not in general a music loving race" (PC 256). Here is a songstress apparently so forceful she is able to sway all who hear her; she is much like one of Kafka's own sirens. She alone is able, through her power of song, to render the inhabitants blissful; she alone can relieve them of daily life's repetitive doldrums; she is the high priestess of song. But the narrator begins to doubt his own apparently undeniable initial statement when he admits that her song is perhaps more nearly a whistle. As the story-essay develops, even her whistling becomes, for the narrator's ears, so weak that little of it remains. Since her song was her power, the narrator, now aware that her song was sham, is no longer dominated by her; the rest of the population, the mice-folk, remain under her sway. Able to see—in this case, hear—clearly, the narrator can avoid her blinding power, and the concept of authority becomes farcical.

The fragment "The Sirens" demonstrates the superficiality of authority: "These are the seductive voices of the night; the Sirens, too, sang that way. It would be doing them an injustice to think that they wanted to seduce; they knew they had claws and sterile wombs, and they lamented this aloud. They could not help it if their laments sounded beautiful" (PP 100). This is not to say that authority as seen by Kafka is not a fearful thing. But, valued highly as it is, it attains its power merely from the weakness of the people over whom it is manifested, it cannot exist in its own right. When the maximum potential of a series of external experiences is realized as they sweep into the protagonist's own little limited world, the actualized concept of authority appears overwhelming. The protagonist is powerless to stop it. Seeing himself helpless and apart, blinded by his own guilt, he cannot see the guilt of others around him, others with whom he could commiserate and thereby avoid feeling alone. But because guilt is individual, much as the lack of action that caused it was individual, so too is the realization of the guilt and its consequences individual and separate.

The protagonist has come a long way from the moment of his birth; he has lived through crises without being able to act in accord with the situation. He has discovered, he has thought, he has been overwhelmed, and now his moment has come, or, more correctly, his hour has come. In the fourth part of this life cycle, the protagonist is at last about to act; he has been prodded sufficiently. But Kafka's characters cannot react normally, for they are still blinded by the pain of the blow with which they were struck when the unified external world intruded into their own. Assertive motions may therefore appear forced and distorted, although the distortion is not apparent to each protagonist, who still believes himself to be acting within the context of his old world. At last, however, the protagonist feels the absence of context in a world void of related objects and beings. He senses the need to legitimize his existence, to justify his mediated self-image, but to do so is impossible. Only by lying to himself can he possibly achieve what he believes to be legitimacy—whereupon legitimacy itself becomes the lie. He struggles to assert himself, not by saying "I am right," for accusation makes him uncertain, but by insisting, "I must do something"—it makes no difference what. He may even be able to fool himself into thinking he has in fact redeemed himself. Or he may, in a state of naïveté, never realize the seriousness of his situation. Therefore, because all the protagonists are able to understand their conditions at least preconsciously, they realize their need for, and carry out, the drive toward self-assertion.

Karl Rossmann of *Amerika* is still trying to assert himself as his story ends. Rossmann is the American dreamer. The whole novel illustrates the principle of assertion; here is the story of a young man who must prove himself after he has been forced to leave his home because he has made a servant girl pregnant. Even through his pre-America ordeal (the realization that his life must change, the pondering over the choice of the method for changing it, the arrival in New York), he has for a number of reasons been able to retain his naïveté. The most important of these has been the double shift in his landscapes. He has left not only the Old World, but also his own old world in the usual Kafka sense. This change of both physical and psychological contexts has obscured to him the real impact of his new world situation. There is another difference between Karl and the other Kafka protagonists, that of age. Gregor Samsa is prepared to become a bug, for he has been in the uninvolved pupa stage for many years. Much the same is true for K., Josef K., and the others. But Karl is only sixteen, and his crime, the accident of making a servant girl pregnant, was not an act caused either by his will or by his lack of it. Karl was seduced, for Karl was not in control of the situation. Certainly his misdeed was not as great as Josef K.'s or Gregor Samsa's. Karl comes to America to assert himself. America is the naïve world where all is possible, where the least sophisticated self-image can be justified. When justification can be found, it is salvation, since it makes the mediated image real. Whether that image is one of a land whose streets are paved with gold, or a land in which the most naïve ideals are blessed with success, the image implies an actualization of hope, an American dream. An unreal place in Kafka's mind, America is a country where self-assertion will be justified.

In the same vein, but for a different reason, the ape before the academy is able to achieve his own dream, to retain his own naïveté. The ape is lucky; the process that breaks men and makes them into dung beetles gives him human identity and innocence. The ape is born into the world of men; he experiences the moment of awakening and the onslaught of totality. But because his apehood caused him to lag behind by two stages in the development toward human form, the process leaves him in the same state of naïveté as that which Karl never left. The ape begins to assert himself, as a human might if he were born full grown, but in the beginning the ape possesses the mentality of a two-year-old child. His first lesson is to learn to spit; his second, to smoke. These abilities, for the ape, are the two highest human achievements. The only real differences between the ape and the men who surround him are: (a) that he licks the spit off his face, whereas the men evidently let the ape-expectoration stay on their faces, and (b) that the ape cannot tell when his pipe is full. The ape's greatest problem arises later when he tries to imitate men as they drink; he cannot stand the smell of liquor. But he is able to overcome even this deficiency, as are most men in order not to be different from others.

The American dream, in Kafka's terms, is self-assertion with the appearance of success. During a character's attempted assertion Kafka's writing most often appears humorous, for assertion is attempted where no real assertion is possible, in a void, without a defined context. Even when apparently successful in its American-dream sense, the attempt seems grotesque to the reader, who cannot be wholly integrated into the structure of Kafka's story. The action, the struggle to assert oneself, is incongruous with the situation; one sees the protagonist acting in a confused, Chaplinesque fashion. By putting the highest courts in back alleys, or by allowing the first acts of man learned and copied by an ape to be spitting, drinking, and smoking, Kafka controls both social situation and metaphysical universe and allows humor to penetrate the objective world of his characters. He thereby also leaves himself open to interpretation by social critics when in reality he has not transcended his own principle of viewing through the eyes of his characters.

If *Amerika* is to be considered a comic novel, it is because all the action relates to Karl's attempts at self-assertion in an America as naïve as himself, naïve even in its evil and its decadence. If *The Castle* and *The Trial* are also to be seen as novels with large elements of humor, it is because the greatest part of the action lies in the vain and irrelevant attempts of K. and Josef K. to assert themselves in worlds from which they have been disconnected. Yet the simultaneous terror, which is constantly apparent and which alone remains visible to most Kafka readers, hides the humor and emphasizes the disconnection. The reader, having lived with the protagonist through the first three steps of his life cycle, often cannot adjust to the humorous struggle for assertion.

After having re-enacted the arrest scene for Fräulein Bürstner, Josef K. leans over and greedily busses her, then violently kisses her throat. His animal-like action and the passivity of Fräulein Bürstner are completely out of context, especially in their unexpected immediacy; they appear ridiculous. Yet his sexual advances were altogether unlike his earlier sex life, in which he paid scheduled weekly visits to Elsa, the prostitute. His life thereafter follows the same abrupt contextless pattern.

Much like his counterpart in *The Castle*, Josef K. learns of a part of his fate on the telephone. It is then that he consciously decides to fight out his case in court. He wants to end the foolish proceedings as quickly as possible; he wants to be certain that they *are* completed, so that his case will not be brought up again. When he arrives at court, he of course makes a fool of himself in the eyes of the spectators and the judges. The reader who sees the incongruity of Josef K.'s actions laughs also (albeit, since he is sympathetically disposed to Josef K., somewhat uncomfortably), not only when others laugh but also when hearing Josef K.'s felt need to mention the trivial: " 'I have no wish to shine as an orator,' said K., having come to this conclusion, 'nor could I if I wished. The Examining Magistrate, no doubt, is much the better speaker, it is part of his vocation. All I desire is the public ventilation of a public grievance. Listen to me: Some ten days ago I was arrested, in a manner that seems ridiculous even to myself, though that is immaterial at the moment' " (T 53–54). A few moments earlier someone in the audience had applauded and yelled out, "Bravo." Despite his unnecessary pointed denial, Josef K. *is* orating and continues to do so for the next several pages. Whenever he comes to a point he does not understand, but which is nevertheless critical to his case, he calls it "immaterial" and thinks he has thereby dismissed it. Later he argues against the counsel of other characters from whom he has sought advice; he also rejects the words of the prison chaplain, who tells him, in effect, that it is too late for him to do anything more.

K. also encounters other characters, but in a much more passive manner than had Josef K.—necessarily, for the demands K. makes are much greater, and so come much closer to the impossible. Josef K. demands only justification in a world of mediated values; K. insists on speaking with the highest authorities themselves, with the men who control the castle. Such a demand approaches hubris. K. speaks to Frieda, the mistress of one of the men who work for the castle (Klamm), to Barnabas, to the Mayor, and to Barnabas's sister, but no one can help him. In order to justify himself he must speak to the direct representative of the castle itself, but, as the story progresses, he gradually lowers his demands and will accept an interview with one of the minor employees, Klamm. Even this, however, in the words of the landlady, is to ask for the impossible. Frieda says to her: " 'You see what he's asking for.' 'You're a strange person,' said the landlady, and she was an awe-inspiring figure as she sat more upright, her legs spread out and her enormous knees projecting under her thin skirt. 'You ask for the impossible' " (C 62). While she is speaking, K. reaches out and pulls Frieda onto his lap. The landlady goes on to tell him that this method of approach is wrong; there may be a way of achieving his goal, but this method is incorrect: "I don't deny that it's possible once in a while to achieve something in the teeth of every rule and tradition. I've never experienced anything of that kind myself, but I believe there are precedents for it. That may well be, but it certainly doesn't happen in the way you're trying to do it, simply by saying 'No, no,' and sticking to your own opinions and flouting the most well-meant advice" (C 67). To say "No, no" is wrong; K. should instead admit his disconnection from the castle and try to reattain his naïveté. But the only known attempts to do so took place so long ago that they have attained the stature of legends. He cannot, and so should not try to, communicate with the castle people; they are part of the old world with which he can have no further association.

In "The Judgment," Georg Bendemann too tries to justify himself by rejoining the context of the old world; he must at least assert himself against his father. The old man shouts at Georg that his friend from Russia need not come to visit them because the friend already knows everything a hundred times better than does Georg. In his enthusiasm the old man gets carried away. "He knows everything a thousand times better." Then Georg tries to justify himself by mocking the old man. As might be expected, because this is the wrong way to seek legitimacy, it is Georg who appears the fool. " 'Ten thousand times,' said Georg, to make fun of his father, but in his very mouth the words turned into deadly earnest" (PC 62). The words are Georg's own death knell, his final sign of importance before he is condemned to death. They epitomize the unsuccessful attempt at self-assertion.

In "The Metamorphosis," too, Gregor Samsa's beetle-body makes an attempt: he hears his sister playing the violin and promises himself that she will play only to him, that he will even take advantage of his situation and use his ugly body to ward off anyone who tries to take her from him. He drags his body into the room where his sister is playing and succeeds in disgusting everyone present; the action is his last, the only one of importance in his attempt at self-legitimization; he dies soon thereafter. The huge beetle lumbering about is at once funny, horrifying, and quietly sad. For it, and for the others, real justification is impossible.

The life cycle of the Kafka protagonist draws to a close once the illusion of possible justification has been dispelled. The realization that nothing remains leaves the reader with the despair for which the work of Kafka is universally acclaimed. Once the impenetrable structure of the external world has been perceived, only death remains. Before death can take place, however, a final process must be recognized and then quietly discarded. Because the protagonist's attempt at legitimization has been turned aside forcibly by the world's authority, that is, by the total possibility of things beyond him, he sees his death looming before him and realizes it is too late to continue to act, too late even to avoid acting. Like the moments of birth and impact with totality, this is a phenomenon of the instant; the external impenetrability is recognized by the protagonist for the first time as the element of death that has existed in him from the moment of his physical birth, that has developed as he has grown, invisible to him until his moment of awakening, his moment of existential rebirth. When that rebirth takes place, the element of death grows into his consciousness much as it matured in his body. His guilt developed out of his failure to act, his failure to exorcise the metaphysical death from within himself. The death expanded like a cancer; by the time it first makes its appearance it is too late for possible future action. The protagonist's inability to realize that it is too late until after the fact lends the moment its final irony. It is then accepted silently, without fuss. The protagonist returns to his earlier passivity and accepts whatever is to come. Should he appear in motion after this realization, then he is *being* moved; he is no longer in control of the movement.

After Josef K. has ended his talk with the prison chaplain, who has told him the parable of the man before the Law who did not act, who himself was dying before he could realize that it was too late, he continues his death-in-life while accepting it to be no more than that, and on the evening of his thirty-first birthday, just one year after his arrest, the two men come for him. He has been waiting for them without having been told of them, without really knowing they were coming. They walk together: "It was a unity such as can hardly be formed except by lifeless matter" (T 281). Death-in-life has almost completely taken over.

The ape too realizes his situation; it is also too late for him to return to the life he once knew, the life he has forsaken for human

death-in-life. In his rich naïveté he believes himself to be an ac-
complished being. Despite the apparent triviality of his accomplish-
ment (as he goes on to point out), his achievement has been great
because his ability allows him to travel on the paths of humanity. He
would never be able to realize the parallel between his newly
achieved position and Georg Bendemann's abnegation of all that he
is and was, Bendemann's neglect of his home and family. The ape is
trapped on the middle ground—he will never be human (he sleeps
with a half-wild chimp), and he can never be an ape again. He has
left his old world but never gained the world of man. He is disconnected from the landscape of his environment and now knows it is
too late to do anything. His own eyes must contain a glance comparable to that displayed on the face of the female chimp: ". . . the insane
look of a half-broken animal in her eye" (PC 184). Just as the mediocrity of the average citizen is death for Josef K., so it is death-in-life
for the ape.

It was Gregor's sister, the one whom he had thought would play
only for him, who locks him into his room for the last time. For
Gregor, too, the time comes. It is too late for him to feel love for his
sister, too late to feel even a desire to move. Passively he may think
about his tiny legs and wonder how they were ever able to move
his huge bulk of a body, but he can do no more. All that is left for
him is to lie in his room, on the floor, in degradation, covered with
dust, and acknowledge the death awaiting him. The night recedes,
the world outside grows light, and Gregor the beetle-man dies. As
he was lying there, he thought of the apple lodged in his back. It did
not bother him; but the reader is not told that it *no longer* bothers
him, rather that "Den Apfel . . . spürte er *schon kaum*"(E 125; my
italics)—the apple *already hardly* bothered him. The phrase shows
that the time even for pain has gone by; it is too late for anything.

Georg was once innocent, old Mr. Bendemann says. He was innocent only in that he had never done anything wrong; the man who
does not act can never be guilty of a committed misdeed. So too the
"I" of "The Vulture," beset by the bird that tears at his feet, will not
act now just as he has not acted in the past. As with all of Kafka's objects, it would of course be possible to call the vulture a symbol of

something specific, but to do so is unnecessary. The vulture is nothing more than a vulture, and as such it is a powerful destructive force. It is to be known by the function it performs, which in this case is to rend the flesh from the feet of the protagonist. The protagonist is approached by a strange gentleman, who explains that one shot would kill the bird and so let the tortured man escape. The gentleman says he can return in half an hour with a gun, if the protagonist can wait that long. After some thought, the latter beseeches the gentleman to go home for the weapon. But the half-hour is too long to wait, because "during this conversation the vulture had been calmly listening, letting its eye rove between me and the gentleman. Now I realized that it had understood everything . . ." (PP 149). It is too late to help the protagonist; the mistake has been to wait so long. Now he must pay. There can be no salvation from passivity, for this is the guilt of noncommission.

Once a Kafka character realizes that it is too late, nothing remains but to die. When the metamorphosis is complete, he has no further control over his life—therefore he cannot himself be expected to emphasize his death. These deaths complete the life cycle; they are essential to it. The final instant is at hand when the protagonist can be content that at last it is too late.

In the end both Gregor Samsa and Georg Bendemann loved their parents, the authorities that in great part had been the cause of their condemnation. Gregor Samsa "thought of his family with tenderness and love" (PC 127). Georg Bendemann says "Dear parents, I have always loved you" (PC 63). In the end, with death, they have achieved a legitimization, although not the one that earlier they had felt they must attain to achieve their self-justification.

Each is ready for death when it comes, because each knows the immediate cause of, if not the more generalized reason for, his guilt. The specific context, the emblem Kafka employs to particularize the cause of a character's being condemned, may appear trivial in comparison to the punishment demanded. But the particular cause is only a symptom of the general reason; the same guilt underlies them both, they are differentiated only by degree. Bendemann's father has spelled it out for his son: Georg has forsaken the father, the mother, the friend, even the fiancée. Georg does not know the reason for his guilt, he does not realize his unconsciousness of the needs and hopes of others. In the same way, though Josef K. knows he is guilty, he does not know the reason, the context in which his guilt belongs. The chaplain has explained it to him in the parable of the man before the Law. At first arguing against it, K. at last understands the analogy and awaits his executioners, those who will punish him for his immediate guilt. Even so, at the very end he still considers the possibility of a last-minute reprieve; he still does not understand the deeper, the more general, reason for his impending execution. He realizes only that the shame will outlive him—the memory of his metaphysical life will transcend even his physical death. He can never understand that he was guilty for his death-in-life. With the ape, the paradox of death is embodied in his deification of death-in-life as mediocrity. His story might be considered a prelude to "The Metamorphosis"—the pre-life of Gregor Samsa. From ape to man to insect, the metamorphosis completes itself.

At the last moment Josef K. realizes he is supposed to be his own executioner; he finds he cannot kill himself, not from unwillingness but from physical inability. Georg Bendemann will not die until he is condemned to death; passively he lets himself slide into the water under the bridge. The officer in charge of the harrow lets the machine finish him while he lies motionless inside it ("In the Penal Colony"). The very non-act of fasting allows the Hunger Artist to die of starvation. Passivity, as metaphysical equivalent to inaction, unites with its physical counterpart as either the cause or the correspondent of the protagonist's death.

The paradox of death plays possibility against actuality. In several fragments that depict only the end of the life cycle, Kafka demonstrates this paradox with the kind of slick, impenetrable terror that characterizes the surface of his fiction. The Messiah will definitely come, but he will come after the end has passed, "not on the last day, but on the very last" ("The Coming of the Messiah," PP 81). What is to be done in the eternity between the last and the very last day, no one is ever told. The possibility that the Messiah will come remains, and so the protagonist must yearn; but his hopes will never be fulfilled. His own immediate actuality, the new world, he can escape only through death. The other possibility—escape through some uncaused metamorphosis into the easily explainable world of parable ("On Parables," PP 11)—can never occur; it is a leap from one context into another, an unverbalized hope that a protagonist may at best envision, but never realize. So the first man tells the second that the former has lost the bet in the one way in which he (the former) could rid himself of his daily cares, rid himself of his mediocrity; he has lost in parable. In reality—that is, within his own mediocrity—he has won. The only way out of the paradox is to incorporate it into actuality, into the integrated impenetrable structure of the external world. This happens in the parable, "Leopards in the Temple" (PP 93), when the repeated destruction of the temple by the leopards is finally incorporated into the ceremony. (The parable, appropriately, has no protagonist.) But none of Kafka's heroes are capable of controlling circumstances to the extent of organizing the world they live in. The paradox of death is predictable: it achieves significance when it fits into the general external structure, when it becomes part of the world into which no protagonist could penetrate, and of which he has become for all future protagonists an integral if totally passive element.

Development within Kafka's stories can thus be characterized as a structural thrust toward completion: completion of a life cycle, completion of a narrative structure. For Kafka's protagonist there is no way out. Naïveté means imprisonment within an American dream, within nonconsciousness. Action is nearly impossible, passivity is weakness. Authority condemns but cannot guide. Movement is visible, but it is activity separate from and irrelevant to the landscape against which it takes place. Kafka has described what he has seen; he has not analyzed it. He is aware that his narrating protagonists have not seen clearly, that they have structured their reported view. But there is no one to explain to the reader the completely subjective nature of the Kafkaesque vision to which he has been exposed.

2. A Derivation of Meaning from Point of View

ONLY A DETAILED EXAMINATION of subjective vision can accurately explain the several meanings of the term *Kafkaesque*. These meanings are rarely distinguished by interpreters of either Kafka's works or the works of others whose themes seem to parallel Kafka's own. The meaning of *Kafkaesque* depends entirely on what part of a Kafka-like world the person using the word is gazing upon as he verbalizes his perception; hence it is a confusing term. But one must differentiate between the use of a confusing term and the confused use of a term. Too often critics and reviewers, unable to understand the complexity or the apparent keylessness of an artistic work, label it Kafkaesque. Such an attitude implies that difficult creations deserve no more than catch-all terminology; the attempt here must be to discard the confused use of the term and bring some order to its meaning.

As any number of commentators have demonstrated, the apparent thematic parallels between Kafka and the other writers, both earlier and later, are numerous. Kafka's ideas are hardly original. Although

his narrative technique was unique, others before him had wrestled
with the problem of man's separation from his environment. Kafka
was the child of his time, rooted in the values of the past but overcome by the phenomena of the moment. Yet, although he reacted to
the same stimuli felt by his contemporaries, his vision was more precise; it transcended the specific themes of his day and was transformed into stories told in a unique idiom. What critics interpret,
alternatively, as loneliness or alienation (all too often adding the
extreme value judgment that Kafka's world itself is absurd), was described by Kafka as nothing more than a separation between man
and his environment. Certainly an industrious reader, using the
stories as a Rorschach test, can render a Kafka protagonist lonely,
alienated, or even absurd, but such a reading is artificial, imposed by
a reader whose standards demand that the text provide nineteenth-
century completion, interrelation, and connection. Kafka's protagonist describes a world filtered through his narrating consciousness
and leaves consoling interpretation up to the reader. As Susan Sontag
notes: "In most modern instances, interpretation amounts to the phil-
istine refusal to leave the work of art alone. Real art has the capacity
to make us nervous. By reducing the work of art to its content and
then interpreting *that*, one tames the work of art. Interpretation
makes art manageable, comfortable."[1]

What, then, is this idiom that renders one so uncomfortable, that
since the appearance of Kafka's works has forced readers to interpret Kafka in a myriad of ways? Heinz Politzer states it succinctly:
"What distinguishes an actual Kafka story from a Kafka-like dream
is the style of the story."[2] In the style lies the impossibility of a
phrase-by-phrase, analytic, interpretative explanation.

The difficulty in describing Kafka's stylistic procedures is caused
by the lack of a way into the story. The unity of narration, the sustained point of view, forces the reader to remain, as Laurent LeSage
has said, "walled up in the narrator's consciousness, never permitted
to consult with the author or to depart even momentarily to get an
outsider's look at the situation." Friedrich Beissner explains that "the

[1] Susan Sontag, *Against Interpretation*, p. 8.
[2] Heinz Politzer, *Franz Kafka: Parable and Paradox*, p. viii.

Kafkan unity of meaning in the narration does not allow the narrator to manipulate his characters like a puppeteer or to explain the external facts and the external course of events to the reader through some knowledge he possesses by virtue of his detachment . . ." One has before him, in Kafka's works, merely a picture—the picture of a pure fiction. "In his *Gespräche mit Kafka* Gustav Janouch records a remark which deals with this problem quite unequivocally. In a conversation concerning the short story, *The Stoker,* the writer said the following: 'I was not describing a person. I was not telling a tale. Those are only pictures, only pictures.' This is not just a feature of one short story, it concerns a method, it has a bearing on his work in its entirety. In Kafka's writings we do not find Prague as, say, one finds Lübeck in Thomas Mann, for he [Kafka] 'was not depicting a town.' "[3] Mann attempts to reproduce a pre-existent reality; Kafka's close realistic descriptions of details begin to create a picture. Mann paints landscapes—Lübeck, an Alpine sanatorium—whereas Kafka creates isolated details suggesting landscape. Whether it be Prague or a country village or America matters not at all, because the created fiction alone is present; one has no recourse to any original from which to enter into the Kafka story.

There remains only one further possibility—the unity of meaning itself. The internal point of view of which LeSage spoke is the key to the work's style. The reader must be able to see the events with the narrator's eyes and, on that level to limit himself to the narrator's limitations. For the narrator's vision, total in its realism, is one with the style; the narrator can do no more than describe what he sees and what he believes he feels in reaction to what he sees. No explanation is forthcoming either for the picture viewed or for the reaction felt. The protagonist of the story is one with the narrator, even when, as Beissner says, the character speaks of himself in the third person.[4] The reader, in order to realize this unity in point of view, must place

---

[3] Laurent LeSage, *The French New Novel,* p. 27; Friedrich Beissner, "Kafka the Artist," published by W. Kohlhammer Verlag, as translated in *Kafka: A Collection of Critical Essays,* ed. Ronald Gray, © 1962, Prentice-Hall, Inc., Englewood Cliffs, N.J., p. 142 (all quotation from this article by permission of the publisher); Emanuel Frynta, *Kafka and Prague,* p. 11.

[4] Beissner, "Kafka the Artist," in *Kafka,* ed. Gray, p. 18.

himself in the position of the narrator and perceive the world with equivalent eyes; the reader must be led through the story by the narrating consciousness. Read from an external point of view the story would be misunderstood; the fabulation can be recognized as a unified structure only when the narrating voice is recognized as itself a fictional entity. The reader who cannot limit himself to the protagonist's point of view is made to feel uncomfortable. His only recourse to any previously known rationality is to interpret the phenomena he experiences in terms he can understand; and there he makes his mistake.

Within Kafka's vision all is equally valid; the hierarchy of observations that exist in normal empirical contexts cannot be related to Kafka's descriptions. If one wants to speak at all of empiricism with regard to Kafka, it must be in Eliseo Vivas's sense: "Kafka's empiricism differs radically from that which is fashionable today—that which constitutes the foundations of scientific naturalism—since the latter has been devised in order to deny the evidence which experience presents of its lack of self-sufficiency, while Kafka through an empirical examination of human existence is led to assert its dependence on transcending factors."[5] Kafka's empiricism depends, that is, on the conscious mind that reports human existence.

The pattern of most of Kafka's stories is a repeated constant. Speaking of The Metamorphosis, Johannes Pfeiffer says: "Leaving out of consideration the last five pages . . . , all events are seen with a quite dictatorial one-sidedness through the eyes of Gregor—the main character who dominates everything. Any attempt to disregard this fact, so vital for the meaning of the whole story, and to transfer this center of gravity to the family, disturbed and distracted by Gregor's transformation, amounts to arbitrary distortion." And not the stories alone: the novels are equally controlled by this unity of view.[6] No didacticist, no interpreter, is available. Whether the struc-

---

[5] Eliseo Vivas, "Kafka's Distorted Mask," in Creation and Discovery, p. 40.

[6] Johannes Pfeiffer, "The Metamorphosis," in Kafka, ed. Gray, pp. 53–60. "The reader will . . . see . . . from this unitary point of view, the impressive coherence of the great novels, in which characters other than the main one also appear. . . . if the reader of The Castle takes the account of the landlady of the Bridge Inn doing this or that as implying that the land surveyor K. hears her

ture of the entire narrative or merely one word is to be examined, no help will come from the author. Yet each word present has its purpose, each word can be explained without being interpreted. Choosing an unusual example from among Kafka's words and over-elaborating upon it, Gunther Anders points out that Kafka

> . . . uses the word "Odradek" to describe an object the function of which seems to lie in its having no function. But the introduction of this "meaningless" object with an apparently meaningless name is, in fact, as meaningful as the introduction of falsely labelled objects. This object puts us in mind of those many things and machines which modern man has to use day by day, even though what they accomplish seems to have no direct bearing upon what man really desires and needs. In countless ways modern man comes into contact with mechanical devices the workings of which are unknown to him and towards which—since their relationship to the complex of human needs is infinitely remote—he feels himself a stranger . . .[7]

Despite his insistence in talking of "modern man" as some generalized homogeneous mass, Anders correctly relates functionless labels on functionless objects to all labels on all objects and underscores the arbitrariness of a human vision that is forced by its nature to label things, correctly or falsely, in order to grasp them.

But one must examine in its entirety one of Kafka's stories in order to determine whether these generalizations are valid. Heinz Hillmann does this, but rather crudely, when he examines several fragments from the collection *Hochzeitsvorbereitungen auf dem Lande*;[8] Heinz Politzer employs this principle of integrated analysis and demonstrates Kafka's narrative integration—with great subtlety in the first chapter of his book on Kafka, the chapter dealing with the short narrative "Give It Up!"

---

say it, he will have gained a good deal in artistic understanding. Nothing happens without K.; nothing happens that has not some relationship to him, and nothing happens in his absence. Everything that happens, happens to him. And everything is told as clearly and as unclearly, as distortedly and as precisely, as he himself perceives it in his disappointment, his vexation, and his weariness. The 'writer' does not stand beside him, explaining, teaching, and reflecting" (Beissner, "Kafka the Artist," in *Kafka*, ed. Gray, p. 26).

[7] Gunther Anders, *Franz Kafka*, p. 2.

[8] Heinz Hillmann, *Franz Kafka: Dichtungstheorie und Dichtungsgestalt*, pp. 113–152.

Among the most typical of Kafka's fictions, "The Judgment" employs narrative consciousness almost completely; at the instant it lets up, the exception has proven the rule. From the beginning, the narration of "The Judgment" is analogous in its blinkered vision to the other stories: to understand Georg one must stand in his shoes. Beissner points out that "this story is clearly imbued with the retrospective thoughts of Georg himself, who 'on a Sunday morning in the very height of spring' has just finished a letter to a friend who has been living abroad for some time past, and is sitting contemplatively at the window." Partially relevant but not essential to a discussion such as this is that Kafka's own understanding of the story demanded that everything be seen from Georg's eyes. The conclusion is impossible to avoid if the story is to be understood: Beissner notes that the narrator "has completely transformed himself into the lonely Georg, even when he talks about him in the third person. And Georg is, from an external point of view, the only character in a story that is—to all intents and purposes—a monologue."[9]

Georg's vision of the world, as the story describes it, should not be confused with the concepts either of first or of third person point of view. That it is not third person point of view should by now be obvious; the story cannot be understood from outside itself. That it is not first person is also obvious—not only is the "I" of such narration absent, but empirical, "realistic" first person narration is also undiscoverable. A first person narrator usually tells a story as it happened in the past, in which case he has nothing to learn as the story progresses. (Although he can pretend he is learning, for consistency's sake he must be aware of everything from the beginning—the best example might be Ford Madox Ford's *The Good Soldier*.) Or he tells the story as it happens, in which case he is totally ignorant that a story is unfolding, and simply records events, learning with the reader as the events take place (the novel in journal or letter form is the nearest example of this). But in the work of Kafka, the narrator does not, as far as the reader knows, learn anything. He is merely an observer, as ignorant at the end as he is at the beginning.

[9] Beissner, "Kafka the Artist," in *Kafka*, ed. Gray, pp. 23, 25.

The narrator's metaphysical awareness of his impending psychic death is nothing more than an acceptance of his final moment. The action has shown him nothing (which is to say, in no way can the reader ascertain if the protagonist has learned anything), for the narrative has dealt only with the conscious faculties of the protagonist, objects have been described only as the protagonist sees them at the moment. Although the narration is totally subjective, the reader can also view the protagonist's action objectively: the protagonist is seen seeing and, at the same time, what he sees is described to the reader.

Almost any narrative demonstrates this principle. As long as the story is read through the filter of the narrator's consciousness, the reader remembers the narrator's consistent unawareness of his own limited, prejudiced reporting. One knows what is happening only according to the narrator's subjectivity; the external world is rendered incomplete, edited by the narrator's eye. Consequently, the events that shape Kafka's fiction can be comprehended only if one remembers that their significance derives from point of view.

It is difficult to distinguish in importance the several events of Josef K.'s or Georg Bendemann's life if one does not see from within the character's consciousness his reaction to events as he lives them. Incidents it may otherwise appear arbitrary to stress become, when seen by the reader, natural emphases in the life cycle of Kafka's characters; they stand out when the reader recognizes their function within the internal narrative. Only Gregor Samsa himself, for example, could know, at the instant of his awakening, that his dreams had been "uneasy." And with the opening words of *The Trial*— "Someone must have traduced Josef K."—it should be immediately clear that Josef K. is explaining to himself the background of the situation in which he has so suddenly found himself. He alone is capable of claiming he had done nothing wrong—". . . for without having done anything wrong . . ."—and he protests too much. An omniscient narrator would have attempted to bring back to Josef K.'s mind the many minor misdemeanors he might at one time have committed; only Josef K. himself would immediately claim absolute innocence.

The short parable "In the Caravansery" goes far toward establishing the nature of narrative consciousness, for it shifts, at about the
center, from general statements of the situation to a personalized
point of view—from the third person pronoun "one" to the definite,
first person "I." An early phrase does parenthetically add to an
observation, "or at least so it seemed to me" (PP 110), but its impact
is lost in the consistency of the "one" phrases that follow. The narrative begins with a description that is very personal, very limited by
the point of view describing the caravansery. Phrases such as "What
was unpleasant, now . . ." and "It looked almost as though . . ." (PP
113) take all attention away from any possible "I" in an attempt to
generalize, impersonalize, and thereby verify the events and situations. But it is most definitely a single consciousness at work, describing and dominating in accord with its own prejudices. When the
narrator verbalizes his presence, the subjectivity of the previous
description becomes apparent and relaxes the tension between the
actual nature of external situations and the manner in which they are
described.

K., attempting to reach the castle by telephone, moves in his mind
from pondering over his situation, his separateness from the castle,
to a realization that things have indeed changed, perhaps irremedi-
ably. Trying earnestly for some time to have the voice at the other end
believe him, he finally gives up: "He felt like laying down the receiver. He had ceased to expect anything from this conversation"
(C 28). Formally, the narrator rather than K. is speaking here, yet
the thoughts are K.'s—they cannot belong to an omniscient narrator.
Similarly, the castle, which K. knows to be the seat of those who
control his destiny, is for a moment early in the narrative nothing
more than a few interconnected small houses; but as the novel develops the *Städtchen*, the small town, takes on monstrous proportions
until in K.'s mind it really is seen as a castle, or at least as a *Schloss*
that locks him out.

Especially in indirect discourse the third person pronoun "he" can
be replaced by the first person pronoun "I"; the many imperatives
of personal necessity fall more easily into the first person pattern.
Yet one rarely thinks of oneself in the first person. One may voice an

"I," but when thinking of oneself a mental picture of oneself most often replaces the pronoun. This form of objectification is presented fictionally by Kafka through *erlebte Rede* (*style indirect libre*), twice removed because it is difficult for the reader to stand exterior to the situation if the narrative itself is controlled by an internal point of view. For example, when Josef K. realizes he must fight his case in court, he decides to do so without a moment's hesitation. The immediacy of his decision and the proximity of his mind are startling only if the reader remains outside Kafka's point of view—only such externality will allow the equation that calls this passage "Kafka-esque" (descriptive but meaningless) and labels the technique "absurd" (anthropomorphization). ". . . his mind was made up, to keep the appointment on Sunday, it was absolutely essential, the case was getting under way and he must fight it; this first interrogation must [*sollte*] also be the last" (T 40). An imperative combined with a conditional leaves the reader behind if he is unaware of the reinforcing point of view. Gregor Samsa thinks in much the same way. In *"The Metamorphosis,"* the early shift from obvious, conscious *erlebte Rede* to a third person narration conceals for unwary eyes the continuation of a single voice:

What has happened to me? he thought. It was no dream. His room, a regular human bedroom, only rather too small, lay quiet between the two familiar walls. Above the table on which a collection of cloth samples was unpacked and spread out—Samsa was a commercial traveler—hung the picture which he had recently cut out of an illustrated magazine and put into a pretty frame. It showed a lady, with a fur cap on and a fur stole, sitting upright and holding out to the spectator a huge fur muff into which the whole of her forearm had vanished! (PC 67)

Later, at the moment of his death, no retrospective glance is possible for Gregor. His narrating consciousness reports only the present moment, the moment of overweaning weakness: "This did not surprise him, rather it seemed immaterial that he should ever actually have been able to move on these feeble little legs" (PC 127).

Josef K.'s death too is seen from his own point of view. The gentleman does not lay his hands on Josef K.'s neck, rather (from Josef K.'s point of view) the hands lay themselves on his neck: ". . . an K.'s

Gurgel legten sich die Hände des einen Herrn" (P 239). But action by anthropomorphized hands is valid only if anthropomorphized by Josef K. He also watches his death as he dies, and comments himself that his death is like a dog's—the last phrase of the novel is his last thought. He cannot mention the instant of his death, for it is his conscious mind that reports the proceedings: to the dying moment of his conscious mind, "It was as if the shame of it must outlive him" (T 286).

The country doctor is perhaps the most blind and the most pathetic of Kafka's narrators; his intense self-centeredness destroys any chance he may have for seeing his own weaknesses with objective clarity. The story, told in the first person but in the past tense (the present tense later establishes a frame) is an example of Kafka's use of the retrospective point of view wherein a narrator places himself back in the situation through which he has lived, while remaining as blind to his reactions as when he first lived through the story. The narrative has a frame—the doctor is apparently relating the events on his way back to his own village on a ride that appears to take forever—but the frame is not discovered until the end. As the doctor retells the story, his retrospective narration begins to take on the tone of a compelled confession, but one that allows the doctor merely to relive, without self-analysis, his recent past. It could not be otherwise, for even in his final despair he is too involved with himself in his immediate situation to abstract some truth about the relation between himself and his patient in the country.

The doctor considers himself a misunderstood martyr, devoting his life to unappreciative country folk who neither understand nor really respect him, but the reader comes to realize that the doctor uses his self-assigned martyrdom to excuse himself from other responsibilities. Called to a patient during a severe blizzard, he discovers that his horse has died during the night. In anger he kicks at a pigsty door; it opens and a man, apparently a groom, appears and offers the doctor two powerful, fiery horses and a carriage. The doctor accepts the offer as his due, not at all questioning the source—at least no question is present in the details he bothers to mention. In exchange for the horses, the man must have the doctor's servant girl;

as she helps the groom harness the horses he bites her cheek. The doctor is furious, yet consciously he finds what for him is a sufficient excuse: the man is a stranger. Actually to whip the groom would mean not going to the patient through the blizzard, not being the martyr with a single-tracked mind; it would mean taking some responsibility for the servant girl. So he accepts, in silence and consciously happy, the groom's barter: " 'Get in,' he said then, and indeed, everything was ready. A magnificent pair of horses, I observed, such as I had never sat behind, and I climbed in happily" (PC 137). Although at this point he still claims that Rosa, the servant girl, is coming with him, he lets slip his acceptance of the deal already concluded in his mind: Rosa flees "with a justified presentiment that her fate was inescapable" (PC 138). Paying lip service to his responsibility for Rosa, he attempts to convince the reader of his confession that in fact he has been forced to come to a decision within this conflict situation, and duty to his patient has won out.

So concerned is he with the decision he has just made that the trip to the patient, to which he has not been paying attention, seems to take place in a matter of seconds; he does not report the thoughts that keep his eyes from seeing the passing countryside, and he is immediately present at the ill boy's farm. Even as he examines the boy his self-centeredness, his concern for his own problem, blinds him to the situation at hand, and he literally does not see the boy's wound. The boy, who asks the doctor to let him die, is according to the doctor "gaunt, without any fever, not cold, not warm, with vacant eyes, without a shirt"; the doctor sees nothing more. His mind returns to the horses, to the groom, and then finally back to Rosa; he has refrained from thinking about her for as long as possible, but her memory breaks through to his conscious mind. Nevertheless his attention shifts quickly back to the miserable situation in which he finds himself; he refuses a glass of rum, then accepts it, ignores the warning of the horse's whinny outside, and reaffirms in his mind that the boy is quite well. Immediately thereafter his thoughts turn only to himself; he bemoans his fate: "I was no world reformer and so I let him lie. I was the district doctor and did my duty to the uttermost, to the point where it became almost too much. I was badly paid and yet generous and helpful to the poor. I had still to see that Rosa was all right, and then the boy might have his way and I wanted to die too. What was I doing there in that endless winter!" (PC 139–140). His momentary wish to die, a motif picked up later, remains consistent with a desire to extricate himself from what begins to appear as a decision with which he has not yet come to terms. Seeing no illness in the boy, his guilt at having abandoned Rosa chagrins him; his lament never ceases.

The domination of his conscious mind by thoughts of Rosa is re-emphasized by the horses' whinnying outside. All of a sudden, as if a blanket had been pulled away, he sees the boy's rosy wound; the association of color is not accidental. Having become at last aware of the boy's illness, he presumably exaggerates the wound as if to make up, in his mind, for time and description lost to thoughts only of himself. The description, growing in grotesque detail as the nar-rator's eye moves closer toward the wound, corresponds to the in-creasing guilt of having betrayed both responsibilities. He is un-aware of it consciously, but everything he now feels and hears is filtered through his overpowering guilt. His failure both as a doctor and as a man, from the point of view of his guilt, leaves him feeling naked and helpless. Having admitted his naked helplessness, his refusal to be dominated by fear allows him to believe himself in control of the situation, so that when it seems to him the people in the house carry him, naked, to a place in the bed beside the ill boy, he remains composed, equal to the situation.

Having coped with the boy as best he can (not well, considering the wound he has described), he feels the need to save Rosa and redeem himself as a man. He rushes to his horses, hoping the return to the village will be as quick as the trip out, but his mind is on the goal, and the ten miles back pass with the slowness of eternity; nothing but the impossibility of rescuing Rosa comes to his mind, rendering his actions on both sides of the conflict failures.

Like "A Country Doctor," "The Judgment" is the story of individu-al failure. Georg Bendemann has finished a letter and is sitting by the window. The moment is tranquil; there is little emotion. It is a time when statements may still be accepted with a reasonable assurance of their validity. At least, if one is to have any information at all, any assurance that something more than, as Beissner says, mere "dreamlike inner life" is in question here,[10] one must accept the probable "facts" that Georg is recently engaged, that Georg has just written a letter, telling of his engagement, to someone he calls a friend who has moved to Russia, and that Georg lives in the same house as his father, who is in another room at this moment. More need not be assumed; these "facts" are agreed upon by all elements in the story.

Georg's first glance is directed toward the friend. After some cursory and, we assume, factual comments (except for asides, which explain that the friend had run away, that the friend's presence in Petersburg is useless, and that the friend has directed his life toward permanent bachelorhood), Georg's mind begins to interpret. The narrative explains that the friend has gone in the wrong direction: "What could one write to such a man, who had obviously run off the rails, a man one could be sorry for but could not help" (PC 50). Here Georg himself is obviously talking, although the artificiality of third person narration distances the thought at first. The friend is in Russia, certainly, but only from Georg's interpretation of his friend's situation in Russia does one learn that his position is unpleasant. From the facts given, the disparity between any reality they possess and Georg's interpretation of them becomes evident. The friend may indeed be in a bad financial situation, he may indeed be wasting his life in Russia, the skin of his face may indeed be growing yellow in indication of a disease—but if all this is true, one knows it neither from what the friend tells the reader, nor from what the friend tells Georg, but from Georg's interpretation of what his friend has told him (or, one must assume, as from the yellow pallor of the skin, from what Georg has seen; but Georg has not seen his friend for some years). Georg has already filtered the facts through his mind and presented the reader with his own conclusion. But interpretation of scattered facts is a common enough characteristic of a human mind that creates form and pattern—rational explanation—from briefly

---

[10] *Ibid.*, p. 25.

glimpsed, partially seen circumstances. Georg cannot yet be blamed either for concealment of information or for mistaken interpretation.

But when Georg implies his friend is beyond help, he has overstated the situation in order to avoid involvement and responsibility. It is Georg himself who has brought the argument to a point where the friend now has, in all probability, "neither friends or a country of his own any longer, wouldn't it have been better for him to stay abroad just as he was? Taking all this into account, how could one be sure that he would make a success of life at home?" (PC 50). Georg feels the friend is beyond help, but whether the friend is actually beyond help is at best a moot point. The inadequacy, the inability to cope with a situation, is not necessarily the friend's, though of course it may be that also; it is at least as much Georg's own fault. Georg has taken the friend's words—that the latter is out of touch with business problems in his old country—and turned them against the friend. The implication is that the friend would be alone wherever he went, but it is Georg who has made of this possibility a value judgment and labeled such aloneness bad.

By the end of his rationalization Georg has portrayed his friend not only as weak and alone, but also as unworthy of help. The whole case has been built of a few statements from the friend, which Georg has interpreted. Assuming that his own interpretations were correct, he has reacted according to them alone, thereby discrediting the friend and forcing him to remain as alone as Georg has already judged him to be. The rejection of the friend could well be a rejection of Georg's idea of the friend. Georg pushes the friend yet further from him, further than the remotest acquaintance, although the friend himself remains unchanged.

Georg continues to cite evidence and interpret it. The friend alone, and not he, is the cause for the rupture in their relationship: it has been three years since the friend's last visit. The friend, says Georg, attributes his long absence to political circumstances in Russia. Georg claims, in a necessarily exaggerated tone, that hundreds of thousands of Russians do travel peacefully (*ruhig*) abroad. Georg's constant voice is again apparent: first, he is not sure how many Russians are abroad and so grasps at an inexact, general figure; second, he never can know if the Russian travelers are truly *ruhig*. Probably he is right, and the friend is merely offering potential political upheaval as an excuse for not wanting to visit Georg, but in his reading of the excuse Georg is interpreting his friend's actions. Out of guesses originating in himself he prejudices further the case against a so-far innocent friend.

Extremely important is the sentence immediately following this charge that the friend is afraid to travel. It reads: "But during these three years Georg's own position in life had changed a lot" (PC 51). The switch to Georg himself (without so much as a change of paragraphs) in the very sentence following the final accusation against the friend strongly suggests that Georg's mind is on himself, having switched to himself so directly that even while using the idiom of friendship he has been talking about himself. Instead of running the paragraph on, he could have easily begun a new paragraph after the statement about the hundred thousand Russians; the preceding information had been a continuous whole, dealing only with the friend. A less subjective text would make the logical shift into a new paragraph after mention of the traveling Russians, but here no such shift can be found, for Georg's thoughts, as narrative and as self-justifying consciousness, continue in the same vein.

The friend enters the narrative again briefly, only long enough for Georg once more to misinterpret his actions. Two years ago the friend had learned of Georg's mother's death, and had "expressed his sympathy in a letter phrased so drily that the grief caused by such an event, one had to conclude, could not be realized in a distant country" (PC 51). The dryness of the note, another judgment by Georg, is seen as the man's unfriendliness in order to justify Georg's own unfriendliness. Yet the letter Georg is about to mail is as dry, as unfriendly as he imputes his friend's to have been. Georg himself has said it was impossible for him to write anything of consequence— nothing more than words one might write to a distant acquaintance. That the friend's nature should so closely correspond to Georg's constantly shifting needs is appropriate, since the friend is wholly Georg's creation. Although he may actually exist in Russia, his many attributes are of Georg's own making. At this point in the story, the process of the invention has not yet become clear, however.

The final sentence of this paragraph, the one beginning "Perhaps during his mother's lifetime . . . ," is characteristic and very important to the physical composition of Kafka's style.[11] It is one sentence made up of five sentences. There are no relative clauses—the several phrases between the first *perhaps* and the final period are all complete sentences, each capable of standing alone. The effect of running several sentences together is linked closely with a repeated return to the opening word, *perhaps*, three times within those five sentences: by using *perhaps*, Kafka attempts to refrain from giving the character the certainty of the absolute knowledge of causation. Kafka is not explaining that all these *perhapses*—the father's loss of aggressiveness, the possible good fortune—have brought about the success of the father and son in business. Georg can never be held responsible for having said so, yet he has nonetheless established these possibilities as the actual causes that both Georg and the reader's mind accept without further question. But the reader can only assume them to be true, he can never prove them so. The third *perhaps*, which Georg has decided to fortify by explanation, is the one expressing the possibility of good fortune—the vaguest, most difficult *perhaps* to define. Physically noticeable changes, such as the father's decreased control, could be accepted by the reader as describable, explainable phenomena; merely citing "accidental good fortune" explains nothing—the term is only a gloss, a phrase that conceals certain further, but here unmentioned, events. Yet Georg decides to elaborate—one is uncertain of his reason. Georg will not, apparently, accept the possibility that it is his own promotion to the company's command that has provided the soundness of their business activities with an added advantage. At any rate, the structure of the sentence obscures the lack of causality. Description of the situation only as it appears on the surface must set aside all explanations of causality, be they valid or not; causality is lost within the

<hr />

[11] In the German text, the sentence beginning "Vielleicht hatte ihn . . ." In the English text, the sentence is a paragraph by itself.

undivided phrases, which, if properly punctuated, would form five sentences. Instead, the one-sentence structure forces the reader to think ahead toward the conclusion; he is aware of the lack of logic only when he has finished the sentence, when his mind is allowed a chance to reflect. Lack of causality disappears into the commas; full stops would have permitted the reader to pause and ponder the development's validity.

Immediately thereafter, the letter of condolence is mentioned in a brief relative phrase, again with the word *perhaps*. The letter, one now learns, probably asked Georg to come to Russia. It was therefore a warmer letter than Georg initially implied; at least, if Georg can admit that such a letter arrived, his memory of it (when he is not attacking it as being cold) is no longer so opposed to it. Its imputed coldness may well have resulted from the usual uncomfortable tone of condolence, which Georg had interpreted as his own mood demanded. Here it is again Georg who remains cold in his letters, not even telling his friend anything of the expanded business—his apparently kind, helpful friend who had invited him to come to Russia specifically to expand his business—precisely his own kind of business, as the friend had emphasized. Furthermore, Georg feels uncomfortable by the necessity to explain *now* that his business has expanded: ". . . if he were to do it now retrospectively that certainly would look peculiar" (PC 52). Such an explanation seems peculiar to Georg himself; at no time does Georg say that the explanation would look peculiar to the friend. The reader has no proof that it will; he has only Georg's fear that it might.

Worthy of speculation, too, is the content of those letters Georg has been writing to his friend over the years. Georg gives the impression that the friend is in Russia, yearning for connection with hometown acquaintances. The friend, it appears by Georg's own indirect admission, is far from such a state; only Georg's continued misinterpretation of the few available facts leads him to believe so. Georg assumes he knows the picture of the hometown that his friend has built up while in Russia. The irrelevancies about which Georg talks in his letters, picked up by the friend, show that the friend has no more connection with or interest in his hometown than what Georg writes him. (And, advancing one step further, the friend has no more connection with Georg than the letters exchanged by the two; the only remaining proof of the friend's reality are the letters received from him.) The reader is left with only Georg's assumption that the friend is interested in the hometown; in much the same way, the earlier part of the story, the speculation about the friend, has emanated from the character and nature of Georg.

Georg refuses to write of actual events, of what is really taking place about him—of what might be of more than artificial interest to his friend. Georg holds back the news that he has become engaged until the last moment; he engages in small talk rather than speaking seriously about himself. When he finally decides to write the letter about his engagement—too late for his friend to make plans to come all the way from Russia for the wedding—he shows once more a superficiality of thought that the friend could well understand as coldness toward him (the same dryness and coldness of which Georg has accused his friend). Georg refers to his fiancée with the hackneyed phrase, "a girl from a well-to-do family" (PC 52, 53), which he uses when thinking of her himself; such a phrase tells his friend nothing and shows the reader merely that Georg has an inordinate desire for propriety, in marriage as in the rest of his life. He decides to write after all only when, together with his fiancée, he has considered all the pros and cons of such communication and concluded that it could cause no harm.

Immediately after deciding to write, he thinks to himself: "That's the kind of man I am, and he'll just have to take me as I am . . . I can't cut myself to another pattern that might make a more suitable friend for him" (PC 53). The points of understanding have now become reversed; Georg assumes that his friend sees him in a way other than he is, and he (Georg) refuses to act according to his idea of his friend's idea of him. The reversal, which at this point in the narrative still appears acceptable in a quick reading, forms much of the background for the first part. Georg, a not highly conscious being, is acting the part that in his own eyes appears to be himself; this part, he imagines, is not what his friend sees, but Georg refuses to accommodate himself to this friend; and when, later, the existence of the friend (outside Georg's unimaginative mind) becomes highly dubious, the reader who is uncertain on which of several shifting grounds to stand loses his balance completely and thereby loses the thread of the narrative—unless he can follow it from within Georg's mind. In writing to his friend, Georg is already so much on the defensive against an apparently nonexistent offensive that he appears to fight a shadow. After repeating the only description of his fiancée that he can muster —"a girl from a well-to-do family"—he dismisses any attachment the friend might have to her by saying that she is one "who only came to live here a long time after you went away, *so that you're hardly likely to know her*" (PC 53; my italics). Such offensive division is hardly necessary, but it does set up the conclusion of the letter, wherein Georg implies that, since there is no connection between the friend and the girl, the friend need not come to the wedding. At long last Georg has extended the invitation to the friend, but in the most backhanded, halfhearted way; he adds as the letter's last words: "Still, however that may be, do just as seems good to you without regarding any interests but your own" (PC 53). The phrasing is polite, of course, but the undertone says, "Be selfish; we all are." The selfishness Georg implores his friend to maintain is Georg's own, which he assumes exists in all others. Nor is this the matter of kindness that Georg makes it appear to be; rather it is his selfishness imposed onto the friend—Georg has, after all, waited until too late to invite the friend to the wedding.

So the introduction ends; Georg places the letter in his pocket and goes into his father's room across the hall. He has not been in the room for months. Although such absence from the room is unusual, it is on the whole natural enough if he had been involved with himself for so long a time. His already implied selfishness and the fact of his recent engagement are sufficient reason for his absence. Then why mention it? Why go even further and mention a couple of excuses for not being in the room recently? Assuming, as one by now must, that Georg himself is the narrating consciousness, there are two probable reasons. First, he does so in order to draw attention from himself, for otherwise a reader might return to the previous pages in his search of an explanation. Second, Georg has to underscore his several months' absence; there must have been dozens of other daily acts Georg had not committed in the past months, and, if a thing is not done, there is normally no need to mention it. Not doing a habitual or likely act becomes important in a world where each act is noted, where each viewed phenomenon is worthy of description. Georg must mention an act omitted, but as he does so he finds himself once more on the defensive. No one is arguing with him when he says that he and his father spend the evenings doing what each one prefers— "In the evening, *it was true* ["zwar"], each did as he pleased . . ." (PC 54; my italics)—yet in his discomfort he feels compelled to defend himself against an unseen antagonist.

The first disarrangement in his daily scheme to awaken Georg from his reverie is the darkness in his father's room. He is, all of a sudden, on the alert, whereas just moments before he had barely acknowledged the greeting of a friend who passed on the street by his window. He notices his father is reading a newspaper held far away from him. The father has difficulty seeing. Georg's only thought is, "My father is still a giant of a man" (PC 54), as he sees the old man coming toward him; to the reader the thought sounds strange within this context unless two preconceptions are realized. First, it must be assumed that Georg had always conceived of his father as a giant of a man. It is a reasonable description, for the old man had attained some stature, both in the business and in the home when Georg's mother was alive; any possible decline in his father's literal and figurative stature could only have taken place after the death of his mother. Second, the expression of such a conception assumes that Georg may for the moment have doubted his father's stature as businessman and parent/invalid, either because he had seen correctly and the size of his father's body and influence were actually decreasing, or because he had seen incorrectly and merely desired a decrease in the father's stature, a wish he now thinks to have been in vain. Doubt of his previous opinion must still be occupying his mind when in the subsequent conversation with his father his mind follows only one track:

"And you've shut the window, too?"
"I prefer it like that."

"Well, it's quite warm outside," said Georg, as if continuing his previous remark, and sat down. (PC 54)

Georg is talking, making words, but he thinks neither of what his father is saying nor of his own speeches. He pays little attention to his father's statement; the conversation of one passes by the conversation of the other. This lack of relation emphasizes once more Georg's self-centeredness (possibly the father's also, but we are less interested in him at the moment; also the father seems to be reacting as if he were an extension of the son). But the implication from the phrase is that Georg has continued his own previous remark, a remark that is in fact no more connected with his present statement than it was with his father's comment. The conversation has a twofold irrelevance: Georg's comment is unrelated to his father's words and bears little relation to his own previous phrase.

An embarrassing conversation between Georg and his father ensues; Georg cannot meet his father's eye. The first part of the conversation is controlled by Georg, who talks about his friend in Petersburg. The father limits himself to interjected questions, the answers to which are already implicit, or even explicit, in Georg's previous comments. When Georg speaks of his friend's character, he tells his father that the facts he is mentioning are already familiar to the father: " 'Oh yes. To your friend,' said his father with peculiar emphasis. 'Well, *you know, Father*, that I wanted not to tell him about my engagement at first. Out of consideration for him, that was the only reason. *You know yourself* he's a difficult man' " (PC 55; my italics). He tries to force "facts" onto his father, hoping that it was still possible that he had been correct before—that his father's stature of mind had declined. Even in these few words he is on the defensive, suggesting that his silence about the engagement until this time was totally out of consideration for the friend.

But the father has a direction of his own; he has been listening and at last interrupts; his voice is questioning and doubting. To this point Georg's voice alone has been heard; those few phrases of the father's until "Georg, listen to me!" are repetitions of Georg's words. The father's voice sets up a point of reference outside Georg's narrating mind; as such it has a double relevance. First, it suggests strongly that Georg is not telling the whole truth, neither to the father nor, by implication, to the reader: the father has doubts about Georg's friend. Second, the father himself cannot be trusted by the reader, for he interprets observed incident and situation with Georg's own facility —which, as a human being, he must. He refers, for example, to what has happened since the death of his wife (Georg's new authority in the business, Georg's engagement, Georg's distance from the father— everything is Georg's) as "things that aren't right" (PC 57) ("un-schöne Dinge" [E 59]). The only new phenomena are Georg's actions, which the father is interpreting negatively.

No sooner is the backhand accusation implied, however, than the father switches emphasis from Georg's recent actions to his own passive situation. The plot is like Georg's own, first seen in the nar-rative when Georg talks about his business responsibilities. Here the father combines from three to five sentences in one, and with each phrase shifts his emphasis from Georg to himself. The shift covers the movement from "unschöne Dinge" to the business to the father's con-dition. Drawing Georg's mind from the accusation made earlier, the shift allows the father his element of surprise when, in returning to the "unschöne Dinge," he can ask the son, quite blatantly but still in a semi-friendly manner, "Do you really have this friend in St. Peters-burg?" (PC 56).

Georg at last understands that his father sees the fabrication; he understands that all that follows will be different from his previous life. Georg is now on his own in a new world. His only immediate reaction is embarrassment, and his words are only tangentially rele-vant to the father's question: "Never mind my friends. A thousand friends wouldn't make up to me for my father" (PC 56). Were Georg of normal mind his attitude would be typical of the gentle evasions one hands the senile to avoid fuss. But he is defending his fabrication, he is challenged by his not yet senile father. In the next paragraph Georg attempts to shift their conversation from the question; he tries to make doubletalk sensible by using familiar subject matter. The shift is from the friend to a thousand friends to the father—on this last the emphasis is made and remains. The flow of language is smooth, but the paragraph contains five different subjects. Georg attempts, by subtle switches of emphasis, to slide them all by his father's admittedly weakened mind; he forgets totally his initial reaction to his father, that he is "still a giant of a man." The steps away from the subject are fivefold: 1) a thousand friends won't make up for his father; 2) the father is essential to the business; 3) the father must change rooms; 4) the doctor will come; 5) all the foregoing can wait, rest alone is needed.

The father, however, spoken to as if already senile, neither accepts the flow of argument nor follows Georg along any of the five false leads. He pronounces clearly that his son in fact has no friend in Petersburg, but then he weakens, possibly out of kindness to the son, possibly out of his own lack of total conviction now that his mind and body control have weakened. The weakness is sufficient to suggest to Georg that he could re-establish the fabrication of the friend. Groping for a moment of security in his present state—disconnected from the world that, he had convinced himself and others, alone was real—Georg attempts to reassert the original world. He does not realize that floundering only worsens his situation and, instead of returning him to the comfort of the world he had known, is merely the first step toward a total intrusion of the new world, from which there will be no escape. Georg attempts to use his old devices. He knows the reason for his presence in the room is to force rest upon his father, whereas he had, in fact, come in merely to tell the father about the letter. Only if the father were truly senile would he have approved of the letter, in which case he would really have needed rest. However, Georg's now saying his father needs rest represents nothing more than his hope transposed into words of feeble sympathy, into a weak attempt to return his father to the subservience established earlier.

Even the technique is not new. "Just think back a bit, Father" is totally reminiscent of "You know, Father" and "'You know yourself'" some pages back. Georg again switches subject; here his method is more subtle. His argument can gain in intensity only if he is able to force his father, who is definitely weak, to think he is beginning to forget. Georg points out that three years (that is, quite a while) have passed since the friend was last seen. The father disliked the friend;

therefore he may have forgotten him, he may have pushed the friend
out of his consciousness. Twice at least Georg had kept the father
from seeing the friend when he was visiting. But was he really visiting? An invisible friend is as good as none at all, and the reader has
only Georg's word for the friend's presence—Georg whom one cannot trust. Then the shift takes place: the father's dislike is understandable, says Georg, attempting sympathy for the father by way of
a reaction the father may never have had. Next the son expresses
pride in the friend. Surely the father remembers such moments when
he and the friend did meet; the son remembers well how proud
he felt. There is no reason for Georg to mention the pride except as a
further attempt to shift emphasis, to create a character at the moment, impressionistically—a detail here, an incident there. No logic
or reason unites the sentences, and there is, in all probability, no
unified individual to whom they pertain. Georg concludes the attempt
to stir the father's memory by claiming that the friend was the source
for one of the father's own stories, thereby trying to undermine by
infiltration his father's crumbling conscious powers.

During the explanation Georg is drawing his father's mind further
from the subject they had been discussing by undressing the old man
in order to put him to bed. He notices his father's dirty underwear
and feels responsible for it; the relevance of dirty underwear at this
point in the narrative becomes clear when the reader once more
recalls that he is seeing with Georg's eyes and accepting with his
mind. Georg feels no honest responsibility for allowing his father's
underwear to remain unwashed; at best he would (and does) say
he felt responsible; he might even convince himself that he thought
he felt responsibility. Still looking out through Georg's eyes, everything appears all right again when he has placed his father in the
bed. The vision of the world is still Georg's; all in fact is not well.
The father, ignoring Georg's attempts to end the conversation, insists on cutting back to the subject at hand. The conversation once
again shows both protagonists ignoring each other. This time the
father will not stand for it.

The old man reacts violently at last, wrenching all control from
his son. He tears the fiction of the friend from Georg and assumes it

himself, exaggerating the "facts," interpreting the "incidents," and adding to the fiction misinterpreted frustrations of his own that had been previously unconnected with the friend issue. The father has grown old. Either he really believes most of the fiction he is inventing, or he pretends to believe it; either is possible, but only his verbalization, his seizure of control, matters. He is not as doddering as Georg would like him to be; he overaccepts the friend story, but, knowing only what Georg has told him, he interprets the "facts" and adds his own.

Georg realizes that his situation has grown more perilous; there is now no way back to the secure world of his desk by the window where he had written the letter. The whole has become a *Schreckbild*; Georg no longer controls it. The father suddenly knows the friend too well; Georg has never before conceived of his friend in such terms. Georg's control even of the image of a friend is gone. Totality from the outside has intruded, the friend is part of it, and Georg has no contact with him. "Lost in the vastness of Russia he saw him. At the door of an empty plundered warehouse he saw him. Among the wreckage of his show cases, the slashed remnants of his wares, the falling gas brackets, he was just standing up. Why did he have to go so far away!" (PC 59). Georg's addition to the *Schreckbild* as mobilized by his father retains the image of the friend, but the image is falling apart. Georg has created the image (whether he has created the friend also is not the question), and now the creation has gotten away from him, has been used against him. The made image, once a unified whole, has been convincing only to Georg. The friend stands in the midst of his junk; imagistically, so does Georg.

Once the matter of the friend is seen as a question of image founded on need, several phenomena should be recognizable to the reader. First among these is the narrator's ability to verbalize Georg's great fear of his father. "Georg shrank into a corner, as far away from his father as possible. A long time ago he had firmly made up his mind to watch closely every least movement so that he should not be surprised by any indirect attack, a pounce from behind or above" (PC 60). The fear is deep-seated, dating back many years.

The father continues to play with the image as a fiction of his creation and to play a personal role in relation to the fiction. He stabs Georg to the quick with each new thrust. When he says he was the friend's representative, Georg can read the statement symbolically and can accept it as the truth: just as his relation to the friend in Russia is a lie, so is the relation to his beloved father.

Georg makes a final attempt at self-assertion by calling his father a comedian. But his father has laid this trap for him; the words are no sooner out of Georg's mouth than he regrets them, realizing the mistake. The whole has been a matter of comedy—play-acting by both of them—and Georg has named it so. The father agrees, responding in kind. He gets up high on the bed; Georg fears and even hopes the father will topple over and smash to the ground like a statue of a dictator, not like a human being; Georg has always seen his father in such a way and in the moment of crisis cannot switch the idiom.

But the father does not topple. Instead he shows himself to be even stronger because he has taken control over the image of the friend: ". . . your mother has given me so much of her strength that I've established a fine connection with your friend and I have your customers here in my pocket" (PC 61). Georg alters the figurative use of "pockets," in which the father has all of Georg's customers, and turns it into the literal "He has pockets even in his shirt!" (PC61). Georg's last vain attempt at making the father appear ridiculous in the eyes of a nonexistent third party to whom some form of justification might seem necessary succeeds only in drawing himself in the ridiculous terms by which he had hoped to portray his father. He himself becomes significant—incapable of running a business, incapable of self-control, and realizing neither.

The sting of the sentence is lost by the juxtaposition of the sentence that follows. Kafka, possibly not completely conscious of the need for the author to remain out of his story, allows himself, as creator, a comment: his personal intrusion into the narrational tone, and therefore into the domain of Georg, the narrator himself, gives the reader a moment of confusion. The two sentences read: " 'He has pockets even in his shirt!' said Georg to himself and believed that with this remark he could make him an impossible figure for all the world.

Only for a moment did he think so, *since he kept on forgetting every-thing"* (PC 61; my italics). Such a generalization goes far beyond anything Georg could say, especially about himself; the phrase is objectively true, it is Georg seen from the outside. And the outsider reporting it, a voice previously unheard and not necessary here, is Kafka.

But despite the intrusion, the narrative continues. The father has now wholly taken away from Georg control over the friend fiction: "I've been writing to him, for you forgot to take my writing things away from me" (PC 62), the father proclaims, rendering the fiction ever more absurd and himself more foolish in the process. Georg can no longer even argue with the old man, but he makes one last and spurious attempt at self-assertion, adopting even greater exag-geration than his father has used. The father shouts, talking about the friend: " 'He knows everything a thousand times better!' 'Ten thousand times!' said Georg, to make fun of his father, but in his very mouth the words turned into deadly earnest" (PC 62). And Georg succeeds only in making himself ridiculous once more.

By this time self-assertion is no longer possible; the only remaining realization is that everything has come to an end. The father accuses Georg of his one real sin, that sin for which he has been responsible from the beginning of his life and from the beginning of this narra-tive—his self-centeredness, his selfishness. Georg, once an innocent child, has become a devilish human being. At last the relationship to the fiancée also becomes clear: Georg has disregarded everyone to whom he owed responsibility—mother, father, created friend, even the fiancée Frieda, whom his father has mistakenly judged earlier as Georg's only center of attention—in his own self-centered life. He has lied to the fiancée about the friend, he has centered attention away from themselves and onto an external object, the friend, so that his and Frieda's attention could be aimed at himself alone as the sole communicant with the supposed friend. The father too has witnessed these events. He has misinterpreted the symptom, but diagnosed the disease.

The father sentences the son. The father is not sane, he is rather the declining, doddering old man who plays with Georg's watch chain while Georg carries him to bed. But neither is he insane. He knows he is being fed lies by Georg, but he does not try to avoid them. Instead he turns them around and forces them backward at the son, exaggerating them. His sentencing the son to death is an exaggeration also and, just as Georg is incapable of successful argument against his father by further exaggeration and elaboration (one thousand, says the father; ten thousand, says the son), so is he unable to negate his father's condemnation to death (an exaggeration) and must accept the judgment (further exaggeration). He brings to a logical conclusion his father's case.

Georg's last words—"Dear parents, I have always loved you" (PC 63)—are possibly true. But they are an interpretation of his feelings, they represent sensations Georg does not understand. The words may well be correct; the reader will never know. And the last words of the story—"At this moment an unending stream of traffic was just going over the bridge"—are Georg's also but they are his as narrator. They are his final observation; as he drops toward the water the traffic will always seem endless, but the life cycle will be complete.

Part II: BECKETT

3. The Form of Consciousness: Modified Patterns

WERE ONE TO ASK a collection of apparently intelligent readers and critics, their consensus would be that Beckett's fiction is without form; their consensus would be wrong. The all too easily confused relationship between form and plot would be at fault. If there is no apparent story, if the page presents nothing more than apparently disassociated gibberish, how can one speak of a form? And, many add, why should one bother? The answer to the second question becomes apparent as one responds to the first. There are plots that may not immediately appear to be telling a story. Martin Gerard points out that "plot is a device in which elements of surface realism and artificial drama are concocted into a scenario. . . . In Beckett's work the form is indigenous to the material; it has an analogical relationship to the meaning."[1] This is a newer kind of scenario; the camera of fiction stands at the necessary focal point and the subsequent form will be the camera's own. Realism is after all the goal of all art, and

[1] Martin Gerard, "Molloy Becomes Unnamable," *X: A Quarterly Review* 1, no. 4 (October, 1960): 315.

from the Beckettian point of view nothing is more real than the world
as seen from the eyes of a very average human being. In *Happy Days*
Winnie is not a suffering existential human being; she is, in all like-
lihood, neither more nor less than an average housewife. She claims
her days are happy; perhaps they are. Each Beckett character is able
to cope with his world because each day differs very little from each
preceding day and will differ almost not at all from the day to follow.
Within each day repeated action of some sort gives to the world, if
not meaning, at least the order of habit. "The existential experience
is thus felt as a succession of attempts to give shape to the void; when
nothing can lay claim to final, definitive reality, we enter a world of
games, or arbitrary actions structured to give the illusion of reality."[2]
If one generalizes all experience sufficiently, all experience will be
seen as a series of patterns or, perhaps, as one great pattern. In the
process, one must give up the specific pictures that differentiate one
moment from the next. And for the process of generalization to be
viewed by the reader, the author's narrating consciousness must pre-
side throughout; without this consciousness there will be no established point of view through which the patterns can appear. This is
not the generalization of philosophical fiction, however, for philosophical generalization implies abstractions immediately present in
the work, placed there by an author, a process alien to Beckett's
novels. In Beckett, generalization appears in the form of repetitions
that must be the result of continuous observance from one vantage
point, since objects appear and disappear with a regularity that the
mind translates into a pattern. For the Unnamable, events and people
pass by with repeated circularity. The narrator of *How It Is* lives
through the same corresponding patterns during three time periods
that may be generalized as a string of periods equivalent to those
which preceded and those which will come. Malone tells himself
stories that correspond through his own generalizations with the pattern through which he lives as he narrates.[3] The variation between

[2] Martin Esslin, introduction to Martin Esslin, ed., *Samuel Beckett: A Collection of Critical Essays*, © 1965. By permission of Prentice-Hall, Inc., Englewood Cliffs, N.J., p. 19.

[3] Even for the earlier heroes the same generalization may be made. "There
is an infinite number of possibilities for such games and series, such as patterns

stories lies in there being no form except as the repetitions are en-
forced into a pattern by the conscious mind and as such patterns are
shown to have relevance to the viewer, both conscious mind and the
reader. Thereupon the narrating consciousness becomes the point of
view, demanding of the reader that he place himself in the shoes of
the narrator in order to understand the world as viewed. This world,
when accepted by the reader, relates the patterns of a Beckett hero
to the reader's own world; the patterns seem to be asking him to
interpret as he reads in order to attempt an understanding of the
Beckett vision. In the succession of Beckett narratives the limits of
viewed horizon for each become increasingly generalized, the vision
more introspective; but the introspection never recedes into the unconscious. The reader's mind must coincide with the narrator's in
order to comprehend and so to create each form and each pattern.

To interpret these patterns as truths is a mistake. The characters
of the plays and stories simply *are*; they affirm no truth, they deny
no meaning. Each is the interiorization of his own universe, but one
can only begin to guess the nature of that universe from the few clues
extracted from that character's motions and words.[4] Beckett depicts
no more than ordinary encounters and ordinary situations—situations modified, of course, by his own idiom. His people, if more ar-
ticulate than the average housewife, are no more conscious. The job
set up for the writer is to lay bare the patterns inherent in the material with which he is dealing, in Beckett's words, "to find a form that
accommodates the mess, that is the task of the artist now." In that
sense each of his characters is an artist; the world itself is already
there, within the artist: ". . . the work of art is neither created nor

---

of existence. While none of them can lay claim to *meaning* anything beyond
itself, they nevertheless are worth our attention: they may not express reality
in terms of something outside itself, but they *are* reality, they *are* the world to
the consciousness which has produced them and which in turn *is* what it experiences" (Esslin, introduction to *Samuel Beckett*, p. 19).

[4] Hugh Kenner says of Beckett: "He stated that he knew very little about the
race of literary beings he called 'my people'; no more, in fact, than appears in
the books; this led to an ancedote about an actor who in despair threw over
the part of Pozzo when the author was unable to enlighten him on a dozen points
concerning the character's age, race, occupation, social status, education, philosophy of life . . ." (*Samuel Beckett: A Critical Study*, p. 10).

chosen, but discovered, uncovered, excavated, pre-existing within the artist, a law of his nature" (P 84). Or, as Christopher Middleton says, "Beckett's prose depicts the naked, the essential, . . . and furthermore with the imperturbable rhythm that animates all true works of art."[5]

There is form to Beckett's work, imposed on it by the author's vision or by the attempts of his "people" to render sensible their everyday experiences. Since the form is created by action in time, since the movement is temporal, the form must be considered as ritual, the repeated action of human event. Kenner has cited the example of Emmett Kelly to depict the path prescribed by ritual in Beckett's sense, and Fletcher adds that "one . . . expects, with the same assured anticipation with which one greets a clown, the Beckettian hero, in every tale, to execute certain ritual gestures, to submit to certain regular happenings."[6] The ritual of the character, the repetitions of his actions and the movement in the world he sees, slowly impresses itself onto the mind of the reader; it is a never-ending process in which stimuli from the page—the words of the narrating consciousness—force their way into the reader's own conscious mind. "Throughout Beckett's work this process is repetitive to the point of exhaustion. He must break every connection in order tentatively to establish new ones, which in turn will merge and alter, and this must be done by saturation so that the isolated assents of the reader's brain will give way to the reflex's pervasive recognition."[7]

The form I have been discussing is reminiscent of that which dominates Kafka's work—the pattern of the unsuccessful quest. It differs from Kafka's in its elimination of any tight relationship between the several steps that make up its progress—and the flow of circumstance into obstacle into defeat lies at the root of what certain critics have called the dreamlike nature of Beckett's prose. Beckett's quest,

[5] Christopher Middleton, "Randnotizen zu Romanen von Samuel Beckett," *Akzente* 4, no. 5 (October, 1957): 409.

[6] John Fletcher, *The Novels of Samuel Beckett* (London: Chatto and Windus, 1964), p. 28. All quotation by permission of the publisher.

[7] Josephine Jacobsen and William R. Mueller, *The Testament of Samuel Beckett* (New York: Hill and Wang, 1964), p. 43. All quotation by permission of the publisher.

unlike Kafka's, appears to be unmotivated, at least by any specific and personal cause. Certainly Moran is asked to go out to look for Molloy, and Molloy himself has begun the whole thing by journeying forth to see his mother, but such reasons are insufficient to explain the bulk of what follows. Instead of an explanation, the narrative becomes a line extending both forward and backward from the initial moment of nonmotivation. The content therefore is doubled: the normal and expected forward motion is present; but at the same time the narrative is interlaced with numerous suggestions of possible reasons for the quest's actually taking place; because these are intertwined with the forward movement, the whole may at times give the appearance of stasis. At the very least the apparently contradictory directions lend the narrative its tone of doubt as it attempts to explain itself. The original moment is followed by an initial (minor and external) impasse. Molloy is taken by the police, the old woman ceases to bring Malone his soup, the roar overwhelms Sapo's head—in each instance the hero is dominated by some external authority he cannot escape. Yet at the same time, at the moment, it appears as nothing more than a momentary hindrance. By the time the second impasse appears, however—the first having been disregarded or eliminated by accident—the hero's desire to continue has weakened substantially, so that his lack of will becomes accessory to external authority's effort in blocking the continued quest; forward thrust is weakened by the hero's accession to the demands of the impasse. As movement toward the goal slows down and begins to die, with it dies movement in the other part of the line, the movement toward some explanation for the existence of the quest itself. It is then not far to the fourth step in the process, when the hero realizes he is no longer interested in his project, when, although he continues to drag himself along, there is no longer any chance of his ever reaching his goal. All practical aspects of the quest are lost; at best a shell remains.

What shape the form of each quest takes has been debated at length: are the lines straight, or are they circular? In Moran's narrative, for example, it could be argued that, since he returns at the end to the beginning, the whole is circular in form, yet to conceive of it in this way weakens the story, for it denies ultimate temporal progress within the context. If the whole process is seen merely as a framed story, its development is far clearer.

Now there are two kinds of frames; either the frame is established beforehand (as in both halves of Molloy), or it is recognized at the end. But there is also the other kind of narrative, the one that takes place at the moment of recital. In the discussion of each passing moment—the mode of narration of Malone and of the Unnamable—the simultaneity of remembered and passing phenomena blends into an immediate narrative and eliminates the necessity, still present in Molloy's reminiscences, of the double trajectory—developing fabulation and search for explanation. Ruby Cohn says of the trilogy (counting "Molloy"/"Moran" as two narratives), ". . . the first two are accounts of quests in the past; in the second two the accounts *are* the quests."[8]

As Beckett's work develops, the pattern of the quest becomes ever more apparent; by generalizing his events and situations, he allows the reader, through each narrating consciousness, to delineate its outlines.[9] As the narrative proceeds, the futility of the whole quest becomes apparent, if not to the narrator, at least to the reader. The quest is omnipresent in the narrative, linking all disparate parts, from the apparent indecision of Molloy as the viewing narrator—

I don't work for money. For what then? I don't know. The truth is, I don't know much. For example my mother's death. Was she already dead when I came? Or did she die later, I mean enough to bury. I don't know. Perhaps they haven't buried her yet. (Tr 7)

—to the final forward thrust (ironically denied by its situation) of an affirming unnamed being: '. . . perhaps they have carried me to

---

[8] Ruby Cohn, *Samuel Beckett: The Comic Gamut* (New Brunswick, N.J.: Rutgers University Press, 1962), p. 115. All quotation by permission of the publisher.

[9] Germaine Brée, "L'Etrange Monde des 'grands articulés,' " in *Configurations Critiques*, no. 8, ed. Melvin J. Friedman. Mme Brée compounds the pattern by suggesting that it further involves a brief fight between the narrator and someone he meets. Though this is correct for several of the narrators, it cannot be generalized to include them all. She calls these protagonists "characters charged with a mission and endowed with a voice" (p. 89), and goes on to say, "The stories told are appreciably the same, unfolding in an increasingly simplified, epic and cyclical pattern that Beckett presents us with frequently: a trip, a search or an encounter, a fight, a separation, a return" (p. 94).

the threshold of my story, before the door that opens on my story, that would surprise me, if it opens, it will be I, it will be the silence, where I am, I don't know, I'll never know, in the silence you don't know, you must go on, I can't go on, I'll go on" (Tr 414).[10] Thus, the writing, "in spite of illogicality and surface chaos, bears no relation to the automatic writing of the surrealists, for the quest theme structures all the novels, down to the most apparently irrelevant detail."[11]

Implicit in the suggestion that one quest structures all Beckett's novels is the conclusion that his characters are the several incarnations of one protagonist. This is not to say that Molloy is Moran is Murphy is Watt is Malone or that each novel is a simple reiteration of the previous one or a plan for the next, but that the presence of a single quest structure implies that the life cycles of the several protagonists are closely parallel, at least in their outlines. The reaction of Molloy to his situation cannot differ from any reaction felt by the Unnamable, save by circumstances of situation. The pattern lived by each is traceable from *Murphy* onward. The narrative technique of *Murphy* and *Watt* (as well as of the unpublished *Mercier et Camier*) differs greatly from that of the trilogy, yet the essential narrative pattern remains the same: Melvin Friedman notes naïvely (and the description gains in irony outside his text) that "Murphy is curiously unexperimental." Nevertheless, Murphy's cycle, without the complicating secondary and retrospective episodes, is not different from Molloy's.[12]

---

[10] The doubt in the English version is absent in the French, which reads: ". . . dans le silence on ne sait pas, il faut continuer, je vais continuer" (I 262).

[11] Ruby Cohn, "Still Novel," *Yale French Studies*, no. 24 (Fall, 1959), p. 49.

[12] Melvin Friedman, "The Novels of Samuel Beckett: An Amalgam of Joyce and Proust," *Comparative Literature* 12, no. 1 (Winter, 1960): 51. According to Jacobsen and Mueller, ". . . the fact that all of Beckett's work—plays, verse, and novels—is in reality one unified work, . . . must be grasped in order to bring Beckett's genius and its nature into focus. This is one *magnum opus,* which must be examined in depth and intensity. . . . We are examining, in Beckett's universe, the Beckett protagonist; this unique figure of which all alter egos are the mask— a giant, amorphous, frightening creation, whose image dominates every word Beckett has written. This omnipresent figure should be referred to as Malone, Molloy, Estragon, Watt, etc., only in specific contexts. In its omnipresent whole it contains their composite identities, and it must be equally omnipresent in the reader's mind, seen as hovering vastly over the shoulders of its fragmented personalities" (*The Testament of Samuel Beckett*, p. 5).

Murphy: The Point of Departure

The clear-cut outline of Kafka's progression is gone; only its shadow remains. Beckett's structure exists only in the broadest sense, and yet its presence cannot be denied. It is not an academic addition, superimposed by minds incapable of coping with the formless universes of novels. The reciting voice is enclosed within its subjectivity. The quest is generalized, and always unsuccessful; Beckett's patterns are comparable, but their sharpness has been diminished; movement flows forward, physically and temporally.

In *Murphy* the flow appears under the guise of a "curiously unexperimental" form. The novel's narrator, an omniscient author, controls all the strings of his puppets and allows them little that will give them the semblance of living people, but this is his aim. *Murphy* is, for its hero, a search for quiet and peace of mind; for Beckett, the novel is an attempt to find a form in which his characters can exist. The unapparent seeds of the future novels are already here, for from the beginning everything is interrelated: the search motif is present before the formula of quest is voiced. At this point in Beckett's development, repetitions and small forms are matters of artistic play. Beckett toys with correspondences and cross-references, experimenting with the surfaces presented by Joyce's far more profound and complex interrelationships. And yet the patterns are important to Beckett. He plays, for example, with the number thirteen: M, the thirteenth letter is the first letter in the names of the majority of Beckett's protagonists; there are thirteen chapters to *Murphy* and thirteen parts to *Echo's Bones;* later there will be thirteen *Textes pour rien* and thirteen *Poèmes.* And it is no coincidence that Murphy is the name chosen for this early protagonist, a name "probably not pure Irish, but a pun upon the Greek *morphe* meaning 'form,' which is both what Murphy is seeking for himself and an indication of how he will serve Beckett—as the prototype of future fictions."[13] Or, as Raymond Federman says, "This novel can be read as the first step of an epistomological quest whose purpose is not the discovery of some

[13] Cohn, *The Comic Gamut,* p. 54.

philosophical or psychological truth, but the negation of all concepts formulated by man to rationalize his existence."[14]

Murphy, hoping to find his peace of mind in his own room, rocking slowly but building himself up into a violent rock approaching ultimate pleasure, is not allowed his pleasure by Celia, who demands that he find a job so that she need not continue in her profession, that of prostitution. Further, she insists that he marry her. To both these demands Murphy is and remains opposed.

"What do you love?" said Murphy. "Me as I am. You can want what does not exist, you can't love it." This came well from Murphy. "Then why are you all out to change me? So that you won't have to love me," the voice rising here to a note that did him credit, "so that you won't be condemned to love me, so that you'll be reprieved from loving me." He was anxious to make the meaning clear. "Women are all the bloody same, you can't love, you can't stay the course, the only feeling you can stand is being felt, you can't love for five minutes without wanting it abolished in brats and house bloody wifery. My God how I hate the char-Venus and her sausage and mash sex." (Mu 29)

But Murphy lives by the horoscope compiled for him by Ramaswami Krishnaswami Narayanaswami Suk, which has just told him, among other details:

Lucky Days. Sunday. To attract maximum Success the Native should begin new ventures.
Lucky Numbers. 4. The Native should commence new enterprises, for in so doing lies just that difference between Success and Calamity.
Lucky years. 1936 and 1990. Successful and prosperous, yet not without calamities and setbacks.

.   .   .   .

"Can you work now after that?" said Celia.
"Certainly I can," said Murphy. "The very first fourth to fall on a Sunday in 1936 I begin, I put on my gems and off I go, to custode, detect, explore, pioneer, promote or pimp, as occasion may arise."
"And in the meantime?" said Celia. (Mu 27)

In the meantime he promised to avoid all phenomena against which the horoscope had earlier warned him: fits, publishers, quadrupeds,

[14] Raymond Federman, *Journey to Chaos: Samuel Beckett's Early Fiction*, pp. 57–58.

the stone, Bright's disease and Grave's disease, also pains in the neck and feet. It might be added that *Murphy* was published in 1938, the bulk written in 1937. Murphy successfully avoids this first impasse in his search for quiet and peace of mind.

But Celia does convince him that, if she is to remain with him, they must find an apartment in which they can live. Their possible cohabitation is a wedge into the peace Murphy hoped would be his forever, so he applies for a custodian's position at the Magdalen Mental Mercy-seat, a mental institution near London, in order to escape from her. He accepts it also, despite his fear of working, because the words *lunatic* and *custodian* appeared in his horoscope, and because he feels himself more qualified for it than its present holder, Ticklepenny, a homosexual "distinguished indigent drunken Irish bard" (Mu 63). "Murphy . . . was inclined to think that the arrangement would find immediate favor, assuming that Ticklepenny had concealed no material factor in the situation, such as liaison with some high official, the head male nurse for example. Short of being such a person's minion, Murphy was inclined to think there was nothing Ticklepenny could do that he could not do a great deal better, especially in a society of psychotics, and that they had merely to appear together before the proper authority for this to be patent" (Mu 66). There at M.M.M., Murphy is at least happy; if he has not found a real goal in his quest of peace, he at least settles for a satisfactory facsimile. No real goal would allow Ticklepenny to interrupt the beauty of a stupor achieved by rocking on his chair; but on the other hand, Murphy can enjoy and settle for partial satisfaction: ". . . in effect Murphy's night was good, perhaps the best since nights began so long ago to be bad, the reason being not so much that he had his chair again as that the self whom he loved had the aspect . . . of a real alienation. Or to put it more nicely; conferred that aspect of the self whom he hated" (Mu 133).

In this early search for patterns and form, however, the quest is little more than motif; it only begins to give structuring power. The germs are present, but the idea of failure remains dispersed among Beckett's several puppets; they do not belong primarily to Murphy. In the end Murphy dies, his chair standing empty and his last wish unfulfilled. He had asked that his ashes be flushed down a toilet at the Abbey Theater, preferably during a performance, but one of his friends, Cooper, who is carrying the paper bag with Murphy's remains, gets drunk and in a brawl throws the contents of the bag in the face of his opponent. "It bounced, burst, off the wall on to the floor, where at once it became the object of much dribbling, passing, trapping, shooting, punching, heading and even some recognition from the gentleman's code. By closing time the body, mind and soul of Murphy were freely distributed over the floor of the saloon; and before another dayspring greyened the earth had been swept away with the sand, the beer, the butts, the glass, the matches, the spits, the vomit" (Mu 187). Despite Murphy's less than glorious demise, it is his friends who bear the heaviest weight of failure. Before he died "Murphy then [was] being needed by five people, outside himself. By Celia, because she loves him. By Neary, because he thinks of him as the Friend at last. By Miss Counihan, because she wants a surgeon. By Cooper, because he is being employed to that end. By Wylie, because he is reconciled to doing Miss Counihan the honour, in the not too distant future, of becoming her husband. Not only did she stand out in Dublin and in Cork as quite exceptionally anthropoid, but she had private means" (Mu 138). And furthermore, " 'Our medians,' said Wylie, 'Or whatever the hell they are, meet in Murphy' " (Mu 146). They are linked totally with Murphy and their failure is his; Murphy's death renders their individual semiquests unsuccessful.

Watt: Progression Backward

Ruby Cohn has remarked that "like Kafka's *Castle*, *Watt* is a novel of the failure of a quest," and that "Beckett is unconcerned with guilt and redemption, mercy and justice, crime and punishment. Beckett holds the terms of our sentence to be self-evident: we have been born. Condemned to this world, Beckett and Watt examine its reality. The progressive decay of Watt's senses keeps pace with the disintegration of his reason . . ."[15] The constant nonmetaphysical

---

[15] Cohn, *The Comic Gamut*, p. 68; Ruby Cohn, "Preliminary Observations," *Perspective* 11, no. 3 (Autumn, 1959): 123.

forward motion is present here, although in this novel Beckett plays
games with the several simultaneous forward movements in his
search for a satisfactory form. Three worlds exist simultaneously, and
the order this forward movement displays, while overall another unsuccessful quest, is specifically established according to which world
dominates at the moment. The three, as Raymond Federman notes,
are: ". . . the material world (traditional fiction), where seemingly
rational characters are confronted with external reality, with facts
and tangibles; the Knott world, where the hero (Watt) and other
fellow servants struggle to disentangle elements that are as irrational,
as illogical, and as evasive as fiction can permit; and the world of in-
sanity, where human and heroic alike are driven when they fail to
reconcile the outer with the inner world, or when they fail to understand the Knott world."[16] Such intertwining of apparent realities
lends the narrative a halting, if progressive, movement forward; the
order of things is complicated by the fact that the last quarter of the
story is narrated before the third quarter, a situation itself confused
by Beckett's lie that begins the fourth chapter. "As Watt told the beginning of his story, not first, but second, so not fourth, but third,
now he told its end. Two, one, four, three, that was the order in
which Watt told his story. Heroic quatrains are not otherwise elabor-
ated" (W 214). In fact, the chronological order is one, two, four,
three. Nevertheless, the story is paced through its paginated order,
and either progression reveals the pattern of the quest.[17]

   The first difficulty Watt encounters is the problem of finding Mr.
Knott's house; this is compounded by his unique method of forward
propulsion, commonly (and for lack of a better term, in this case
also) called walking:

Watt's way of advancing due east, for example, was to turn his bust as
far as possible towards the north and at the same time to fling out his right
leg as far as possible towards the south, and then to turn his bust as far as
possible towards the south and at the same time to fling out his left leg
as far as possible towards the north, and then again to turn his bust as far
as possible towards the north and to fling out his right leg as far as possible

   [16] Federman, *Journey to Chaos*, p. 97.
   [17] See Cohn's *The Comic Gamut*, pp. 90–91, for a further discussion of this
order. She finds the epistomological order to be 2, 1, 4, 3.

towards the south, and then again to turn his bust as far as possible towards the south and to fling out his left leg as far as possible towards the north, and so on, over and over again, many many times, until he reached his destination and could sit down. So, standing first on one leg, and then on the other, he moved forward, a headlong tardigrade, in a straight line. The knees, on these occasions, did not bend. They could have, but they did not. No knees could bend better than Watt's, when they chose, there was nothing the matter with Watt's knees, as may appear. But when out walking, they did not bend, for some obscure reason. (W 28–29)

The description ends with: "The arms were content to dangle, in perfect equipendency." In its detailed discussion of the several actions involved in walking, such a description appears to be a very careful analysis of the action called walking; in reality, it is nothing more than a close description of only the tiniest part of the walking process. The narrating consciousness (like Molloy's or Malone's to come) is attempting to wrench order from apparently chaotic movement; such a description depicts the need for this kind of narration, which edits while describing; only by editing out the momentary irrelevancies can an order be discovered. "To find a form that accommodates the mess" amidst the surface tumult, that is Beckett's attempt. His is not objective description, for objectively he would be required to describe everything visible in Watt's action. There is no attempt to achieve photographic reality in the one-picture-worth-a-thousand-words sense, for here, not a thousand but merely (so to speak) 212 words have been used. The description, although probably quite relevant to the legs, busts, and knees of Watt, excludes much else about him, rendering the passage a caricature, albeit an ordered caricature, of Watt walking. And the process, used by all novelists to characterize their creations, becomes for Beckett the instrument for explaining the narrator. In a novel such as *Watt* the result is purely humorous, for the reader, uninterested at this point in Beckett's personal struggle to find a form, has little curiosity about the narrator; the reader focuses his attention on what the narrator himself sees: Watt's organized flailing of legs and head. Hence, in *Watt*, the description of Watt walking adds little to one's understanding of Watt himself; through its ability to make the reader laugh it draws his attention away from the larger pattern, patterns that become more apparent in the later, leaner, more streamlined narratives.

Despite his unorthodox ambulation Watt arrives at the house of Mr. Knott; he strives to fill an institutionally proscribed role; his function there he never understands. He attempts to establish the "whatness and potness" of Mr. Knott's pots, to understand situations described to him and situations he experiences, but he finds he must abandon such questions. In the process of describing these moments and their aftermath, Beckett allows himself the tangent of simultaneous tribute to and satire against one of his masters; these together, by suggesting Watt's subsequent lack of memory about the events, imply the beginning of Watt's own giving way before the impasse in his search.

This need [to discover the meaning of situations] remained with Watt, this need not always satisfied during the greater part of his stay in Mr. Knott's house. For the incident of the Galls father and son was followed by others of a similar kind, incidents that is to say of great formal brilliance and indeterminable support. . . . But what was this pursuit of meaning, in this indifference to meaning: And to what did it tend? These are delicate questions. For when Watt at last spoke of this time, it was a long time past, and of which his recollections were, in a sense, perhaps less clear than he would have wished, though too clear for his liking, in another. Add to this the notorious difficulty of recapturing, at will, modes of feeling peculiar to a certain time, and to a certain place, and perhaps also to a certain state of health, when the time is past, and the place left, and the body struggling with quite a new situation. . . . And some idea will perhaps be obtained of the difficulties experienced in formulating, not only such matters as those here in question, but the entire body of Watt's experience, from the moment of his entering Mr. Knott's establishment to the moment of his leaving it. (W 71–72)

But before any answers can be discovered, chapter three begins; it has skipped a period of time and tells of Watt already transferred to an asylum. Chronologically, it is chapter four. The discourse is narrated in the first person by an inmate named Sam, who describes Watt's early days at the place. Watt's search, then, has been doubly interrupted. The chronology has been interrupted by this apparently unrelated, certainly unconnected chapter—the original tale, the quest, is eliminated, never to end, since the real chapter three must now end the book. Nor is the original quest successful according to the chapter that in terms of page numbers follows chapter two, for Sam tells of Watt's lack of success. Federman explains that

there are then two possible endings to Watt's tale: Watt in the asylum, or Watt back in the material world. These two endings are rendered even more ambiguous by the presence of an addendum which suggests that the novel could not be completed, or at least could have been told differently, and consequently should not be taken at face value. Introduced by a curious footnote ("The following precious and illuminating material should be carefully studied. Only fatigue and digust prevent its incorporation." [p. 247]), the eight page addendum, rather than clarifying the novel, adds to its structural confusion, and yet appears essential to a narration that cannot find its own logical exit. In its seemingly unfinished form, Watt offers itself as a literary fraud, since it is never known how the protagonist ends his quest or for what reason he undertook it.[18]

But "fraud" is valid in fiction; artistic creation transforms "reality," causes it to be seen anew. Certainly the story could have been told differently; it will be in the several novels that follow.

The first among these is *Mercier et Camier*, Beckett's first novel in French, which he has never allowed to be published. Fletcher claims it to be "chiefly interesting as the first thorough working out of the journey theme."[19] Since more than the seeds of this theme have already been discussed, it now becomes possible to turn to *Molloy*.

Molloy: Double Vision

Like *Waiting for Godot, Molloy* embodies a double structure. In *Godot,* as in *How It Is* to come, the structural division enforces without directly demanding the anthropomorphic notion of days as measurable by man and their implied recurrent patterns. Much the same may be said of *Molloy.* Each half mightily reinforces the other, yet with a difference: act 2 of *Godot* is essential to *Godot* for the unity of the whole, parts 2 and 3 explicate part 1 of *How It Is,* but the two units of *Molloy* are capable of, and successful in, standing by themselves. Nevertheless, as partners, they can be said to represent the private and the public selves of Molloy; in this way they underscore the structure of the quest and the nature of narrative consciousness.

---

[18] Federman, *Journey to Chaos,* p. 106.
[19] Fletcher, *The Novels of Samuel Beckett,* p. 118.

Read together, each part grows beyond its individual success; without the unity of the double focus, the force of Beckett's statement could be lost, especially if *Molloy* is not read with the two subsequent volumes of the trilogy.[20]

Although scholarship exists to "prove" that the Molloy and the Moran episodes are virtual equivalents, it is neither necessary nor even possible to posit such an absolute parallel. To note with Fletcher that the repetitions are refracted according to the vision of each narrator is sufficient: "Very few events or items from Part I are repeated in Part II with no alteration: usually they are, as it were, refracted, and it is when their superficial difference gives way under analysis to a realization of their fundamental similarity that Beckett's best effects are obtained, and we feel that two men of very different character are fulfilling a simple destiny." Both Moran and Molloy live through the described similar details, but "more important than such minor occurrences are the parallels carefully established between the journeys of Molloy and of Moran,[21] not only parallels of patterns within the two halves of *Molloy* but also parallels between this volume, the others in the trilogy, and the novels past and yet to come.

Within each section, too, there exists an order and symmetry suggesting that Beckett has at last found a satisfactory pattern for the lack of success of his several knights-errant. Moran's life, for example, "has the cruel order of habit: he bullies his servant, torments his son, goes prudentially to Mass, masturbates systematically, and is proud of his garden. The mad barren precision of his life is one of Beckett's best things . . ."[22] This second section of *Molloy* is a favorite for proving the circularity of Beckett's narratives, but the narrative returning at its conclusion to the beginning establishes nothing more than a framed structure. Certainly it is not impossible to talk of a circular quest, in which the protagonist returns to his starting point

[20] Only in 1965 have Calder and Boyars and Grove Press published the trilogy in one volume. No Editions de Minuit single volume has, to my knowledge, yet appeared.

[21] Fletcher, *The Novels of Samuel Beckett*, pp. 131, 132.

[22] Frank Kermode, "Beckett, Snow and Pure Poverty," *Encounter* 15, no. 1 (July, 1960): 74.

at the end of his journeys, and he could very well return out of failure, but, just as there is no circularity in the frame stores of Gottfried Keller and Joseph Conrad, there is no need to superimpose such
structure here. It is possible that a mind suffused with the *motif* of
circularity in *The Unnamable* could transfer it as *structure* to Moran's
episode, but the interpolation adds little even to a metaphysical interpretation of the narrative and distracts from its essential purpose;
allowing the reader to forget the priority of the quest and the deterioration of that quest's hero. Especially true in the Moran section,
the chronology of deterioration belongs as much to the included
frame as it does to the tale of Moran's travels. When Moran begins
his narrative in the present, within the time of the telling, he is still—
or appears still to be—in good physical shape, but reliving the events
through their narration results in the decline of Moran, both physically and within his consciousness. Much like *Watt* in structure, the
Moran tale depends on temporal relationships between adjacent descriptions.

Beginning with the first episode of *Molloy*, probably the best
realized of Beckett's novels and the prototype of his narrative quest,
the pattern of apparent nonmotivation and the compulsion to begin
the superficially trivial journey mingle in Beckett's idiom. Molloy,
having discussed the possible relevance of two characters A and B
(A and C in his English translation), who themselves appeared to
be on a journey (for they passed by and were never seen again),
suddenly begins: "But talking of the craving for a fellow let me
observe that having walked between eleven o'clock and midday (I
heard the angelus, recalling the incarnation, shortly after) I resolved
to go and see my mother. I needed, before I could resolve to go and
see that woman, reasons of an urgent nature, and with such reasons,
since I did not know what to do, or where to go, it was child's play
for me, the play of an only child, to fill my mind until it was rid of
all other preoccupation . . ." (Tr 15). His mother is the goal he never
reaches, as he has explained in his first words. As he narrates, he lies
in the bed his mother vacated at her death, a death that may have
taken place before or after his arrival; he has no idea when. "The
truth is I don't know very much" (Tr 7). He begins his journey—

with difficulty, since one of his legs is useless, making it difficult to pedal a bike—and is almost immediately accosted by the police. According to pattern, the first impasse is minor, yet Molloy is dominated by external authority. Although he is taken to police headquarters, it is only a matter of form and time before Molloy is thrown out and accused of wasting the police's time by having done nothing wrong; the impasse is avoided and Molloy continues on his way.

His search becomes thoroughly sidetracked, however, when he kills a dog belonging to Lousse (or perhaps her name is Sophie); she demands that Molloy help her bury it, an act which because of his bad leg he cannot accomplish, for he has no other leg to stand upon when he attempts with his good leg to drive the shovel into the ground. After the burial he is invited to the woman's house, where he spends perhaps fourteen days in a cubicle, all his possessions including his clothes having been removed. Thereafter he stays for a long time with Lousse, and the quest for his mother becomes ever dimmer. At one point, talking of love and the actions of love, he says: "Was such an encounter possible, I mean between me and a woman? Now men, I have rubbed up against a few men in my time, but women? Oh well, I may as well confess it now, yes, I once rubbed up against one. I don't mean my mother, I did more than rub up against her. And if you don't mind we'll leave my mother out of all this" (Tr 56). The stories, "all this," include not only the anecdote being told at the moment but the whole fabric of Molloy's narrative. It is too late to return the mother to the story. Molloy's own desire to find his mother grows dim; he is apparently no longer interested in the quest, since the effort demanded of him is too great. Consequently, Molloy begins to wander, regardless of the goal: there is no end, nor is he curious about one. Only the process retains import, only the forward movement counts. "And far more than to know what town I was in, my haste was now to leave it, even were it the right one, where my mother had waited so long and perhaps was waiting still. And it seemed to me that if I kept on in a straight line I was bound to leave it, sooner or later. So I set myself to do this as best I could, making allowance for the drift to the right of the feeble light that was my guide" (Tr 65). As he drags himself out of the town to become a part of the landscape, Molloy does occasionally think of his mother. Once, in a cave, the memory of her nags a little, but it is soon forgotten or at least not mentioned again. When, in the end, he can pull himself no further, although ahead of him he fancies he sees a town that might be—but surely is not—the town of his mother, he notes the irrelevance of questions dealing with metaphysical subjects, such as the problem of the end of one's search, to a man in his condition: "In any case, whether it was my town or not, whether somewhere under the faint haze my mother panted on, or whether she poisoned the air a hundred miles away, were ludicrously idle questions for a man in my position, though of undeniable interest on the plane of pure knowledge" (Tr 91). All practical aspect of the quest has gone by for Molloy. There is nothing left for him but to die, which, however, he does not do, since he is discovered by an unknown hand that ultimately takes him to his mother's room, where the narrative begins.

Moran's story parallels Molloy's, if not in specific events, then at least in its march toward the destruction of a narrator. Moran, an agent of Youdi, has an apparent reason for beginning his search for Molloy: he was told to do so by Gaber, Youdi's lieutenant. But beyond this no motivation is given. Moran does not know why Molloy is wanted, nor does he know what to do with Molloy should he find him. For his journey he decides to take along his son Jacques (which is Moran's name also). The son provides Moran with the original impasse in the journey's forward movement, for Jacques wishes to bring with him the album containing his best postage stamps. The encumbrance would be too great for Moran, and he will not allow Jacques the album over which the latter has spent many gloating hours. As a compromise Moran agrees to let his son take with him the album of duplicates, but young Jacques transfers his good stamps to the duplicate album in order to deceive his father and to have with him his beloved favorites. When Moran discovers the deception, his fury delays the beginning of his search. But not until they have actually been on the road for several days does Moran begin to weaken: his knee begins to pain him. Unable and unwilling to continue, he sends his son to buy a bicycle. His lack of desire to go on forces on him the role of accomplice in the impeded success of the search, for at the moment he begins to weaken the whole project loses relevance. When his son departs, Moran in self-pity commences his decline to that remembered figure, a lump on the landscape, like Molloy, his goal. Moran has become so distracted from the course that, upon the return of his son, he can only embroil himself in a violent disagreement with Jacques, who leaves him. The scene itself has no memorable incidents, and yet it marks an end to Moran's interest in the quest, since his son alone can assist him in the lonely struggle toward Molloy. Just as some helping hand was given to Molloy, out there in the dark, to bring him to his mother's room, so Gaber finds Moran and orders him back home: "He said, Moran, home, instanter" (Mo 217). Throughout a whole winter he struggles toward home, alone, without the help of his son or of Gaber. His quest has proved a failure.

Malone Dies: Narrative and Reinforcement

Malone and his creation Sapo/MacMann enact once more the quest that fails. Two narratives—the tale of the telling and the tale told—intermingle; Malone's desired end for the simultaneous and intermingled quests appears to be his own death. But Malone's goal in reality is less the desired presence of death than it is the need to continue speaking—filling up time with sound to give the impression of lived-in duration, until he can die. Even if Malone expects and verbalizes a wished-for death, he fills the majority of his time creating something new, making people where none before existed. Nevertheless, at the beginning Malone does send the reader along a track that only parallels the main direction of the narrative; Malone claims that he wishes simply to die, and that the entirety of what is to come—the story-telling—is merely a matter of passing time until such a moment as the arrival of death eliminates the need to continue. As his end approaches, Malone still finds the breath and the need to say, "Je vais quand même essayer de continuer" (Ma 196).[23] No Beckett character allows his end to take him passively, and few in

[23] Beckett translates the phrase without referent, "Try and go on" (Tr. 142), so that in English Malone may be speaking either to himself or to MacMann.

fact find their end in death, as part of the plot lies in the need to continue, even after all has been said and lost. From the beginning Malone's function has not differed from that of the present moment: "Live and invent. I have tried. I must have tried. Invent. It is not the word. Neither is live. No matter. I have tried. . . . For I was already in the toils of earnestness. That has been my disease. I was born grave as others syphilitic. And gravely I struggled to be grave no more, to live, to invent, I know what I mean" (Tr 194). And he must continue to invent in the hopes that it will serve at least the purpose of filling up time; perhaps in the process something more will come of it.

The two simultaneous narratives reinforce as well as intermingle with each other; Sapo/MacMann and Malone must live through the same essential pattern because they are the creations of authors closely related. Fletcher sees the repeated straightforward movement of the novel as "a fragment of fiction . . . followed by a fragment of self-examination, and vice versa, to the end; and an important theme is the ambiguity of what constitutes the fiction and what does not."[24]

Malone begins his own narrative by mentioning that he will soon be dead—he has the feeling. Although he knows that the rest of his life will be totally passive, he cannot accept the unpleasantness of lying in dead silence awaiting the outcome of inaction. He must talk. And so he establishes his program, his search for words to fill in time. He struggles to tell his tales, but his attempt is undermined. At first only external authority in the form of the asylum or the home in which he spends his days and nights exerts its strength to weaken him and deprive him of his goal: the old woman who brings him his daily soup ceases her diurnal visits. But slowly the narrative follows the earlier established patterns. Malone loses his pencil, but he is not distressed, despite its being his only tool for recording his stories, essential if he is to continue at all. More important to him than the pencil, however, is his stick; it is an extension of his body, lacking only the prehensile proboscis that would allow him to pick up fallen objects. His stick is the object closest to him—he keeps it in his bed, under the blankets; ". . . there was a time I used to rub myself against

[24] Fletcher, *The Novels of Samuel Beckett*, p. 191.

it, saying, It's a little woman" (Tr 247). It is so well protected that for
it to slip from his grasp is highly improbable; yet, out of fear of falling, he lets it go. Losing the stick begins the final phase of deterioration, placing him at the brink of the end he has expected from the
beginning of his narration. Soon thereafter a stranger pays his visit—
possibly the undertaker. Malone pays lip service to an attempt to
continue struggling, but in reality he no longer has the desire, and
therefore, as predicted Malone dies.

Malone's own progress toward death is reinforced by the tale he
tells of the boy Sapo who grows into the man MacMann. But Sapo's
quest has no apparent goal—he is a dunce. His parents expect great
things of him, but he is doomed to disappoint them. "They thought
of him as a doctor for preference. He will look after us when we are
old, said Mrs. Saposcat. And her husband replied, I see him rather
as a surgeon, as though after a certain age people were inoperable"
(Tr 189). He goes for long walks instead of studying for his *bac-
calaureat*; his head is filled with great roaring sounds, and when he
looks at objects he merely describes them, he does not interpret or
abstract. Malone describes at length Sapo's lack of direction and
ruminates over its possible reasons. Sapo consciously refuses to abet
his parents' hopes for him and complies with the impasse before him,
which more and more becomes one of his own making—of his own
laziness it might be said, were it not that Sapo's orientation differs
completely from hopes held for him by his parents and by Malone.
In the end, Malone ages Sapo and changes his name to MacMann in
an attempt to disguise his failure; in the episode with Moll, Mac-
Mann demonstrates his total lack of interest in achieving any goals,
either human or animal. As MacMann's story draws to a close,
Lemuel in Malone's narrative gains dominance over MacMann. "It
was as though the Saposcats drew the strength to live from the
prospect of their impotence" (Tr 189). The same might be said of
both Sapo/MacMann and Malone.

An Unnamable Voice: The Way It Is

The Unnamable, like *Malone Dies*, is a narrative account of the
present; and, together with its predecessor, this last novel in the

trilogy establishes as a large bulk of its content stories wrenched from the imagination and told at the very moment in which they are being created, as if they were from the past. But where Malone's stories merely reinforced his own quest, those of the Unnamable are the structure itself of the "I's" narrative consciousness. The present moment is sustained from the opening "Where now? Who now? When now?" (Tr 291) to the closing "I'll go on" (Tr 414); and the quest through which the Unnamable has lived has not succeeded, not yet. Its search is for silence, yet it cannot cease to speak. It describes what externalities it can and, being a human mind, can occasionally be sufficiently self-conscious to wander outside itself— though not very far—in order to glance back at itself and watch the quest continue. The general pattern of quest begun, external impasse encountered and overcome, new impasse with internal compliance thereto, deterioration of the original quest, and final failure, is still present, but its outlines have become blurred. A character, evolved down to nothing more than a head on a trunk without limbs, stuck in a jar, may appear to be a step in the direction of the silence to which the voice could at least acquiesce; yet, although its wish is present, it cannot do so. The search for silence is the search for freedom from the obligation of continuing speech, a search for the moment when all will have been said. It is the search for the impossible, for there always remains another word, another clarification, another possibility. The writer's art is limited to the observance of narrative consciousness; his world is as large as any, and as filled with possibility: "I should, I had, I were, I could, I must have—they are all hypotheses which can be increased ad infinitem. Each 'Perhaps' hints at the possibilities of a whole novel, each 'But' introduces a counter-move, each 'Or' leads into a new bifurcation."[25]

Therefore the stories—both the ceaseless, apparently arbitrary stories of the Unnamable and the three parts to the narrative of Pim —must flow into the pattern of the whole. Fletcher notes that "it is only 'the search for the means to put an end to things, an end to speech [that] enables the discourse to continue.' There can be no possibility

[25] Dieter Wellershof, "Failure of an Attempt at De-Mythologization: Samuel Beckett's Novels," in *Samuel Beckett*, ed. Esslin, p. 103.

of an end to speech, for such a cessation would entail the end of existence itself. Everything therefore, fictions and fables included, is grist for the mill." And the mill demands more and more—the more that is spoken, the more numerous become the possibilities of variation and new tangents. The greater demand for new matter is reflected in the movement of the narrative: as the probability of a successful conclusion to the quest diminishes, the voice tries ever harder, becoming more and more disconcerted; as limits of possibility fall, the direction of the quest becomes blurred and failure can be the only outcome. Fletcher explains: "The formal principle which governs *The Unnamable* is that of accelerated forward progression. The prose slowly gathers momentum as the pages turn. Early on, for instance, the division into paragraphs is dropped, and the prose is unbroken from that point onward. Thereafter full stops become less and less frequent, and the last of all is found three pages from the end, making one long sentence of the final fifteen hundred words of the novel."[26] In the novel, style is dominated totally by the point of view together with the forward thrust that such a position demands; the constant sound-filled present is inescapable: "Non-arrival, non-having, frustrated union with one's goal—there they are all reduced to the briefest formula. The torso is the shrunken remnant of the narrative and at the same time the narrator himself, who tried to broaden himself imaginatively in his narratives and who has now returned to himself."[27]

Much of the same might be repeated for *How It Is*, in which the syntactic device of punctuation and the rush of language through paragraphic nondifferentiation used in *The Unnamable* is eliminated, leaving what appears to be unpunctuated verses ranging in length from five to ten lines—prose poetry in novel form. Yet *How It Is* is narrative prose rather than an epic poem; it is a natural conclusion to the developing line from *Murphy* and *Watt* through the trilogy. All outlines of the search's pattern have been obliterated, but the search itself remains, narrated from three separate perspectives:

[26] Fletcher, *The Novels of Samuel Beckett*, pp. 187, 192.
[27] Wellershof, "Samuel Beckett's Novels," in *Samuel Beckett*, ed. Esslin, p. 102.

before Pim, with Pim, after Pim. As Raymond Federman notes, "It has acquired such momentum . . . that it could easily go on for an infinite number of parts, simply repeating the same process, the same images, the same words and gestures, just as the two tramps of *Waiting for Godot* could repeat their useless comedy to infinity."[28] Yet these three moments are bound; they are limited and framed within the mind of the narrator who explains that all his narratives are lies, invention, every one of them. Something did happen, it is true, but the truth bears little resemblance to his own narrative. Once more the stories are grist for the mill, and once again the pattern—what remains of it—is carried through by the substance of internally invented narrative.

if all that all that yes if all that is now how shall I say no answer if all that is not false yes

all these calculations yes explanations yes the whole story from beginning to end yes completely false yes

that wasn't how it was no not at all how then no answer how was it then no answer HOW WAS IT screams good

there was something yes but nothing of all that no all balls from start to finish yes this voice quaqua yes all balls yes only one voice here yes mine yes when the panting stops yes

.   .   .   .

all this business of sacks deposited yes at the end of a cord no doubt yes of an ear listening to me yes a care for me yes an ability to note yes all that all balls yes Krim and Kram yes all balls yes (H 144–145)

Aside from the obvious parody of the end of *Ulysses*, the fictions have been within Beckett's quest pattern. If one wishes, it is possible to abstract out the journey toward Pim; the difficulties encountered externally; the acquiescence to the moment with Pim; the narrator hoping that the goal had been reached and his consequent discovery that it had merely been obscured, that something other than being with Pim must have been the goal, for at the end another is crawling forward in the mud to be with the narrator. The cycle can continue forever, and the goal will never be reached, for there are always new

[28] Raymond Federman, "Beckett and the Fiction of Mud," in *On Contemporary Literature,* ed. Richard Kostelanetz, p. 260.

goals beyond those first thought to be the ends. The abstraction veri-
fies, but it is unnecessary; the dominating movement etches its impression.

But these events did not happen; they are figments of the narrator's
imagination. Something like them did occur, but the recited facts
have only the most general relationship to the real events, whatever
they were. And of course it matters not at all that the story told was
not the true one, for all stories are the same if they are told by a
narrating mind with consistent obsessions. Had *How It Is* been punctuated, it would have been possible to interpolate Beckett's earlier
words: "I don't know why I told this story. I could just as well have
told another. Perhaps some other time I'll be able to tell another"
(STN 25). The meaning would not have shifted.

Krapp: Dramatic Texture and Narrative Form

The already complex question of a distinction between Beckett's
"stories," as opposed to the form taken by his narratives, is compounded further when he presents his voices in a visual/verbal medium. It is therefore necessary to make, from the outset, a distinction
between the story one gets from a play and the narrative presented
at the moment of performance.

For Beckett, as for Kafka, only the images perceived have even
the chance of being valid. What is not seen need not be happening,
need not have happened. When an event is reported the audience
knows nothing more of it than that it was reported. The imagination
of the reporter, be he character or author, alone is available; it alone
can be experienced as an existent phenomenon by the audience. Beyond it, one can be sure only that the reporter is describing less than
a complete picture: the world is too complex for words to contain
more than an image of reality, as Beckett constantly makes clear.
The reporter can have forgotten, he can be purposely distorting, he
may be lying, he describes according to his predilections and prejudices. Hence it is impossible to know if Gogo and Didi saw Godot
yesterday, or last week, what he told them at the time, whether he
was coming today, whether he told them anything, or if in fact they
ever were told to wait for him at all. We know only that two men are

waiting for someone called Godot because they say they think they were told to wait. Within that many parentheses the play quickly makes specific interpretation impossible and gains the breadth of Beckett's formal patterns. An audience learns the story of *Waiting for Godot* because it is reported in the play; but the play's sequence of events, that element in the play which the audience follows visually, is not the "story," as it "actually" happened; it is rather Beckett's pattern of movement/impasse/movement/impasse with internal compliance and deterioration. The narrative form of the plays does not differ from the narrative form of the stories, but the presentational dimension, the dramatic element, serves a different function. The same distinction between surface and story underlies the difference between all narrative and all theater. *Narrative* is the statement of events as they "actually" occurred; *theater* (or, for the novels, the *structure* or *pattern*) is the relationship of events as they are presented.

Theater can present elements of several structures simultaneously. In a sense, a tightly constructed prose narrative also expresses more than a single element at a time, but in the final analysis all prose narrative is temporally linear, at least for the reader. The reader follows the narrative's evolution in the time it takes him to progress through the book, and when he turns back to a previous page the return is conscious and willed. A dramatic production is a more limited experience for its audience and at the same time more complex. If one missed the implications of a speech in the first act, it is too late to go back after the intermission—it is too late once the words of the speech have been spoken. On the other hand, the texture of performed dramatic narrative is often richer than prose narrative: several narratives are usually taking place at the same moment, all of them visible to the audience. Not only may numerous characters individually be living out patterns with which the audience is concerned, but also these patterns will be evolving on different levels and at different paces. Further, some patterns will be presented to the audience in any of several modes of action, whereas other patterns will appear in the form of dialogue. Juxtaposed differences in similar patterns, evolving in the same way but made visible at earlier or later moments in their progress, provide a play with tension. The more complex the interrelationship between patterns, the tighter the drama.

Beckett's rational post-Renaissance Western man, withered to a narrative's protagonist, has thought his way into deterioration. Beckett's stories present the intellectual extreme of the Cartesian *cogito, ergo sum*. Each Beckett protagonist has thought himself through rational meaning and out the other side, into incompetence. The mistake of the character has as its source the Aristotelian limitation of beginning with oneself, of never transcending oneself, of denying the Other. The lack of interconnection among characters creates for each protagonist a narrating consciousness that perverts, distorts, and in the end destroys its possessor, who can go nowhere with it. The logical goal would be a return to the world of other men, a return to situational interrelationships; but a single narrating consciousness is forever separated from other consciousnesses that, in the Western post-Renaissance tradition, also respond to their self-aggrandizing duty, their attempt to think, to narrate, and therefore to be. The obvious resolution lies in beginning not with *cogito*, but with what Anthony Wilden calls *locquor*, with some form of interrelationship, of discourse with any and all Others.[29] When intercommunication of some sort is attained, the isolation at the center of each narrating consciousness would be transcended, and the link to an external point of reference established.

Beckett fails to make this link in the narrative of his stories. But his plays achieve their fascination and power precisely because they play the isolation of each individual consciousness against the formal interrelationship between protagonists: each character has a sense of *locquor* imposed upon him by the dramatic format. Even if the intention of such intercommunication remains invisible to the characters themselves, it does become apparent, though not necessarily explicit, to the audience. The plays succeed because they provide the audience (never the characters) with a satisfactory alternative to frozen isolation. The theater of intercommunication, of which

[29] At the time of this writing, Wilden's essay is still in manuscript. It will appear in *General Systems Yearbook*, 1972.

Beckett is not part but within which his techniques become clear, stresses discourse as process.[30] The Ibsen/Shaw/O'Neill theater of realism stresses linearity, the *cogito*, isolation. The material of Beckett's plays is drawn from the theater of realism, linearity pushed to its extreme. But the simultaneous structures of Beckett's plays depend on principles of the theater of intercommunication: the discourse between elements is as important as the single elements themselves.

Krapp's Last Tape provides a highly satisfactory illustration of the form of Beckett's narrative, of the movement toward deterioration. Its brevity denies it no complexity, but the complexity is more self-contained than in an equally brief section from a longer play. The two characters of the play, old Krapp and his tape recorder (or old Krapp and the younger, recorded Krapp), interact almost not at all. For purposes of analysis it is handy that the second character is inanimate and technological, thereby casting into sharp profile the moments of interaction; the contrast would be unavailable if the second character had a mind of its own. Of course, in a sense the tapes from thirty years ago do (or did) have a mind, the mind behind the spoken words, but of these we can know nothing. If the tapes are recorded memory, their reports from the past have to be taken by the audience at face value; we simply cannot know if young Krapp lied or distorted or perverted when he recorded them years earlier. The only sense of mind available grows from Krapp's reactions to the tapes—primarily his attempt to forget by dulling his mind with alcohol (my interpretation of his apparent offstage drinking) while simultaneously trying to remember by having played the tapes to begin with.

There are two narrative lines; they have similar but not completely simultaneous forms. The first belongs to Krapp of the play, the second

[30] The theater of intercommunication is a dramatic phenomenon emerging in the twentieth century. It opposes the linearity of realism with the simultaneity of incessant spatial/verbal interaction. Its chief practitioners are the German expressionists, the French surrealists, Brecht, Gênet, some of the American off-off-Broadway movement, especially Jean-Claude van Itallie. It does not include most so-called absurd playwrights, who are instead symptoms of the impossibility of continuation for the theater of linear realism.

to the tape recorder and its accompanying ledger. Both narratives present the pattern of alternating movement and impasse with internal compliance and deterioration: they begin at disparate points and, by the end of the play, converge. Each contains within itself elements that can be broken down into smaller replicas of the movement/impasse patterns. This last is important: symptomatic reinforcement of the macrocosmic pattern is essential to determine its repeated and complete nature. That the pattern writ small supports the larger suggests that each complete pattern is itself an impasse. If the largest of Beckett's patterns, a complete story, is the reflection of a universe as he and apparently many another (see the vast amount of metaphysical criticism) see it, then that universe, assuming natural distortion, becomes itself the impasse to successful interrelation. But the implications here are themselves becoming metaphysical and beyond the present scope, the attempt of which is merely to comprehend the structure of an impasse so that it may be fairly and intelligently dealt with.

Old Krapp's realization of the natural pattern proceeds with the following specifics. *Movement*: Krapp is happy, he eats bananas, he laughs, he begins to brood. *Impasse*: He has difficulty in coping with meaning, here only the meaning of the word *viduity*. He finds it is in a dictionary, but he has stopped the forward progression of his project, the listening to a tape. *Movement 2*: He finds the meaning, is happy with it, turns the tape back on. He relaxes, stops the tape for a moment to remember a nursemaid in whom he was interested, turns it on again, begins to be impatient with the words on the tape, stops it three times, twice in order to move it ahead, once to move it back. Each cessation of the taped voice slows down any forward progress, any attempt on his part to understand the past through the just reported moment in his life. *Impasse 2*: In disgust he finally puts the tape off altogether, puts on a new spool and begins to record the reaction of the present moment. The recording, itself a pattern to which I shall return, is useless and clarifies to him the equivalent uselessness of continuation. *Deterioration*: He has neither the strength nor the desire to overcome the last impasse. He turns back to words already heard and discarded from the third fragment of tape he played. The tape ends, and Krapp continues to listen as it whips around the spool, emitting no sound.

The pattern on the tape proceeds simultaneously. *Movement:* The ledger calls the tape a farewell to love. Within this context the audience learns that at the time the tape was recorded Krapp was thirty-nine years old, healthy despite his old weakness, by which he apparently means his drinking. Intellectually he feels himself to have peaked. He ate bananas in those earlier days also. *Impasse:* He remembers the bad experiences of several sexual relationships, but mental association leads him out of the block and on to pleasanter thoughts. *Movement 2:* Young Krapp speaks of a dog and the ball he gave the animal, of his generosity at the time, then of a storm; the first impasse is resolved with the pleasanter memories of what sounds like a good, at least reasonably good, sexual (perhaps love) relationship. The audience hears the conclusion of young Krapp's report first, because old Krapp has moved the tape forward. At the end of the tape old Krapp rewinds it to a moment prior to the last chunk, listens to the several minutes preceding what he has already heard, together with the last minutes again. The preceding minutes put what sounded like a good heterosexual relationship into context and establish *Impasse 2:* He and the girl had been floating gently in a punt on a sunny day. But the day itself was the conclusion rather than the progression of their relationship. Young Krapp reports that he has told her again it was no good going on and that she agreed with him. The sense of forward movement has stopped, at least for young Krapp. They continue to lie in the boat, and the previous sense of the ending, the pleasant motionlessness, becomes instead an impassivity: they do not move, but, under them and all around them, all else is moving. *Deterioration:* Old Krapp removes the tape with his voice from the past, puts on a clean tape, and records a message of finality. The motifs from the old tape reappear, each imaged in terms of decay and irrevocability. The old tape used sentences; the newly recorded tape will be filled with fragments, gasps, many pauses. All progression is finally and fully restrained by the elimination of the old tape; the restraint is abetted by old Krapp, as he makes a new tape. His irritation with the new tape, his sense of its not going anywhere, of its being itself an impasse of a sort, becomes explicit when he throws it off and returns instead to the previous tape, to the ending that the audience has heard several times already; he plays it till it ends, and allows the empty tape to play on and on.

In the end, Krapp's and the tape recorder's patterns coincide: the conclusion has unified the later elements of the several progressions. When both Krapp and the tape's Krapp have run down, the patterns are complete. The best moments, the best years for each, when there was a chance for happiness as a consequence of actions taken, have passed.

In addition to smaller patterns that serve as primary impasses, there are more momentary irritations, which are themselves impasses of a secondary order. Of this second sort, the eating of the banana serves as a sufficient example. *Movement:* Krapp peels and eats a banana. *Impasse:* He slips on the skin. *Movement 2:* He peels another banana, does not eat it, his progression has been slowed. He pockets the banana. *Impasse 2:* He finds the banana later, but rejects it. *Deterioration:* It stays in his pocket, with the unspoken but apparent sense that it will rot there. This slight pattern has no immediate importance—the narrative in no way hinges on it—but it does enrich the texture of the play, through action only, by reinforcing the primary structures and suggesting, as it flits across the senses to the mind, that if all phenomena are similar, then this indeed must be the way it is.

Young Krapp's sexual experience, the first impasse on the tape, can also be broken down in this manner. *Movement:* Old Miss McGlome he finds to be a wonderful woman, he tries to imagine her as a girl but cannot, and he surmises she is from Connaught (a region of western Ireland), more important for its sex-pun name in French and English than for its actual location. The association with her is pleasant, as it is with Bianca, the girl with the warm eyes. *Impasse:* But almost as quickly the audience learns he was glad to be out of that situation. *Movement 2:* The best among these early women was the young and beautiful nursemaid with the "incomparable bosom." *Impasse 2:* When he attempted to speak to her, however, she threatened to call a policeman, and the affair ended before it began. *De-

terioration: All talk of sexual relationship ends until old Krapp makes the new tape. But on the tape the sexual images are as final as the others. Fanny comes regularly, but she is a "bony old ghost of a whore"; he couldn't do much with her. The girl in the boat is not related to the patterned sexual encounters—she is part of another pattern, the more generalized relationship between Krapp and others.

The tape old Krapp attempts to make at the end of the play, his last tape, has an equivalent pattern. *Movement:* He considers himself as he was thirty years ago. *Impasse:* He condemns his past self. *Movement 2:* He considers his present self, at somewhat greater length. Here he discusses his work, his women, and his drinking. *Impasse 2:* He condemns all these. *Deterioration:* When he realizes there is nothing left to say or do, he ceases recording, and instead of cataloguing the new tape carefully with the others he wrenches the tape from the machine and throws it away. The recording process serves as an impasse for the narrative pattern of contemporary Krapp by itself being an impasse; and similar patterns can be drawn from the primary impasses in the two major narrations. All stories are one story, only the telling differs.

In this study of narrative, it is not necessary to examine all Beckett's major plays. The patterns of his life cycle are present in each of them, from *Godot* to *All That Fall,* and from *Endgame* to *Cascando.* In the short pieces of the sixties, Beckett attempts to integrate music into the pattern of his protagonists' experience. In *Eh Joe,* for example, Music is itself a character which, from the stage directions, lives through a similar pattern. Words is a character who himself lives through the pattern in the course of the playlet and also narrates the story of another who lives through the pattern too. Though there are fewer stage directions for the Music in *Cascando,* Words, Music, and Opener also repeat the pattern. All stories are the same story.

4. The Dominance of Point of View

T HE NEW READER of Beckett is impressed—for good or
ill—first by his style, a style that has been measured as "limited,"
"infinite," and at all the steps between.[1] To understand how a style
can be described with such contradictory labels, it is necessary to
adopt the point of view with which Beckett conceived his prose—
what has here been called narrative consciousness.

If a reader is to understand the Beckett novel before him, he must
treat it as he has the work of Kafka—he must realize that as he reads
he stands in the shoes of both the author and of the narrator; but
with Beckett there is another occasionally added dimension. The
paradox of a necessity to achieve the impossible—to express when
there is nothing to be said—demands that the reader, like Beckett
the puppet-master of the early novels, also stand outside and watch
the whole process take place, that the reader, in effect, view himself
in the shoes of the narrator/protagonist. This triple identity of the
reader (not to mention his own) renders him an accomplice in

[1] For specific critical attitudes to Beckett's style, see Appendix 3, section 1.

Beckett's preference for "the expression that there is nothing to express, no power to express, no desire to express, together with an
obligation to express" (P 103). A paradox so constantly present, so
essential to a clear reading of the novels, demands the double point
of view, that of seeing while being seen. Beckett's words—"*Esse est
percipi* ["to be is to be perceived"]. All extraneous perception sup-
pressed, animal, human, divine, self-perception maintains in being.
Search of non-being in flight from extraneous perception breaking
down in escapability of self-perception"—are explained by Esslin to
mean that "self-perception is a basic condition of our being; we exist
because, and as long as, we perceive ourselves. If it is true that for the
artist perception leads to the obligation to express what he perceives,
it follows that for the artist the compulsion to express his intuition
of the world is a condition of his very existence." Such a combination of seeing oneself externally while remaining within the character who sees outward only onto the world that Beckett has created
for him explains in part the inversion of temporality in *Watt*. Cohn
remarks that "Watt . . . is sometimes the observer, sometimes the
observed. Often without sequence or connective, dialogue follows
event, follows reasoning, pushed to an unbearable, seemingly non-
sensical limit." And Kenner, in speaking of *How It Is*, says, "There
is a letter signed 'Sam Beckett' which compounds the difficulties by
carefully referring to the figure in question as 'the narrator/nar-
rated . . .'"[2] Beckett demands primarily that the world be seen from
his narrator's eyes in order to explain the mind of that narrator, in
order to understand that narrator; secondarily Beckett demands that
the reader then look at himself in his new-found position in order to
realize that Molloy or Malone or any named or nameless character
is not alone in his position.

This second demand of Beckett is difficult to distinguish; there is
a great distance between suggesting that according to Beckett the
human position is somewhere in the mud, and understanding the pre-

[2] Beckett's remarks are the opening camera directions for *Film* (C75). Martin
Esslin, introduction to *Samuel Beckett: A Collection of Critical Essays*, p. 3;
Ruby Cohn, *Samuel Beckett: The Comic Gamut*, p. 67; Hugh Kenner, *Flaubert,
Joyce and Beckett: The Stoic Comedians*, p. 68.

cise geography of Beckett's implication; only by beginning with the point of view of narrative consciousness, and thereby seeing through the narrator's eyes, can one begin to make claims about Beckett's metaphysics. Of his style-dominating point of view Middleton mentions that "Beckett is . . . no vague affirming metaphysical, who overlooks all dissonance. He is first of all an inexorable skeptic, a phenomenologist of a madness that is all too human. Therefore his language penetrates to the roots of the most visionary as well as the most banal experience."[3] What Middleton neglects is the impossibility, on Beckett's part, of being a true phenomenologist, one who would describe to the roots the nature of *all* banal and visionary experience. Instead, Beckett's narrators—fragments of himself, as all fictional first person narrators are of their creators—choose that part of the world which best reflects the state of its viewers. If Molloy sits high on his bicycle and can see the policeman before him, he is capable of describing in greater detail than can the Unnamable, whose vision is confined to a horizon of mud. The vision of the narrator limits his ability to cope with his consciousness; if he sees nothing, or little, or abstract qualities, then he, like the tradition of narrators before him, can report no more than what appears to his eyes. As in the world of Kafka, what is described reflects, mirrorlike, the mind of the reporter. Beckett is aware of this from his earliest publications; he praises the manner in which Proust states phenomena not logically, but in the order of their perception—before cause and effect can come into play. And so it is with the consciousness of Beckett's narrators: theirs is a prevocal nonlogicality, a perception of sights and a groping with mental pictures as they begin to turn into concepts, "the sounds the mind makes in actually grappling with words." The development of Beckett's style, from the baroque to the pseudocolloquial, as it must be called, reflects his development from haughty and assumed control to a realization that the way it is differs greatly from his earlier assumptions. The mind is a messy medium, almost as messy as the universe an artist must accommodate through form, and the writer/artist's initial effort lies in rec-

---

[3] Christopher Middleton, "Randnotizen zu Romanen von Samuel Beckett," *Akzente* 4, no. 5 (October, 1957): 411.

ognizing the impurity of his mind. Beckett's effort to verbalize the mind coping with phenomena is his contribution to the phenomenological novel.

That a writer's style must develop from his vantage point for viewing the world is true especially of the writer who is discovering new possibilities for verbal creation—immediacy of discovery cannot be conveyed by hackneyed form. "The work of art helps remove from unseeing eyes the obfuscating veil and transports the reader or viewer to a vision hitherto strange to him. That Beckett's vision is strange is undeniable, as is the fact that the very nature of his art is shaped, naturally, by his way of looking at the world."[4] For the moment, emphasis must be switched from the processes within the mind of a Beckett narrator to the manner by which he perceives those stimuli causing reaction in the mind itself. This epistemology, for Beckett as it was for Kafka, is the relationship between human consciousness and the external world.[5] One does not react equally to all stimuli. Some pictures make a stronger impression than others, some take more time to be understood. Relationships between cause and effect, though possibly valid, make little impression unless they are pointed out. For the most part, a man, as his mind perceives, fits what impresses him into a pattern of his own; if he cannot understand a phenomenon he calls it absurd, for outside his own system there is nothing but a void. Each man's system covers both facts and values; their relationship is established within each person, within each man.

[4] Josephine Jacobsen and William R. Mueller, *The Testament of Samuel Beckett*, p. 77.

[5] "One of the primary reasons for Beckett's obscurity to most readers is his epistemology, his sense of the relationship between the individual consciousness and the whole world of space and time. Most persons assume that their consciousness is a reasonably accurate perceiver of an essentially ordered world and an essentially predictable one, one in which events conform to strict causal laws. Beckett is in revolt against what he envisages as a scientific position which, up to the early decades of the twentieth century at least, led man to assume that he was moving closer and closer to a knowledge of the world of space and time, that certain causes in the physical world lead to certain effects, and that though certain causal relationships may be unknown to us, they do nevertheless exist. Beckett is in revolt also against virtually our whole literary tradition. A reading of the world's literature, certainly up to this century at least, would encourage the assumption of a reasonably clear apperception of a world of cause and effect. The world of Homer, of Dante, of Shakespeare is predictable" (*ibid.*, pp. 60–61).

And, though such a system often keeps an individual from accepting the importance of new evidence for which the system itself has no place (such as the novels of Beckett), each man needs such a system to cope with the daily universe.[6]

Edith Kern explains how Beckett paints his characters in the image of his average reader: "Beckett shows the drama of man as *Dasein* in the Heideggerian sense of the word. Heidegger saw this drama contained in the very world itself. . . . In this way man gives meaning to the world. He neither creates this world nor observes it as an outsider; for he is anchored in it and receives his horizon from it. But he is the small ephemeral intelligence without whom the vastness of Being would remain undifferentiated."[7] Anchored in the world, man cannot see from any point of view other than his own; no externality may be admitted to the category of perceptual validity. A man in a given position sees what he sees, reacts to it, and perhaps deep in his unconscious mind places the newly acquired "fact" in its proper context, but of this process he can know nothing. The writer, primarily a human being and a man honest to an art that attempts to depict reality, can do no more than express what he sees and what he understands about his assimilation of this information. Totally to explain the unconscious is as yet impossible; the novelist of narrative consciousness, limiting himself to the perceptions of his protagonist, presents his audience with nothing more than the conscious mind of a viewing narrator, whereby he implicates the reader. If nothing but strangeness can be perceived about the exterior world, if nothing can be understood about external relationships and little about those between the voice speaking and other possible voices, one must therefore agree with Hugh Kenner, who says that

. . . in extracting all these virtues from the impasse, the impasse of having nothing much to say and no reason for saying it, Beckett succeeds in not at all wasting our time. For since someone else, a character, is responsible

[6] As Jacobsen and Mueller point out, man's mind needs patterns into which all experience can be placed; such patterns help him cope with the phenomena he perceives. Yet the danger of rigidified patterns lies in the evils of habit that patterns breed (*ibid.*, pp. 62–63).

[7] Edith Kern, "Beckett's Knight of Infinite Resignation," *Yale French Studies* no. 29 (Spring–Summer, 1962), p. 51.

for the narration, we are not simply considering buttons, but attending to the intimate deliverances of a human mind, which in finding the buttons of absorbing interest, proves to be itself of absorbing interest, to us. That is what is misleading about quotations from Beckett's novels. The quotations are likely to be about buttons, or stones, or even a photograph of a donkey wearing a straw hat, or else about problems, and these problems of little intrinsic importance. But the context from which they are excerpted is one of intimate human concern; these topics, these questions, have all occurred to a mind, indeed as we encounter them are in the immediate act of occurring to a mind, which appeals to us by its very proximity.[8]

It is the narrating consciousness alone that is of interest. Those who find that characters are apparently no longer relevant to fiction in the works of Beckett and even more in the works of Robbe-Grillet have overlooked the most obvious: the narrating consciousness has become the character, and his adventures alone are chronicled. This consciousness proclaims the impossibility of an expanded, omniscience-seeking vantage point for man tied to a single course, and Beckett's characters live out the cycle of average consciousness. Literature has had difficulty in adapting itself to the idea of limitation; the result has been literature's evolution away from immediate human relevance. Beckett, by accepting the limitations imposed on the writer by circumstance, has with Kafka brought literature, through his own experiments (despite their impracticality), to a point where human consciousness and environment converge. His characters are men who, being human, cope as best they can.

By the middle of the twentieth century we have become skeptical about expansion, and Beckett writes from the cultural context of the mid-twentieth century. All faiths are tottering—religion and science, personality and ideology, family and nation, freedom and imperatives, subject and object—and Beckett's prose totters with them; he even plays up the slapstick comedy, like any competent clown. His plosives echo the puncturing of surface reality by atomic physics and psychoanalysis. Logical Positivists and Existentialists alike insist upon the failure of metaphysics, highlighting Beckett's comic and poignant portrayal of man as *animalis metaphysicum* [*sic*].[9]

[8] Kenner, *The Stoic Comedians,* pp. 84–85.
[9] Cohn, *The Comic Gamut,* p. 4.

Since no expansion is possible, everything must become internalized; since the unconscious is an unknown quantity, all exploration must be limited to the consciousness, the only remaining medium intrinsically man's own. Therefore it becomes not what is said that is of essential importance, but the manner in which it is said; the medium becomes, in Marshall McLuhan's term, the message.[10] The medium establishes the mood.

The task of recognizing man from his voice becomes more difficult if that voice is incapable of discussing matter within his field of vision. The way it is with man's nature reflects the world he inhabits; a removal of man's extensions, his organs and senses of perception, those antennae he has always possessed for reaching out into the world and drawing from it information vital to his existence, removes his ability to talk about his environment and draws him ever deeper into himself. The shifted stress in the new novel, from fictional discussion of the environment to a fictional study of the narrator, more and more becomes the proper place of fiction. The average man's antennae for perceiving his environment, in fact most men's antennae much of the time (sight, reason, hearing, reaction, emotion—once natural endowments) have become stunted by the artificial extensions man has made for himself, by media that have become their own external end for man—radio, television, teaching machines, film, and the like. They are not connected with man except vicariously, and vicarious man has become incapable of perception; he is toughened against possible stimuli. And so, unable to escape from his situation, he accepts his state and must turn to the medium that remains to him, the medium of mood. And it is about mood that Beckett writes. Each of his narratives presents a voice becoming ever more cut away from the stimuli of environment; and no nineteenth-century "literary" discussion is possible if an object, situation, or event cannot be perceived. Only the consciousness remains, a consciousness capable of mood because it still reacts, if merely to the slightest of stimuli, and capable of creating patterns because it must, because it is human. McLuhan's claim that those who call the novel dead are right is

[10] See Marshall McLuhan, "The Medium is the Message," in *Understanding Media: The Extensions of Man*, pp. 23–39.

proved false when the novelist uses the medium of his narration as the message, as the information he is attempting to convey. McLuhan says that many new media can transmit information more easily than literature. "Absurd" writing is a product of the author's trying to cope with his own expendability, says McLuhan. What he does not realize is that literature is still capable of establishing mood, of describing from the point of view of consciousness. Even the film, impure because impersonal, cannot validly establish consciousness. This is left to the new fiction, which preempts McLuhan's war cry and directs fiction into the field of narrative consciousness, which it is only now beginning to exploit.

If Beckett's medium is his message, then it becomes necessary to differentiate between three distinct worlds, two of which are immediately relevant to Beckett's fiction, the third indirectly. There is first of all the objective external world, "objective" here being an abbreviation for something beyond the scope of Beckett's fiction; this world is incapable of being described properly, for there is too much of it that is beyond the pale of perception. The second world is the inner turmoil of subjective consciousness—Moran's, for example, or Sapo's roaring head—which is described by an established mood rather than through objective delineation; it is the controlling tone of the narrative. And finally there is the objectivization of that world —Sapo's, Moran's—which is reminiscent of the objective external world because the mind controls the parts of it that are seen. Any need to describe the external world will choose the momentarily relevant parts of it, for any mood that demands a description of an external world must send the governing stimuli to the consciousness of the narrating voice. The latter two worlds are the matter of Beckett's fiction, but the first is present also, somewhere in back.[11] Beckett rejects any one-to-one relationship between the perceived and the

---

[11] "On Samuel Beckett's planet, matter is minimal, physiography and physiology barely support life. The air is exceedingly thin, and the light exceedingly dim. But all the cluttered complexity of our own planet is required to educate the taste that can savor the unique comic flavor of Beckett's creation. Our world, 'so various, so beautiful, so new,' so stingily admitted to Beckett's work, is nevertheless the essential background for appreciation of that work" (Cohn, The Comic Gamut, p. 3).

described environment after it has been filtered through the human mind, however. Much of the process comes to him from Proust's impressionism. Beckett's relation to Kafka stems from his need to let everything, viewed and expressed, be told in one idiom; there is no differentiation between the observed and the recited, no reflection on it. The idiom is unified within the immediacy of the narrating consciousness and is not separated in its expression; the reader's often-felt sensation of malaise, of inescapability from content, is the result. If one must seek a metaphysical description of such subjectivity, it would appear to be solipsism—and the term is not detrimental to Beckett's fiction.

Beckett's motif—if it can be reduced and abstracted from the novels—is that words are thoughts are emotion, that fiction is our only knowledge and all knowledge a fiction written in a foreign tongue. ". . . that was to teach me the nature of emotion . . . it was to teach me how to reason . . ." comments the Unnamable about his last fiction. But emotion and reason both are clothed in "their" words. Thus there is, finally, no knowledge at all, since there is no defense against solipsism—rationally. But Beckett and his author-heroes are romantics, not rationalists. As such, they are always prey to their quests . . .[12]

In fact, despite the outer appearance of solipsism, the romantic nature of Beckett's heroes, which causes them to begin only with themselves, relates them not to the Cartesian principle, *cogito, ergo sum*, which is followed by rational development (although the Descartes of "Whorescope" is their cousin),[13] but to a narrative consciousness that returns the emphasis to the thing itself as necessarily interpreted by the human mind. Yet, if his writing begins with the existential precept of man anchored without reason to a specific time and place, "Beckett's writings . . . are more than mere illustrations of the point-of-view of existentialist philosophers like Heidegger and Sartre; they constitute the culmination of existential thought itself, *precisely because they are free of any abstract* concepts or gen-

[12] Ruby Cohn, "Still Novel," *Yale French Studies*, no. 24 (Fall, 1959), p. 52.
[13] "Whorescope," a poem of about a hundred lines, is Beckett's first separately published work. It won first prize in a poetry competition the subject of which was Time, sponsored by Nancy Cunnard's Hours Press in Paris in 1930. It deals with Cartesian doubt and the idea of dualism, as Federman notes (*Journey to Chaos*, p. 72).

eral ideas."[14] Unattainable omniscience alone could generalize Molloy's condition into anything beyond himself.

Still in fledgling form, the principle of consciousness is introduced in *Murphy*; Beckett is the puppet-master, but when Murphy is present he fights with his creator for control, or at least for upstage position.[15] From the internality of Murphy's skull, writers about Beckett's work conclude that its nature is essentially Cartesian: that Beckett's narrators reason outward from the self. The direction is correct, but the process—rationality—is not; to imply that *Murphy* is a closed novel because it takes place entirely in the mind of Murphy, that it is an exploration of his mind, exaggerates both the novel's intention and its realization.[16]

Watt is in an analogous, if somewhat more highly constructed, position. "The major achievement of [*Watt*] is to create a tight, compelling and self-enclosed world, with a bare minimum of reference to the cultural and physical worlds of our inheritance. It is for this creation that, years later, Beckett has been compared with Kafka, whose world is comparably closed, absurd, but haunting and disastrous to its hero."[17] The episode of Watt walking demonstrates the ability of point of view to dominate style prior to the establishment of a complete narrating consciousness: there is no speaking mind but

[14] Esslin, introduction to *Samuel Beckett*, p. 5.

[15] Jacobson and Mueller explain it this way: "Before a reader has finished the short first section of the novel, he has three times read the phrase 'as described in section six.' Section six is a disquisition on 'Murphy's mind,' delivered in the comic tone customary to most of Beckett's writing and yet presenting a serious description of the relationship between Murphy's consciousness and the outside world. Murphy's mind saw itself as a microcosm closed off from, but containing everything existing in, the outside world. When the mental concept he had of an action was accompanied by the physical experience of the action, the knowledge was termed *actual*; *kick* was to him actual knowledge, since he possessed both the mental concept and the physical experience of a kick. When mental concept was not matched by physical experience, the knowledge was called virtual; *caress* was to him virtual knowledge. There was no ethical assessment of the forms of knowledge, but an attempted description of them in terms of their position and their brightness: 'The mind felt its actual part to be above and bright, its virtual beneath and fading into dark, without however connecting this with the ethical yoyo' " (*The Testament of Samuel Beckett*, pp. 67–68).

[16] See especially Samuel I. Mintz, "Beckett's *Murphy*: A 'Cartesian' Novel," *Perspective* 11, no. 3 (Autumn, 1959): 156–165.

[17] Ruby Cohn, "Preliminary Observations," *Perspective* 11, no. 3 (Autumn, 1959): 123.

Beckett's, and it moves back and forth between omniscience and first person narrative. In much the same manner Beckett describes the visit of the Galls just after Watt's arrival at Knott's home:

On answering the door, as his habit was, when there was a knock at the door, he found standing before it, or so he realized later, arm in arm, an old man and a middleaged man. The latter said:
  We are the Galls, father and son, and we are come, what is more, all the way from town, to choon the piano.
  They were two, and they stood, arm in arm, in this way, because the father was blind, like so many members of his profession. For if the father had not been blind, then he would not have needed his son to hold his arm, and guide him on his rounds, no, but he would have set his son free, to go about his own business. So Watt supposed, though there was nothing in the father's face to show that he was blind, nor in his attitude either, except that he leaned on his son in a way expressive of a great deal of support. (W 67)

Although the uncertainty will be present later in *Molloy* and the novels that follow, the external view ("or so he realized later" and "so Watt supposed," for example) will disappear. Nevertheless the mind of the narrator who is also the author here embraces all events, still rendering his characters puppets.

Beckett links skepticism to first person narration at about the time he begins to write in French; in the short story, "Le Calmant," the "I" doubts "the landscape he sees, the time that presumably passes, the difference between life and death, and above all reality and the possibility of knowledge."[18] It is a voice that realizes that it makes no difference which story it tells, and so will relate any story because all stories are the same; it foreshadows the voices of the trilogy. Malone's, for example: his doubt too is inescapable, though not so much for him as for the reader. He talks of the old woman who brings in his soup and takes out his pot:

She is an old woman. I don't know why she is good for me. Yes, let us call it goodness, without quibbling. For her it is certainly goodness. I believe her to be even older than I. . . . But it is conceivable that she does what she does out of sheer charity, or moved with regard to me by a less general feeling of compassion or affection. Nothing is impossible, I cannot keep

---

[18] *Ibid.*, p. 124.

on denying it much longer. But it is more convenient to suppose that when
I came in for the room I came in for her too. (Tr 185)

He can know no more, for his circumstances are limited to his room;
there is no external glance he can attain of himself, of her, or of his
situation—no glance either literal or figurative. Both Malone and the
narrator of the novel that follows are in a position analogous to
Murphy's. "The six planes of his room seem often . . . to become the
outer wall of a skull inside which he roams, listening to 'the faint
sound of aerial surf that is my silence'; the Unnamed too speaks of
the 'inside of my distant skull where once I wandered . . . straining
against the walls.' "[19] As the voices seem to change, there is yet no
change in the vision, because the point of view remains constant. No
matter who is speaking, the anchored position of the narrator provides a unity: if for a moment the voices appear fragmented, the
fragments always combine to recreate the whole voice. Esslin says,
"In Beckett's trilogy, not only is the autonomy of the voices that are
heard complete, the voices themselves in turn present and invent
other voices, while the author is reduced to no more than the neutral
field of consciousness into which these autonomous voices emerge."[20]
And in the third section of How It Is the voice notes: ". . . millions
millions there are millions of us and there are three I place myself at
my point of view Bem is Bom Bom Bem let us say Bom it's preferable
Bom then me and Pim me in the middle" (H 114).

The initial instance in which Beckett discovers complete realization of an unsuccessful quest through narrative consciousness is his
first published French novel, Molloy. This novel, standing halfway
along the progression from Beckett's baroque to his pseudocolloquial
style, presents in about equal proportions the two immediate worlds
of Beckett's fiction: it combines creations of the narrator's conscious
mind with the existential rumbling of a mind attempting to cope.
How It Is remains the best example of the latter, Murphy of the
former. In Molloy the two are not only necessarily mixed, they are
also inextricably merged. The world as objective reality appears
rarely; little more than Molloy's struggling mind, meshed with a

[19] John Fletcher, The Novels of Samuel Beckett, p. 153.
[20] Esslin, introduction to Samuel Beckett, pp. 5–6.

world that it assumes from the few stimuli it takes in, appears on the page. Molloy's early statement—"The truth is I don't know much"—is as honest as Moran's last words—

Then I went back to the house and wrote. It is midnight. The rain is beating on the windows. It was not midnight. It was not raining. (Tr 176)

—for the validity of the narrative's relation to the "objective" world, the world of assumed normal experience. Only rarely does an external force impress itself immediately on Molloy's consciousness.[21] A word in this category is "Thanks"; but even that word comes through to Molloy without meaning—it penetrates as pure sound (Tr 49–50). Although being a psychological penetration of the surface consciousness that to the reader is Molloy's mind, the consciousness must attempt to explain the penetration in physical terms—the question becomes one of deafness. Though he grasps the word, he still has no idea why or how he grasped it.

If any statement about events in the external world can be made, they must be general, so composed of hesitations and assumptions, that little importance can be drawn from them; the narrator does not interpret, he merely assumes—if his words are to remain valid he can do no more.

Each went on his way. A back towards the town, C on by-ways he seemed hardly to know, or not at all, for he went with uncertain step and often stopped to look about him, like someone trying to fix landmarks in his mind, for one day perhaps he may have to retrace his steps, you never know. The treacherous hills where fearfully he ventured were no doubt only known to him from afar, seen perhaps from his bedroom window or from the summit of a monument which, one black day, having nothing in particular to do and turning to height for solace, he had paid his few coppers to climb, slower and slower, up the winding stones. From there he must have seen it all, the plain, the sea, and then these self-same hills, that some call mountains, indigo in places in the evening light, their serried ranges crowding to the skyline, cloven with hidden valleys that the eye divines from sudden shifts of colour and then from other signs for which there are no words, nor even thoughts. (Tr 9–10)

---

[21] From this point it is necessary to view Beckett's words in context. For his closed style, context is everything; the internal unity is achieved only when all is recognized as being part of the same cloth.

The constant use of such terminology as "he seemed," "you never know," "no doubt," "perhaps," "he must have," dominates the tone. It becomes necessary therefore to accept a consciousness that will not generalize. The mind of the narrator has only one other alternative: it can merely question the cause of an event it does not understand. Any questions must pertain to what is seen on the surface; nothing below the surface is understood. Here Molloy returns to the things in themselves and refuses to attach value to them. When, however, he does assume a thing or place to have value, it is because he alone is giving it value: ". . . I knew them well, the amenities of my region, and I considered that the forest was no worse, to my mind, but it was better, in this sense, that I was there. That is a strange way, is it not, of looking at things. Perhaps less strange than it seems. For being in the forest, a place neither worse nor better than the others, and being free to stay there, was it not natural I should think highly of it, not because of what it was, but because I was there. For I was there" (Tr 86). But in judging that a place has value because of his presence, he is encroaching on that other world, the world that is born of his coping mind. Although the process of such birth is implicit, it is occasionally possible to see the evolution from the coping mind to the created world, in which correspondences and functions are inverted.

But I have no reason to be gladdened by the sun and I take good care not to be. The Aegean, thirsting for heat and light, him I killed, he killed himself, early on, in me. The pale gloom of rainy days was better fitted to my taste, no, that's not it, to my humour, no, that's not it either, I had neither taste nor humour, I lost them early on. Perhaps what I mean is that the pale gloom, etc., hid me better, without its being on that account particularly pleasing to me. Chameleon in spite of himself, there you have Molloy, viewed from a certain angle. And in winter, under my greatcoat, I wrapped myself in swathes of newspaper, and did not shed them until the earth awoke, for good, in April. The Times Literary Supplement was admirably adapted to this purpose, of a neverfailing toughness and impermeability. Even farts made no impression on it. I can't help it, gas escapes from my fundamental on the least pretext, it's hard not to mention it now and then, however great my distaste. One day I counted them. Three hundred and fifteen farts in nineteen hours, or an average of over sixteen farts an hour. After all it's not excessive. Four farts every fifteen minutes. It's nothing.

Not even one fart every four minutes. It's unbelievable. Damn it, I hardly fart at all, I should never have mentioned it. Extraordinary how mathematics help you to know yourself. (Tr 30)

Far more subtle is the attempt to force what facts are known into some sort of context; the mind struggles with several hypotheses and concludes:

So I will confine myself to the following brief additional remarks, and the first of which is this, that Lousse was a woman of extraordinary flatness, physically speaking of course, to such a point that I am still wondering this evening, in the comparative silence of my last abode, if she was not a man rather or at least an androgyne. She had a somewhat hairy face, or am I imagining it, in the interests of the narrative? The poor woman, I saw her so little, so little looked at her. And was not her voice suspiciously deep? So she appears to me today. (Tr 56)

But the mind of this narrator has difficulty in garnering information in the first place; for example, in speaking merely of the weather in his region he becomes uncertain of its nature. He describes weather patterns but cannot say for certain they have remained as they were. But if certain phenomena are truly characteristic of his region, they would not have changed during an absence. Molloy's statement throws great doubt on his ability to note a true characteristic when he sees one; even his power of observation is undermined. Often it would have been better to remain silent. In a description of Molloy's own arms and legs, he describes the hands and feet as they lie in his bed and attributes meaning to them, meaning that, although probably not the real meaning of his hands and feet, destroys any probable relationship between object and meaning by making farce of any possible interaction. Having hands that are perhaps engaged in love-play with each other is as good a way to account for them as any other, but, because it clearly is impossible in all human terms that this can be the case, the reader accepts it only as being an absurd (both disconnected and silly) reason. In the same way, however, almost any thought or reason would be so considered, for it would have to be achieved in the same manner. Thus Beckett underlines the arbitrariness of relationships between an object and any meaning possibly inherent in it. All meaning is attributed to objects by the minds of human beings—by Beckett, by Molloy, by the reader.

Successful at the task or not, the narrator can be at best a spectator. Molloy, restricting himself to watching (because of his bad leg) as Lousse alone digs a grave for the dog, remarks: "On the whole I was a mere spectator. I contributed my presence" (Tr 36). He can make no value judgments, nor can he measure preferences except in terms removed from actual experience. By not interpreting sensations, he foreshadows much of Robbe-Grillet's work: "I preferred the garden to the house, to judge by the long hours I spent there, for I spent there the greater part of the day and night, whether it was wet or whether it was fine. Men were always busy there, working at I know not what. For the garden seemed hardly to change, from day to day, aside from the tiny changes due to the customary cycle of birth, life and death" (Tr 52). Preferences are ascertained empirically rather than psychologically; Molloy should be saying, "I preferred the garden because I like the flowers." But he judges his enjoyment of the garden by the measurable length of time he spends there, as if he had no entrance into his mind, and further, as if, like his predecessor Watt, someone were describing him in the garden and coming to an empirical conclusion founded on observed fact. Molloy is both observing and observed.

The mind coping with external fact grasps for the least straw to relieve its burden; anything, even an arbitrary chosen direction, will do. "Shall I describe the room? No, I shall have occasion to do so later. When I seek refuge there, beat to the world, all shame drunk, my prick in my rectum, who knows. Good. Now that we know where we're going, let's go there. It's so nice to know where you're going, in the early stages. It almost rids you of the wish to go there" (Tr 19). And the mind is often difficult to follow if one does not realize that it reacts to what the eyes see. If there are apparent non-sequiturs in juxtaposed sentences, it is because the narrator's glance has shifted. A policeman asks Molloy for his papers; Molloy has only a piece of toilet paper. "In a panic I took this paper from my pocket and thrust it under his nose. The weather was fine. We took the little side streets" (Tr 20). Or again, talking of his cell, Molloy says some of the furniture there has disappeared. Interpreted, the situation could be understood in terms of some of the furniture having been removed while he slept, but Molloy will not so conclude. And in that same cell, a man arrives to clean up, to straighten the furniture: then he begins dusting the woodwork "with a feather duster which suddenly appeared in his hand" (Tr 43). There was of course no magic in the sudden appearance of the dust brush—rather Molloy's eyes have just caught sight of it. The point of view alone shifts from one sentence, or from one moment, to the next. There was no emotional reaction to the first; immediately and without division it is followed by the second. The paragraphless form reinforces this total connection of all things through the eye and mind of the narrator. The resulting sensation implies that nothing is more or less important than anything else: all is an equal part of the whole.

Complete union between the mind attempting to cope and the partial world it creates is presented in a passage describing the moon as it passes the window of Molloy's cell. The reader senses the passage of time by watching a kind of movement that can take place only in time: temporal progression—unmeasured time—is established. Molloy's description anticipates much of what Robbe-Grillet will attempt:

I must have fallen asleep, for all of a sudden there was the moon, a huge moon framed in the window. Two bars divided it in three segments, of which the middle remained constant, while little by little the right gained what the left lost. For the moon was moving from left to right, or the room was moving from right to left, or both together perhaps, or both were moving from left to right, but the room not so fast as the moon, or from right to left, but the moon not so fast as the room. But can one speak of right and left in such circumstances? That movements of an extreme complexity were taking place seemed certain, and yet what a simple thing it seemed, that vast yellow light sailing slowly behind my bars and which little by little the dense wall devoured, and finally eclipsed. (Tr 39)

Part III: ROBBE-GRILLET

5. Toward a New Novel: A Theory for Fiction

ALONE AMONG THE NOVELISTS discussed here, Alain Robbe-Grillet has published a volume of purposely theoretical writing. Kafka's diaries and letters, certainly not meant for publication, deal with the events, the day-to-day trivialities of his personal life; any information about his art must be carefully culled from them, and then it usually appears as its own kind of parable. Beckett's essays on Joyce and on Proust and his three dialogues with Georges Duthuit, all written before his presently published novels, these ostensibly deal with subjects other than himself; they explain what Beckett has discovered in the works of Joyce, Proust, and several modern painters but do not allow him to elaborate on what he adds to the innovations of those from whom he learned. On the other hand, although Robbe-Grillet's *Towards a New Novel* (*Pour un nouveau roman*) contains essays he has written about other people—understanding the tradition is essential if an author wishes to grow from it —the book's primary force arises from its apparently heretical outline for a new kind of novel.

And yet the program the book demands is often little more than a description of fiction already written by Robbe-Grillet's predecessors, Kafka and Beckett. Certainly it contains something more—it contains passages lending themselves to interpretations that infuriated and impressed critical thinking for more than ten years.[1] Perhaps only in retrospect can one see how Robbe-Grillet's essays could be misunderstood while at the same time they presented a plan for novels unrelated to interpretations of his theories by others. For just as each of his novels shows an increased subtlety and comprehension of technique, his theory too develops to a point where it eliminates the confusion imposed on it by such critics as Roland Barthes, who, himself linguistically and scientistically oriented, saw Robbe-Grillet's first two novels (*The Erasers* [1953] and *The Voyeur* [1955]) as representing worlds void of human beings except insofar as humans were viewed, much like all objects within the narrative, as things.[2] In the beginning, Robbe-Grillet did not deny this analysis. He could write the novels and sense their importance, but he could not yet abstract and define the theory. So in 1956 he wrote:

Even the least conditioned observer can't manage to see the world around him with an unprejudiced eye. Let us make it quite clear before we go any further that we are not here concerned with that naive preoccupation of subjectivity which so amuses the analysts of the (subjective) soul. Objectivity, in the current meaning of the term—a completely impersonal way of looking at things—is only too obviously a chimera. But it is *liberty* which ought at least to be possible—but isn't, either. Cultural fringes (bits of psychology, ethics, metaphysics, etc.) are all the time being attached to things and making them seem less strange, more comprehensible, more reassuring. Sometimes the camouflage is total: a gesture is effaced from our minds and its place taken by the emotions that are supposed to have given rise to it ... (TNN 52–53)

Although the argument appears to develop into a plea for objectivity in viewing the world, at the same time it admits that such a project is impossible; the inescapability of subjective vision is a dominant note from the beginning. Yet Robbe-Grillet is not talking about his

[1] The essays collected in *Towards a New Novel* began to appear as early as 1953.
[2] Roland Barthes, "Littérature objective," Critique 10 (July–August, 1954): 581–591, and "Littérature littérale," *Critique* 12 (September–October, 1955): 820–826.

way of seeing the world, but about the world itself; the distinction has become blurred for many of those who follow Barthes's comprehension of Robbe-Grillet's novels and theories.

To no small extent Robbe-Grillet himself has contributed to the rampant misunderstanding about his fiction; at the beginning he was more interested in considering the nature of the external world than he was in discussing the techniques he utilized in viewing that world. His bent led him to adapt to literature the dictum that "the world is neither meaningful nor absurd. It quite simply *is* . . . All around us, defying our pack of animistic or domesticating adjectives, things *are there*" (TNN 53). An explanation about the nature of the world from a novice writer is only natural if, as Robbe-Grillet does, he considers himself to be writing "realistically." It is even more natural if he is only in the process of developing his theories about art and its relationship to that world: one must first understand what one is describing before finding the tools for that description. In this respect, a writer's theories about his art begin only after he has begun to write novels; the novels must, by definition (even if not in their stress), be about the world. The theory follows the fact of creation despite an author's possible understanding of the theory before he began to write.

Therefore, when Robbe-Grillet maintained the *presence* of things to be their primary importance, he gave strong argument to those who believed he was going to be working with things in and of themselves.[3] In this early essay, Robbe-Grillet justly claims that the nineteenth-century fictional tradition sees literature as a mode of expression in which the writer defined and delineated his relation to the external world (called by Robbe-Grillet "tragic complicity") by explaining the world in terms of himself, by finding in the external

[3] Renato Barilli, "De Sartre à Robbe-Grillet," *Revue des Lettres Modernes*, nos. 94–99 (1964), p. 107, doubts that Robbe-Grillet has his phenomenology from reading phenomenological philosophy. Rather, says Barilli, Robbe-Grillet's general sense of the *Zeitgeist* has taught him to combine the tension Sartre sees between man and the world with Merleau-Ponty's ideas of human perception. The result has been a kind of fiction unique to Robbe-Grillet, which displays Merleau-Ponty's idea of perception appeasing the Sartrian tension. We know from Robbe-Grillet's own admission that he could never get through Sartre's *L'Etre et le néant*.

world correspondences to his own moods and sensibilities. By carefully using the adjective to anthropomorphize and domesticate his environment (a countryside is "austere" or "calm," depending on the mood to be established), the writer made of it an accomplice for his hero, as well as an accomplice for himself in his attempt to explain his hero. Robbe-Grillet the theorist wished to eliminate such complicity, since ultimately it must eliminate the possibility of any relationship between man and a universe already by definition nonhuman; only the nonrelationship remains, what existentialism calls the gap of absurdity. Robbe-Grillet, not believing that the simple fact of non-connection between man and his environment should be seen pejoratively (absurdly), claimed that a new kind of fiction could develop if the unbridgeable distance between man and his world was accepted as a neutral fact.

Between taking the world as a series of surfaces, which exist in complete freedom from man's domesticating adjectives and have little relevance for man, and taking the world as a unified projection of man's inmost subjective nature (when the heart is clouded so is the sky, the sun comes out when love is rediscovered—or vice versa, if irony is intended), there is the middle ground upon which Robbe-Grillet attempts to stand. But by arguing forcibly against the nineteenth-century complicity between man and his universe, Robbe-Grillet sounds as if he is embracing the view expounded by Barthes's *chosisme*, and evidence for Robbe-Grillet's possible *chosiste* leanings can be garnered from his 1958 article, "Nature, Humanism and Tragedy," to which he prefixes a quotation from Barthes. The article itself, however, is thoroughly denied by both his previous and his subsequent fictions, which, although they do take as fact the equality of everything external, cannot free his heroes from a complicity with the external world. No human can perceive the world in a nonhuman way; no center other than a living eye, or at least a perceiving mind, can validly explain its environment.

The complicity between man and the universe need not be tragic, and if it is not it differs already from any view within the novels of the past. The fiction of Robbe-Grillet dismisses, as his theories demand, the old myths of depth (TNN 56) whose fictions describe at great length what lies beneath the world's surfaces. Robbe-Grillet makes it clear that for him there is no (human) depth in the external world. But there is a depth to man, a psychology man does not understand, which governs much of his life; that psychology is defined analytically by the manner in which the governing psychology sees the external world and by what it finds appropriate to its glance. Whereas nineteenth-century writers of fiction anthropomorphized the universe, Robbe-Grillet allows his heroes their delineations according to what segments of their universe they choose to see and according to the manner in which they see and understand the segments. The universe remains an accomplice of the consciousness that views it. It is still a humanist's universe; the viewer is no less a victim of his own complicity than he is in the novels of Balzac or of Camus. The great difference, however, and the great contribution of phenomenological fiction, lies in immediacy, in its ability to implicate the reader in the situation of the hero without ever explaining what the situation is. Far from being a scientistic literature, a *chosiste* fiction, Robbe-Grillet's novels display a relevant realism that keeps them in the tradition of that fiction which is altogether descriptive of human experience.

The shame is that, in his enthusiasm to formulate the boundaries of a new novel, Robbe-Grillet attempted to begin with too much of a clean slate, and, for the earlier critics, everything was erased. In his essay of 1957, "On Some Outdated Notions," he states that such trappings of the novel as character and plot must be eliminated in the new attempt at writing fiction. Although he claims that plot and character are outdated notions, he himself is working with precisely those two elements of fiction, in a modified form, as were Beckett and Kafka before him; merely his method of approach to these problems has differed from that of the nineteenth-century authors. In Robbe-Grillet's fiction, the emphasis has shifted to a tone that describes the character obliquely by engulfing the whole series of events (plot) within the mood established by the narrative; the whole of a novel is completely relevant to the character about whom the events take place.

Even in the article dealing with tragic complicity, "Nature, Humanism, and Tragedy," Robbe-Grillet undercuts his theory of man's non-involvement with nature: ". . . it must be added that the character-istic of humanism, whether Christian or otherwise, is precisely to in-corporate *everything*, including things that may be trying to limit it, or even totally reject it. This may even be said to be one of the most reliable mainsprings of its action" (TNN 76). Here he is, in effect, admitting what he discovers later in his theory and knows already after the appearance of *The Voyeur*, that one consciousness narrates only what is relevant to itself—nothing else is incorporated. The unity lies in the human consciousness itself, which can relate details relevant only to its own humanity; everything considered by that consciousness is dependent upon it for the kind of existence it will be allowed. Each man is an internalized universe who considers the external world in accordance with his own nature. In this sense, Robbe-Grillet practices precisely what he condemns: his dismissal of the contemporary relevance of nineteenth-century fiction is so broad that he denounces techniques of his own that differ greatly from those of Balzac. Yet, whereas Balzac sought unified external correla-tives to explain his characters, Robbe-Grillet's characters pick tiny segments of the external world, which they draw to themselves; these segments give the only available clues to their natures and obses-sions. And this is the distinction Robbe-Grillet does not draw.

The difficulty from the beginning lies in a distinction between the consideration of things themselves and the *presence* of these things. For the presence of a thing is relevant only to the mind that grasps that presence. If this is the distinction Robbe-Grillet was attempting to make, he allowed himself to be misled by the intriguing ideas of Roland Barthes and the praises of Barthes's followers.[4] It would be too much to say that the *chosiste* critics misinterpreted what Robbe-Grillet was writing about (in his theories), since a sufficient base ex-

[4] Especially Jean Miesch, *Robbe-Grillet*; Olga Bernal, *Alain Robbe-Grillet: Le Roman de l'absence*, who recognizes merely Robbe-Grillet's projected pic-tures, while the reasons for his choices remain a mystery to her; Claude Mauriac, *L'Allitérature contemporaine*, who rarely thinks critically for himself, here following Barthes completely; and Pierre de Boisdeffre, *Où va le roman?* for whom *chosisme* appears in only slightly different clothes; his term is *reification*. See also Ben F. Stoltzfus, *Alain Robbe-Grillet and the New French Novel*, pp. 55–56, for a discussion of other miscomprehensions of Robbe-Grillet's work.

isted for their attitudes. But *Towards a New Novel*, as a volume of critical essays, cannot be viewed as base for *chosiste* interpretations. Robbe-Grillet claims, quite rightly, that the volume presents a collection of essays, thoughts about the novel that have evolved over a period of years. Such a description is quite valid, provided an attempt is not made to draw parallels between the chronological development of his art and of his theory. A further danger lies in forcing his novels into the mold of previous theoretical statements. Robbe-Grillet points out the writer's difficulty in knowing precisely where he is going before he gets there; the work of art evolves as the attitude to it evolves, as the writer works with it. To take a ten-page theory and attempt to fit into it a three-hundred-page novel is a dangerous business; some aspects of the theory will fit the novel, but the novel must, if it is to be of value, contain far more than the theory itself. In his novels themselves Robbe-Grillet warns, indirectly, against the danger of any immediate parallels between objective, that is, theoretical, statements and the "meaning" of the fiction. In *The Erasers*, Wallas interrogates the concierge and concludes that in his story, filled with details, "It is apparent that the author only reproduces all those trifling remarks out of a concern for objectivity; and despite the care he takes to present what follows with the same detachment, he obviously regards it as much more important" (E 192). The words of the concierge, as well as the techniques of the novel, must be seen in their subjective unity.

In the evolution of Robbe-Grillet's theories, there is mounting emphasis on the need for absolute subjectivity to dominate the form and the description of the world perceived. In his 1961 essay, "New Novel, New Man," he openly proclaimed this subjectivity:

"As there are many objects in our books, and as people thought there was something unusual about them, it didn't take long to decide on the future of the word "objectivity," which was used by certain critics when referring to those objects, but used in very particular sense, i.e. oriented towards the object. In its usual sense which is neutral, cold and impartial, the word becomes an absurdity. Not only is it a man who, in my novels, for instance, describes everything, but he is also the least neutral, and the least impartial of men; on the contrary, he is *always* engaged in a passionate adventure of the most obsessive type—so obsessive that it often distorts his vision and subjects him to phantasies bordering on delirium. It is also quite easy to show that my novels . . . are even more subjective than those of Balzac . . ." (TNN 138–139)

Even if the objects seen appear with hard-edged objectivity, they will be the subjective choices of a psychology enforcing its obsessions onto a conscious and recording mind, and they will be colored by the needs of that mind. For example, the paperweight in the office of Dupont in *The Erasers* is a harmless object when it is first described: "A kind of cube, but slightly misshapen, a shiny block of gray lava, with its faces polished as though by wear, the edges softened, compact, apparently hard, heavy as gold, looking about as big around as a fist; a paperweight?" (E 21). But, when Wallas arrives at the end of the narrative to kill Dupont, there is murder in his mind and the same paperweight appears other than it was: "The cube of vitrified stone with its sharp edges and deadly corners, is lying harmlessly between the inkwell and the memo-pad" (E 236).

This kind of subjectivity was already present in Robbe-Grillet's first novel. Perhaps as a counterargument, the example of the tomato can be considered. Geometrically described, this slice appears totally objective:

A quarter of tomato that is quite faultless, cut up by the machine into a perfectly symmetrical fruit.
   The periphereal flesh, compact, homogeneous, and a splendid chemical red, is of an even thickness between a strip of gleaming skin and the hollow where the yellow, graduated seeds appear in a row, kept in place by a thin layer of greenish jelly along a swelling of the heart. This heart, of a slightly grainy, faint pink begins—toward the inner hollow—with a cluster of white veins, one of which extends toward the seeds—somewhat uncertainly.
   Above, a scarcely perceptible accident has occurred: a corner of the skin, stripped back from the flesh for a fraction of an inch, is slightly raised.
(E 152–153)

But its neither appetizing nor disgusting nature underlines merely what has been made clear earlier, that Wallas is not really hungry, that eating is merely one of the functions he pursues as automatically as the automat where he has chosen to eat carries on its preparation of the food: all the dishes offered, for example, are variations of the basic marinated herring. There is a unified, totally objective center controlling all objects and scenes that appear, binding them to a dominating structure; that point of view of narrating consciousness is human from the first of Robbe-Grillet's novels. Roland Barthes in his introduction to Morrissette's *Les Romans de Robbe-Grillet* asks the question, "Between the two Robbe-Grillets, Robbe-Grillet no. 1, the 'chosiste,' and Robbe-Grillet no. 2, the humanist, between the one portrayed by all the early analysis [established by Barthes himself] and the one portrayed by Bruce Morrissette, must one choose?"[5] The answer must be an emphatic yes.

The link between Robbe-Grillet and the phenomenological theory of Merleau-Ponty especially is constant; in a parallel, rather than influential, relationship, the philosopher and the novelist are working at the same kind of problem with differing tools. In *Jealousy*, the manner in which A. . .'s husband sees his wife writing at her desk and the assumptions he must make are filtered through his narrative consciousness: "The shiny black curls tremble slightly on her shoulders as the pen advances. Although neither the arm nor the head seems disturbed by the slightest movement, the hair, more sensitive, captures the oscillations of the wrist, amplifies them, and translates them into unexpected eddies which awaken reddish highlights in its moving mass" (TN 135). Only the surface is visible, only the details of the surface, and one is not interested in what lies beneath it; the perceiving mind alone establishes the mood. Perhaps A... is terrified, perhaps she is nervous, perhaps impatient—the husband can merely guess, and his mood decides for him. *Jealousy*, for example, follows the movements of the eye of the narrator, the husband. If he closes his eyes for a moment and an object or a person changes position, then, when his eyes turn back to it, it will seem to have appeared or disappeared suddenly. Robbe-Grillet underscores this movement with the image of a lizard that fascinates the husband: "On the column itself there is nothing to see except the peeling paint and, occasionally, at unforeseeable intervals and at various levels, a

---

[5] Roland Barthes, introduction to *Les Romans de Robbe-Grillet*, by Bruce Morrissette, pp. 7–16. The book totally negates Barthes's early statements on Robbe-Grillet's novels.

greyish-pink lizard whose intermittent presence results from shifts of position so sudden that no one could say where it comes from or where it is going when it is no longer visible" (TN 122). Or, in *The Erasers*, when Juard is waiting for Wallas, the apparently confused echoes and re-echoes that will dominate the surface of the later novels are present in the train station: "A tremendous voice fills the hall. Projected by invisible loudspeakers, it bounces back and forth against the walls covered with signs and advertisements, which amplify it still more, multiply it, reflect it, baffle it with a whole series of more or less conflicting echoes and resonances, in which the original message is lost—transformed into a gigantic oracle, magnificent, indecipherable, and terrifying" (E 200). With Robbe-Grillet, narrative consciousness is complete. The uncertainty and fear of Kafka have disappeared, the doubts and improbabilities of Beckett have been all but forgotten (they still do hide below the surfaces, disguised beneath such adverbs as *doubtless, perhaps,* and *probably*): but experiments with the purity of narrative consciousness, with a fiction in which the central interest is the narrating voice, have begun to bear fruit.

It is obvious that writers other than Kafka and Beckett have left their influence on Robbe-Grillet; both Sartre and Camus work with objects and situations, especially in their respective novels *Nausea* and *The Stranger*. As Bruce Morrissette reminds one, *Nausea* makes constant use of object descriptions. "Roquentin's depiction of a chestnut-tree root was also an object lesson in the '*être-là* des choses.'" But thereafter comes the difference: ". . . where Sartre freely employs metaphor and draws intellectual conclusions, Robbe-Grillet rigorously restricts himself to the external object."[6] With Robbe-Grillet, there is no reflection. Camus, even in Robbe-Grillet's eyes, removes some of the anthropomorphism from fiction; but, though a purer narrative emerges, the domesticating complicity continues to persist (TNN 86). It remains for Robbe-Grillet to cleanse fiction of arbitrary anthropomorphism before he can bring to it description of an external world that delineates the viewer rather than the world. When he speaks of a need to liberate the human

---

[6] Bruce Morrissette, *Alain Robbe-Grillet,* p. 16.

glance from the categories that limit its value, he knows he demands the impossible (TNN 52); everything is linked to the entire psychology of the viewer. Therefore all preconditions symptomized by his fiction must be based in a comprehension of this basic limitation; but the proper response must also rise from an awareness of an extremely precise reanthropomorphization with which Robbe-Grillet purposely mars his purified fiction. Robbe-Grillet's heroes undergo exactly that Rorschach test in which most critics of Kafka indulge: among generally geometric (objective) descriptions, edges of cubes that are "murderous" appear. But these descriptions no longer dominate the narrator; they are instead his creation. Complicity still exists between man and the world, but, because the descriptions have become humanly controlled, a great part of the liberation Robbe-Grillet demanded has taken place. Certainly the relation is "humanistic," and because all distance between himself and the world is controlled by man (as theorist or narrator), the complicity need no longer be tragic. "It can in any case quite obviously only be a question of the world as my *point of view* orientates it; I shall never know any other. The relative subjectivity of my look serves precisely to define *my situation in the world*. I simply avoid making common cause with those who turn this situation into a kind of slavery" (TNN 94).

6. Internalized Reality: The Subjective Point of View

THERE ARE A NUMBER OF WAYS in which the narrator of a tale can present himself to a reader. Robbe-Grillet's first three novels, *The Erasers, The Voyeur,* and *Jealousy* are told in the third person, yet the importance of each novel lies in its capacity to produce the immediate presence of a narrator. In each novel the narrator exists at every point only within the character relevant to that particular narrative. There is no gratuitous description, no gratuitous object; everything is linked to the central character. Of *The Voyeur*, Bruce Morrissette remarks," . . . even the most 'neutral' and innocent-seeming description of natural objects may contain, imperceptible at first glance but beyond a doubt fully intentional, some formal theme or coincidence of vocabulary that relates the object to the plot, or to the personality of Mathias, or to some aspect of a later action."[1]

In the novels the narrational voice, a unified source of information, becomes the theoretical basis for an image of the world; the voice seems to speak in absolutes. Each voice's primary relevance is to the

[1] Bruce Morrissette, *Alain Robbe-Grillet*, p. 22.

fiction itself, but the situation of the narrator is analogous to that of the chief of police in *The Erasers*: "He dares not reject his assistant's hypothesis out of hand, for you never know: suppose that happened to be what happened, what would he look like then? Then too the obscurities and contradictions of the case have to be interpreted one way or another" (E 196–197). All obscurities and contradictions must be forced into a mold so that they make sense to a perceiving consciousness; the only mold capable of holding the incidents in proper relation to each other is the one formed by the narrating mind.

The first three novels interchange normal characteristics of first and third person narration.[2] Although each novel maintains a first person point of view, the pronoun itself is in the third person; each "I" character (except A... 's husband) designates himself with his own proper name. In *The Erasers*, although the point of view is distributed among several characters, each in his turn follows this rule of self-objectification—the manager of the Café des Alliés, Laurent the chief of police, Garinati, Wallas.

Snatches of conversation, in their banality, record the undecorated sounds of the human voice immediately, as they are perceived. Wallas's uncertainty in the matter of a simple question is recorded together with the exchanged words. His uncertainty in this trivial matter is the weak echo of his far greater uncertainty and one of the novel's structuring motifs, his Oedipal search for his (probable) father (Dupont).[3]

Maison de rendez-vous (1965) in a sense returns to the multi-narrational technique of *The Erasers*; with the apparent exception of the "I" character, who begins the book and returns to its pages at odd intervals, the several "narrators" each see themselves in the third person. Kim, for example, enters the building of Manneret's apartment; with her is one of Madame Ava's dogs. "Kim has only to follow

---

[2] For the most complete discussions of the events of these three novels and *In the Labyrinth*, which establish the background for the several narratives, see Morrissette, *Alain Robbe-Grillet*, and Ben F. Stoltzfus, *Alain Robbe-Grillet and the New French Novel*.

[3] See Bruce Morrisette, "Oedipus and Existentialism: *Les Gommes* of Robbe-Grillet," *Wisconsin Studies in Contemporary Literature* I, no. 3 (Fall, 1960): 43–73.

the dog: in her turn she climbs the steep, narrow, wooden steps, a little more slowly of course, . . . the absence of light constituting a further obstacle for eyes accustomed to the bright sun outside" (MR 102). The difference here is that the novel is dominated by one character alone, the narrator "I" is creating the conflicting snatches of narrative as he sits in his room. The reader knows that it is probably in an apartment house also, for in the quarters above the narrator's room a man is rocking in a chair, to the great irritation of the narrator. The narrator later gives the rocking chair to Manneret when Kim visits him.

Much more remains of the room in which the narrator/doctor of *In the Labyrinth* writes the story of the soldier returning from the war, who carries a box filled with irrelevancies to be given to someone whose name he has forgotten at a place and time he does not remember. The narrator's room contains all the elements from which the story of the soldier grows: a bayonet, a box, tracks in the dust (which become tracks in the snow), filaments in the light bulb, and, most of all, a picture, titled *The Defeat at Reichenfels*, in which the soldier, the boy, and the bartender figure as principles. The narrator weaves a story from these elements, a story almost fulfilling Flaubert's attempts to conceive a *roman pur*, a novel created from nothing. *Maison de rendez-vous* is, in this sense, purer; only a rocking chair links the created events with the narrator's reality.

Like the created characters of *Maison de rendez-vous*, the soldier attains his own point of view, but it is granted him by a narrator who is constantly in the process of forming his hero. Robbe-Grillet's narrator puts himself in the midst of the situation being described. Whereas the events of the first three novels are actually occurring at a single remove—they are the fictions of Robbe-Grillet (everything happens to the narrator)—*In the Labyrinth* and *Maison de rendez-vous* are operating at a further remove. Robbe-Grillet is writing the story of a narrator who is creating the events he is describing. In this respect the structural development of the two latter novels approaches that of the later novels of Samuel Beckett. A story is told by a narrator within the novel who plays little active part in the story being created. But whereas Beckett's narrator would say, "I am now going to create a narrative," or, "No, no, this won't do, this is badly written," Robbe-Grillet's narrator omits the step; the reader is not certain whether Robbe-Grillet or his narrator is telling the story.

The inability to differentiate between "real" and "imaginary" events is not limited to the later novels. Mathias of *The Voyeur* is quite capable of imagining what could happen as he goes out to sell his watches. In his thoughts he has visited a house, has sold several watches, and starts to go. "As he was leaving he wanted to say a few words of farewell, but none came out of his mouth. He noticed this at the same moment he realized the whole scene had been a stupidly worthless one [*sic*]. Once on the road, behind the closed door, his suitcase unopened in his hand, he understood that it all still remained to be done" (V 26). Here is a further remove, a further frame: first person interplay between imagination and immediate reality is disguised behind what appears to be a third person narrative. The interplay itself is presented from the single point of view, Mathias's mind. Robert Champigny notes that

the technique of *Le Voyeur* is the result of an attempt to present everything that occurs (gestures, perceptions, projects, images, memories, calculations) on the same plane. This search for flatness means a reduction of the conditional mood (the alibi) to the indicative, of the unreal to the real: the alibi is unreal, but the images in Mathias' mind are real. It also leads to a reduction of the past and future to an eternal present: Mathias' memories and projects may point toward the past or the future, but they themselves are present. The thoughts and images which crop up in Mathias' mind are thus assimilated to perception.[4]

A... 's husband in *Jealousy* also mixes imagination with past incident and projected possibility. But the element deleted from Robbe-Grillet's third novel is an objectification, at any point in the narrative, of the narrator himself. The narrating voice must be relevant to the story; context forces the realization that it is A... 's husband. He never refers to himself, either with adjective or with proper noun, or with "I" or "he"; his single device for self-reference is the generalizing "one" or the passive voice. The tone of jealousy itself demands the

---

[4] Robert Champigny, "In Search of the Pure Récit," *American Society Legion of Honor Magazine* 27 (Winter, 1956–1957): 331.

conclusion that no one living in the house with A... other than her husband would be jealous of Franck, with whom, to the narrator's mind, A... spends too much time and to whom she pays too much attention. The narrator could be another lover, but the possibility is eliminated by the propriety of circumstances in which the events take place; and A... does speak of her husband, who can be present only in the person of the narrator—never more than three chairs are occupied. The husband will not admit to himself what he strongly suspects is happening between his wife and Franck. "In order to avoid the danger of upsetting the glasses in the darkness, A... has moved as near as possible to the armchair Franck is sitting in, her right hand carefully extending the glass with his drink in it. She rests her other hand on the arm of the chair and bends over him, so close that their heads touch. He murmurs a few words: [she is] probably thanking him" (TN 43). "Probably" forces the reader to doubt the explanation. The husband fools no one but himself.

In a sense, elimination of the personal pronoun in reference to oneself is an honest fictionalized description of the relation between a subjective conception and the objectification of oneself. In speaking, one does say "I." In thinking, such pronouns are rare. Nor does one use the label of a name (with which the external world objectifies all the qualities compounded to describe an individual) for oneself in personal thoughts. Since memory and imagination do not reach a stage of symbolization demanding words, and pictures suffice (much as they suffice to describe what one sees at a given moment), the need of a pronoun or any label for self-reference is not necessary. A...'s husband finds need neither for this nor for labels other than the most simple (A...) in referring to his wife; whether he has reduced their relationship to this single letter or whether the letter suffices to bring to his mind all associations of their life together is not important.

Contrary to Robbe-Grillet's pronouncements, that characters no longer exist in fiction, he has created, as thoroughly as most authors can, characters who may be spoken of as real and full people; one learns about them as they expose their consciousnesses to the reader. And they are each sufficiently conscious to display themselves not only in the functioning of their minds, but also in their ability to watch themselves as they act out given situations. For example, Kim, seeking out M. Tchang, locates him; but he, for a reason at that point unknown, will not make contact with her. She then transports herself in her mind out of the situation and begins over. The second beginning belongs to the narrator. (To claim it belongs merely to Robbe-Grillet would be to beg the question; it is Robbe-Grillet who is creating the mind of an author/narrator whose several attempts at writing a story are all described.) The juxtaposition belongs to the narrator and as much explains his inability to work out a facet of the plot as it explicates the character of Kim. What the reader of *Maison de rendez-vous* has before him are, in effect, notebooks of the imagination for a novel about an evening in Hong Kong. It has been said that watching the evolution of characters in Gide's notebooks for *The Counterfeiters* is as interesting as reading the novel itself. Robbe-Grillet accepts such a sentiment literally and writes a novel about the psychological movement expressed almost completely in the episodes invented by a writer carrying on his occupation. The changing situations of characters in relation to each other, and in relation to time sequences, is nothing more than a shift in the author's conception of characters with which his mind is working. As the shifts and changes proceed, a novel comes into being.

This experiment relates most completely to Robbe-Grillet's first novel: the process of an examination into the death of Dupont changes constantly as new evidence is introduced. Each new hypothesis is a corrective to previous explanation, an improvement that brings complete explanation (of the case and of the novel) closer. Each incorrect analysis clarifies something not only about the case but also about Wallas, for *The Erasers* is primarily his story. The process of the novel, the constant process of change, is a correction by erasure of those "facts" previously assumed correct. As new information is accumulated, both by the novel's investigators and by the reader, earlier information is edited and events are given more valid explanations. What is incorrect is, so to speak, erased.

Because the reality of each of Robbe-Grillet's novels changes under one's eyes, it becomes essential for the reader to find one point in the novel that remains steady. The point of view of the narrator alone will suffice. Of *Jealousy*, Morrissette says, "The point of view, with its rotations, emerges from a consciousness inside the text which the reader must assume, thus placing himself at the observational center."[5] The reader must, in effect, become the jealous husband, thereby himself experiencing pangs of jealousy for this beautiful woman, his wife, a sensuous female with beautiful hair brushing her bare shoulders and back, who wears tight-fitting dresses so that Franck's wife herself becomes jealous and suggests that A... wear something loose there in the tropics. This place for the reader Robbe-Grillet calls a "hollow" in the text. The same kind of missing factor, this time called a "hole," must be recognized in *The Voyeur*. The time during which Mathias kills Jacqueline is a blank both in the book and in Mathias's mind; the latter position must be assumed by the reader for him to realize the existence of this empty space. Only from within does Mathias's avoidance of the events, even silently in his mind, become evident.

The demands of *In the Labyrinth* and *Maison de rendez-vous* are more stringent. The early novels contain events with which memory and imagination can be linked; the later novels are moving so quickly toward the *roman pur* that very little landscape remains. The reader must submit himself so rigorously to the flexibilities of the author/narrator's mind that imagining events on the snow-covered streets of the city in *In the Labyrinth* and sensing the smells of Hong Kong in *Maison de rendez-vous* become the only conscious reality. The narrative implicates the imagination, even though it consists only of generalizations and clichés about Hong Kong. Yet, when related to each other in Robbe-Grillet's carefully structured descriptions, the pictures and images evoke complicity and force the reader into the chair behind the writer's desk, making him a part of the novel.

Robbe-Grillet is not telling stories as much as he is creating characters—not really creating characters, either, as much as creating an atmosphere for a character. An atmosphere remains for only a limited period of time; Robbe-Grillet's novels never take place over a period of more than a day or two. The period of *Maison de rendez-vous*

[5] Morrissette, *Alain Robbe-Grillet*, p. 10.

covers one late afternoon and the subsequent evening. The narrator's recorded episodes attempt to evoke the exoticism of Hong Kong, an exoticism of the city as well as an exoticism of pleasure. Carnal pleasure is present from the beginning, from the moment the narrator characterizes himself with his opening statement, "Women's flesh has always played, no doubt, a great part in my dreams." A crude interpretation of the intent of the narrator could be paraphrased in Genêt's words, that he wrote *Our Lady of the Flowers* merely to maintain an erection. But the intent here is far more complex, for it makes of a possible Genêt-like author merely another character to serve Robbe-Grillet's fiction-making process. The success of exoticism in *Maison de rendez-vous* is achieved without the use of exotic language or unnatural description; the inventive juxtaposition of clichés suffices.

Robbe-Grillet's methods for presenting a scene or situation are relatively simple. That his artist's mind's eye is no camera should by now be obvious.[6] His descriptions edit too completely; they do not begin with panoramas that a camera's image could embrace; rather they choose microscopic details of large scenes and landscapes. When describing the rows of banana trees, for example, Robbe-Grillet omits not only the foreground of the picture but also the spaces between the trees themselves; furthermore, to differentiate between trees is impossible. The importance of Camus's experiments is discernible here: as Meursault tries to recall, "en imagination,"[7] the details of his room, he lets his mind's eye wander from one wall to another, cataloguing, enumerating everything he can recall, the objects as well as the wall's imperfections, and though he carries on this procedure many times he finds that each repeated survey of the same image reveals more details than had the previous. Without verbalizing this difficulty, as did Camus's narrator, Robbe-Grillet leaves to the reader's discovery the incomplete picture before him. Not even

---

[6] For a contrary attitude see Stoltzfus, *Alain Robbe-Grillet and the New French Novel*, p. 111, and the special issue of *Revue des Lettres Modernes*, "Cinéma et Roman."

[7] Stoltzfus reminds one that *des imaginations* is the descriptive term Robbe-Grillet uses for his characters' mental processes (*Alain Robbe-Grillet and the New French Novel*, pp. 145–146).

a six-page description of *The Defeat at Reichenfels* suffices to describe all the elements the picture contains.

Of course, Robbe-Grillet is partly responsible for the confusion. He has quite deliberately called the published form of both *Last Year at Marienbad* and *The Immortal* "ciné-roman," and his collection of brief prose narratives he has named *Instantanées* (*Snapshots*). Since, aside from his theoretical pieces, these represent his only publication besides his novels, it is not difficult to conclude that Robbe-Grillet is merely applying the techniques of one medium to the presentation of another. But the evidence of his fictional heritage stands opposed to carrying the supposition too far; Robbe-Grillet has, of course, utilized techniques from the film, but artists have always sought new forms in neighboring disciplines. It is his ability to edit language, to keep the narrative relevant, that retains his identity as fabulator. What is not relevant is never absorbed, either by narrator or by protagonist. Like Mathias, Robbe-Grillet is trying to sell his product. Mathias hears from the sailor all the details about the family of the sailor's sister: "Mathias, who expected to put them to good use soon, added all these facts to the inquiries he had made the day before. In work like this, there was no such thing as a superfluous detail" (V 23). Nor must Robbe-Grillet allow superfluous details.

The point of view of narrative consciousness is capable of a great deal. It can, for example, converse, as does the husband in *Jealousy*:

> The conversation has returned to the story of the engine trouble: in the future Franck will not buy any more old military *materiel*; his latest acquisitions have given him too many problems; the next time he replaces one of his vehicles, it will be with a new one.
>
> But he is wrong to trust modern trucks to the Negro drivers, who will wreck them just as fast, if not faster.
>
> "All the same," Franck says, "if the motor is new, the driver will not have to fool with it." (TN 46)

Franck's words are reported as direct or indirect discourse, the words of the narrator/husband appear as generalized thoughts, a pedestal to which only "objectively" true statements are usually elevated. Such a technique is successful in its re-emphasis of the feeling that one's own utterances are always valid.

Even in description that might otherwise be deemed purely "objective," Robbe-Grillet's narrators manage to inject a note of doubt. The usual technique is to overstress otherwise innocent situations. So A...'s husband speaks of A... and Franck in town: "It is only natural that they will meet there, especially for dinner, since they must start back immediately afterwards. It is also natural that A... would want to take advantage of this present opportunity to get to town, which she prefers to the solution of a banana truck" (TN 78–79). All this is so natural that there seems little need for the narrator to mention it; yet he does, and implies that much is going on below the surface of his reports. Much the same effect is gained with such words as *no doubt, probably, certainly,* and *perhaps.* Knowing it not to be true, the husband nevertheless notes: "The table is set for three. A... has probably just had the boy add Franck's place, since she was not to be expecting any guest for lunch today" (TN58–59). To show the complicity between A... and Franck, the narrator describes by concealment the reaction of one to another in a certain situation: "A... is humming a dance tune whose words remain unintelligible. But perhaps Franck understands them, if he already knows them, from having heard them often, perhaps with her. Perhaps it is one of her favorite records" (TN 49). Whether the two ever heard it together is uncertain; only the narrator's suspicions are clear. The narrator chooses ambiguity partly in order to avoid accusing A... and Franck without absolute evidence; partly, however, he does not wish to admit to himself the possibility that his wife is having an affair. Evasion on the part of the narrator plays a large role in Robbe-Grillet's early novels. Wallas is unaware that his search is leading him into a situation in which he will have to kill his (possible) father, and so the evasion is perpetrated by the author on the reader only; but Mathias is capable of, and completely involved in, doing so by himself. The last two parts of his narrative involve nothing but evasion: he will not even admit to his own conscious mind what he has done, and the reader must piece the information together from the images that do come to his mind, for not everything appearing in print can be accepted as "truth," not even very limited truth. Mathias's refusal to admit his acts to himself is based in a conscious desire to establish an alibi for himself to cover the time of Jacqueline's rape and murder.

The narrator, seeing A... leaning through the car window to kiss Franck, describes the scene as geometrically as possible. The fact of passion is absent. In much the same way the husband takes his mind off A...'s late return from her trip to town with Franck by considering with almost paranoid exactness the details of the house; the more control he can retain over his mind the greater will be his ability to withstand his jealousy. In much the same way the narrator will shift his glance from A... and Franck to something irrelevant if he believes he may see some hint of tenderness that transcends the relationship of neighbors, or if he already has seen more than he wishes. The description of A...'s hair gives away the narrator's attitude to the scene; since the sensation of jealousy usually corresponds to the realization of imminent (or already determined) loss, the husband must be shown admiring his wife. This is not to say that Robbe-Grillet portrays in the husband a love of A...; love is not necessary for, although it probably deepens, the imagined oncoming loss. At any rate, Robbe-Grillet is content to portray A..., to her husband's eyes, as a sensual, desirable woman—at least her sensuality is prime in the husband's mind. It is difficult to determine if A... is beautiful. One can assume she is attractive to Franck, who visits her even when his own wife is ill, and she obviously arouses her husband, even though he apparently never considers more of her than her hair, her lips, her shoulder and her figure in a tight dress, which suffices.

Much the same technique is used to establish sensuality in *Maison de rendez-vous*. Once the narrator has avowed his partiality for women's flesh, his always incomplete hints at possible perversions are sufficient to retain the sensation of sensuality, which becomes a major element in the tone of exoticism dominant in the novel. Even his obsession for the very tight dresses worn by Chinese women, slit to the thigh, suggests the constant presence of exotic pleasure.

Sensuality is not the only tone, though it is one of the most prominent, that Robbe-Grillet attempts to create in his novels. All atmos-

pheres can be determined by the external (and externalized) "things"
chosen by the mind's eye. Although related to T. S. Eliot's objective
correlatives, such objects cannot achieve any immediate evocation
of parallel emotions; the blue cigarette package, the figure eight, and
the piece of rope in no way add up to Mathias's crime, but they do
point to the obsessive nature of his mind. Robbe-Grillet's success lies
in his ability to lead one toward the necessary background that will
explain the crime, much as Camus makes it obvious that sun, sand,
and sky forced Meursault to kill the Arab. The choice of the "things"
the eye of the narrating consciousness perceives is based in their ability to suggest rather than in their power to equate and define.

The choice of objects most relevant to the perceiving mind and
the manner in which those objects are described establish the state
of mind that controls the point of view in Robbe-Grillet's fiction. The
subconscious mind is projected onto an external world, but this never
becomes a conscious process; the conscious mind merely reports what
it is driven to view. Such a formula allows an identification between
Franck's killing the centipede and his probable affair with A . . .:
"A... seems to be breathing a little faster, but this may be an illusion.
Her left hand gradually closes over her knife. The delicate antennae
accelerate their alternate swaying" (TN 65). As when A...'s hand
came too close to Franck's, the narrator looks away, fearing the over-
display of emotion to which he might be a witness. The implicit
comparison comes almost to the surface when Franck's attack on
the centipede is described again later: "A... moves no more than
the centipede while Franck approaches the wall, his napkin wadded
up in his hand" (TN 82). This motif reaches its climax when the
husband is awaiting the return of Franck and A...; it combines with
the sense of loss to give the centipede enormous proportions: "The
pantry door is closed. Between it and the doorway to the hall is the
centipede. It is enormous: one of the largest to be found in this
climate. With its long antennae and its huge legs spread on each side
of its body, it covers the area of an ordinary dinner plate. The shadow
of various appendages doubles their already considerable number on
the light-colored paint" (TN 112). Every ounce of objective hatred
is expended on the centipede Franck has destroyed just as he has

defiled, in the husband's mind, the purity of his beautiful wife and the sanctity of their marriage.

In the same way the eraser and the girl in the shop (who may be his stepmother) combine to arouse in Wallas the beginnings of sensuality, essential for the novel's structure in which the son kills his (possible) father. "Once out in the street, Wallas mechanically fingers the little eraser; it is obvious from the way it feels that it is no good at all. It would have been surprising, really, for it to be otherwise in so modest a shop. . . . That girl was nice. . . . He rubs his thumb across the end of the eraser. It is not at all what he is looking for" (E 62). Wallas and A...'s husband have a confederate in Mathias, who establishes his own lustful nature in the cafe after leaving the ferry; he sees a natural action of the waitress: "She held her head to one side, neck and shoulders bent, in order to observe more closely the rising level of liquid in the glass. Her black dress was cut low in back. Her hair was arranged so that the nape of her neck was exposed" (V 50). A much more generalized object of sensual thought than A..., the waitress helps explain how to Mathias's mind his perversion and crime become possible. All females, even thirteen-year-olds (perhaps especially thirteen-year-olds, who are less capable of resistance—lack of resistance becomes a motif in *Maison de rendez-vous*), can arouse Mathias's lust.

Emphasis of a narrator's glance also plays its part. A...'s husband watches Franck and remarks: "He drinks his soup in rapid spoonfuls. Although he makes no excessive gestures, although he holds his spoon quite properly and swallows the liquid without making any noise, he seems to display, in this modest task, a disproportionate energy and zest. It would be difficult to specify exactly in what way he is neglecting some essential rule, at what particular point he is lacking in discretion" (TN 46). Having in effect stared at Franck as he eats, the narrator seems surprised that A... has finished her soup without drawing attention to herself; but the attention to be caught is that of the husband, and he was too busy being irritated at Franck to notice. Franck is not actually lacking in discretion; because the husband is bothered by something far more basic than seeing Franck eat his soup, he expresses his irritation within the context of the incident of the moment. In much the same way and for similar reasons Franck apparently grew sufficiently angry at his own wife when Christiane criticised A... for wearing so tight-fitting a dress.

Having limited his glance only to Franck, the narrator (under the author's control) edits his point of view until he forgets completely the presence of A.... Obliquely this may begin to explain possible causes for A...'s probable infidelity, but since that path of inquiry is both impossible to follow and not relevant to the obsession of jealousy that remains the novel's subject, Robbe-Grillet draws the attention back to the narrator's point of view. Only the fact that A...'s plate is stained lets one (the narrator) realize that she has indeed been eating all the time. The matter, as Bernard Pinguad points out, is not that the glance of the jealous husband deforms what he sees so much as it is that he chooses and sees in a limited way.[8] Mathias's eyes, for example, fall only on a limited number of kinds of things; even in a village shop his eye can find the appropriate object—a mutilated naked mannequin.

In one corner, at eye level, stood a window mannequin: a young woman's body with the limbs cut off—the arms just below the shoulder and the legs eight inches from the trunk—the head slightly to one side and forward to give a "gracious" effect, and one hip projecting slightly beyond the other in a "natural" pose. The mannequin was well proportioned but smaller than normal as far as the mutilations permitted her size to be estimated. Her back was turned, her face leaning against a shelf filled with ribbons. She was dressed only in a brassiere and a narrow garter-belt popular in the city. (V 57)

The extreme subjectivity of a narrator's glance defines his nature. But a descriptive narrative needs more than an atmosphere if it is to succeed as fiction; it needs a relevant interrelation of its parts. It is already apparent that all images in these novels emanate from the mind of the narrator; their sources—the glance of the moment, a picture from the memory, the image of a hoped for or feared future event—are totally interconnected. Stoltzfus notes that Robbe-Grillet unites the several imaginative processes. What Robbe-Grillet "seems to be saying is that dream, day-dream, fantasy, imagination, the

---

[8] Bernard Pingand, "Molloy," *Esprit* 19, no. 9 (September, 1951): 424–425.

creative process, are all related; that the factor which differentiates dreams from imaginative creation or fiction is a matter of volition, direction, or perhaps even coherent organization."[9] Precisely this organization is the artist's domain; more than simply searching for new experiences, the act of structuring uses atmosphere-creating words and shapes them into the beginnings of fiction.

[9] Stoltzfus, *Alain Robbe-Grillet and the New French Novel*, p. 83.

7. Structure as Process:
The Temporal Point of View

For ROBBE-GRILLET the form of the fiction is basic. He has remarked to Bruce Morrissette, "What is important for me in the novel . . . is *structure*, or form. This is why I appreciate a 'bad' novel like *The Postman Always Rings Twice*. It is structured. The accident happens twice, in the same way but with different results." Morrissette adds that, for "Robbe-Grillet, a literary work can only acquire its meaning, and hence its value, through form."[1]

But where the specific form was discernible in the works of Kafka and Beckett, Robbe-Grillet's novels are more elusive, at least at first glance. An attempt to apply the formula of the unsuccessful quest to Robbe-Grillet's novels might appear fruitful at first,[2] but in actuality,

[1] Bruce Morrissette, *Alain Robbe-Grillet*, p. 5.

[2] See especially Jacques Howlett, "Thèmes et tendances d'avant garde dans le roman aujourd'hui," *Les Lettres Nouvelles*, February 20, 1963, p. 143. For Ben F. Stoltzfus (*Alain Robbe-Grillet and the New French Novel*, p. 30), the same unsuccessful quest motif becomes part of any demand that the reader become an accomplice of the novel's protagonist; see also, Lucien Goldmann, *Pour une sociologie du roman*, pp. 281–324. Robbe-Grillet himself abets the confusion about his work. He writes in "New Novel, New Man": "How can a work of art

if there is a quest, it is artistic, technical rather than metaphysical. The resultant vague image of quest in the novels merely reflects the technical search for improved methods to display reality. If the pre-defined impossibility of success in a quest as seen in Beckett's work is present in Robbe-Grillet's novels the coincidence is based in each man's experiments as artist rather than in the metaphysical pessimism attributed to him. Robbe-Grillet's novels are not structured by the peregrinations of knights-errant; rather they are shaped by, just as they are relevant to, their creating mind. Only created forms (possibly quests, but there are others also) give meaning to a life.

If the aim of Robbe-Grillet's structures is not to give the novel a traditional form, only the alternative already mentioned, the attempts to establish a mood, remains. Although his may be among the first experiments that strive to capture merely a mood, the endeavor has been an unconscious force in the creation of much fiction, as well as nonfiction. One often reads a novel—the works of Mann, Durrell, or James, of Tolstoy, Balzac, and Proust come immediately to mind—in which, six months later, the events have disappeared from the reader's mind but the taste lingers on. Of course, individual scenes remain, but they remain also long after one has completed a novel by Robbe-Grillet. Only in this respect can one understand what he wishes to maintain by claiming that characters no longer exist, that plot no longer exists in the new fiction: character, except the narrating consciousness, and plot have become subordinate to mood. Mood is not everything, of course; events still abound, and so do people. But the initial stress has changed. By making a narrating consciousness the point of view from which the world is to be seen, Robbe-Grillet allows the forces controlling that mind to dominate also the mood of the novel, to set the tone for that novel. The manner in which Robbe-Grillet structures a mood—dependent entirely on the inner necessity of the character from whose point of view the novel is written—be-

---

claim to illustrate a meaning that is known in advance, whatever it may be? The modern novel, as we said at the beginning, is a quest, but a quest which creates itself its own meanings as it goes along. Has reality a meaning? The contemporary artist can't answer that question: he has no idea. All he can say is that this reality may perhaps have a meaning in retrospect—once the work is finished, that is to say" (TNN, 140–141).

comes the structure of the book. In this way it becomes easier to understand Bruce Morrissette's analysis of *Jealousy*;[3] he demonstrates the order of intensity in which the vision of the husband is arranged, explaining that the highest moment is reached in parts 6 and 7, when the house is empty. Then the husband's mood gains greatest control over him, because he has not even A... and Franck to distract his jealousy. In those two sections his obsession reveals to his imagination pictures of violence and death all born from the jealousy dominating him. In like manner the world of *The Voyeur* exists only according to the structure given it by the mood of Mathias. There is no preconceived order to the universe—only Mathias can give it form. Stoltzfus says: "There exists a pre-established order for Mathias even though it may be absent from the universe. The 'order' stems from all those predisposing homicidal tendencies residing within him."[4] Wallas's Oedipus project fashions the world for him, and the contents of the doctor/narrator's room control his fiction; the narrator's arrangements and rearrangements of characters within events in *La Maison de rendez-vous* are totally under the domination of his fascination with female flesh.

In view of Robbe-Grillet's attempts to create a totally interrelated mood—not to be writing about something, but to be writing something—a number of his readers have concluded that his forms are essentially circular.[5] But to assume circularity merely because the novel begins and ends in the same place—the first four novels retain this characteristic—is a critical superimposition that explains little about the structure. Mood is continuous; a unity of mood given birth by narrative consciousness must by definition return to the same point at every instant.

The structuring power behind Robbe-Grillet's novels is psychological time. In the sense that events as they occur to the mind of the narrator take place one after the other, the time of the novels is totally chronological. Although this concept of time does not explain the interrelationship of conflicting scenes, it must be grasped before

---

[3] Bruce Morrissette, *Les Romans de Robbe-Grillet*, pp. 116–122.
[4] Stoltzfus, *Alain Robbe-Grillet and the New French Novel*, p. 38.
[5] See Morrissette, *Alain Robbe-Grillet*, p. 14, on *The Erasers*.

the novels can be understood. In none does the time of the narrator on a page toward the end of the book actually precede the time on an earlier page; the problem is never one of shuffled pages.

Robbe-Grillet's concern for psychological time comes to him through Beckett (and Joyce and Faulkner) from Proust. Stoltzfus notes: "Time is dislocated—past, present and future blend and overlap . . . in a manner designed to capture not clock chronology, but the inner time sequence of a living being."[6] Robbe-Grillet places his "objects" in this context when he writes:

And, if we consider an "object" in the general sense (*object*, says the dictionary: A *thing presented to the senses*) it is reasonable that there should be nothing but objects in my books; in my life, after all, there is the furniture in my bedroom, there are the words I hear, or the woman I love, something this woman does, etc. And, in a wider sense (object, the dictionary also says: *That upon which the attention is fixed*) other things that would be called objects are *memory* (by means of which I go back to past objects), *plans* (which take me forward to future objects: if I decide to go and bathe, I already see the sea and the beach in my mind's eye) and every kind of imagination. (TNN 138)

Human time forms a human life. With his complex structures Robbe-Grillet merely wishes to prove there is no specific form a tale must take. Form, dependent on the human mind, cannot have a pre-established structure; it takes on the structure of association most relevant to the conscious state of the individual whose story is being told.

The structure of a novel is created by the description of scenes and events presented by the mind that dominates them; therein Robbe-Grillet's novels begin their difference of function. Formerly, "[it was] trying to reproduce a preexistent reality; now [it] proclaims a creative function" (TNN 145). This is again Beckett saying of Joyce, "He is not writing about something; he is writing something."

Since Robbe-Grillet is creating a narrating consciousness, and since that consciousness moves forward chronologically as the book progresses, the thing created cannot be seen simply as a completed piece of work, existing merely in one's hands as one holds the book. Instead, implicated in the actions of the protagonist, the reader

[6] Stoltzfus, *Alain Robbe-Grillet and the New French Novel*, p. 14.

moves forward with the narrative through descriptions that are controlled by a constant state of flux; the narrative gains the fourth dimension of time. If the lines of description seem to cross each other impossibly the effect can be due only to a forward movement in time—description in the fourth dimension, so to speak.[7] The essential sensation is one of process; the processes of the mind accumulate in an order based only on related association, but they are structured to establish the essence of the mood that dominates the mind of the narrative from beginning to end. Much of the close description in Robbe-Grillet's novels therefore pertains less to the thing described than to a process of which the thing forms a part—the paperweight that gains murderous edges as Mathias approaches his goal is part of the process of Mathias's mind. The reader assumes an obligation to keep shifting his own point of view as he reads. The genius of Robbe-Grillet lies in his ability to keep track of what is human within that process of change.

Structure is thus based on point of view and is totally subservient to it. Objects are placed subsequent to earlier objects because they are perceived afterward; three kinds of perception remain—memory (either correct or false), immediate event, and hoped-for or feared possibility.

In *The Erasers* Wallas's time is essentially linear, with occasional flashbacks to his youth—he remembers his mother and the walks he took in towns like the one in which he is conducting his investigation. An occasional hint of simultaneity of time can be found in Robbe-Grillet's juxtaposition of the thoughts and actions of other characters, but there is no reason to assume this is anything more than a momentary shift in point of view to add depth to the novel. *The Voyeur*, on the other hand, though still retaining its linearity, relies much more heavily on memory (valid and false—Mathias

---

[7] ". . . the lines of the drawing go on accumulating, and it becomes overloaded, they contradict each other, and change places until the very construction of the image renders it more and more uncertain. A few more paragraphs, and when the description is complete, you discover that it hasn't left anything permanent behind it: in the end it has become a two-fold movement of getting created and getting stuck, and this ambiguity you also find in the book on every level, and more particularly in the sum total of its structure, and this is where the *deception* inherent in the writing of today originates" (TNN 145–146).

needs an alibi) and especially on projected possibilities. *Jealousy* establishes chronological irrelevance; its structure is based solely on the depending mood of jealousy in the mind of the husband. The development is based on a shift from early incidents, reported more or less as they occur, to later incidents that, especially in parts 6 and 7, are born in the mind of the narrator. Likewise, *In the Labyrinth* is created in the mind of the narrator. He lives his own chronology as he writes, animating and projecting elements from the picture on his wall and combining them with the objects in his room; the soldier attains life (and death) according to the imagination of the author/doctor.

Maison de rendez-vous is a far more complex work. It is structured like *Jealousy*, except that its frame exists within the narrative. The chronology is linear, the created images are relevant only to the mind of the author who is writing, or attempting to write—probably a novel is his ultimate aim. His obsession for sensuality and the possibility of exotic pleasure are the forces driving him to his descriptions; as the images he creates becomes more turbulent (by suggestion usually), the reader can feel the narrator's mind succeeding in its efforts: the height of the novel (and the depths of perversity) is reached when the narrator suggests the ultimate end of Kito, the little girl prostitute, whose flesh is literally eaten in a ritual sacrifice and feast. But even this horrible scene belongs to the mood of the mind that created it, a mood that sees Hong Kong as the location of sensuality. Exoticism is part of everyone's picture of Hong Kong and explains why Robbe-Grillet chose for his background a city about which any reader would have preconceived notions. His narrator repeats several times, "Everyone knows Hong Kong," and Robbe-Grillet himself said, "Everyone knows Hong Kong. My novel is based on this, on the fact that everyone knows Hong Kong. We, each of us, have a Hong Kong in our minds."[8]

In the reader's and narrator's head the scenes are created, modified, rejected or accepted, remodified. To transpose these shifts onto the page or onto film demands a series of intricate technical devices.

[8] Cited by Jean Alter, *La Vision du monde d'Alain Robbe-Grillet*, p. 78.

Morrissette says that Alain Resnais, who shot the film of *Last Year at Marienbad,* "prepared an elaborate chronological table of the scenes, placing them at various levels of time and reality, including a Monday to Saturday 'last year' sequence, a Tuesday to Sunday 'present' series, with first- and second-degree flashbacks, as well as scenes lying in a 'timeless' zone outside any chronological schematic."[9] Perhaps this is necessary to understand simply that time is the only obstacle between the narrative consciousness and the reader; the technique functions like the windows of the house in *Jealousy*: "The windows are perfectly clean and, in the right hand leaf, the landscape is only slightly affected by the flaws in the glass, which give a few shifting nuances to the too uniform surfaces" (TN 70). As objects and situations are filtered through longer periods of time, they too appear different; Renato Barilli explains that "one of the laws of Robbe-Grillet's universe is precisely that of the continual and serial variation of described objects; *'similar but different'* is the effective formula..."[10]

The manner of movement from one object or scene to another to a third and back to the first can be described as a series of incompleted analogues. An incompleted analogue allows a shift from one object to another, linked by the juxtaposition of features similar in the two objects. The association is made by the mind, which finds a detail in one item analoguous to a similar aspect of another. Through incompleted analogues Robbe-Grillet achieves a flow from scene to scene— the analogy is described rather than named. The closeness of psychological association is usually reflected in the syntactical nature of the shift: a strong analogy can take place within a paragraph, occasionally within a sentence; a weaker analogy demands the mind wait until the end of the paragraph. The link is again the enclosed point of view, which leaves off one description and begins another without mentioning the changed subject. Therefore an early analogue in *In the Labyrinth* need not be precise, because there are so many details in

---

[9] Morrissette, *Alain Robbe-Grillet,* p. 36.

[10] Renato Barelli, "De Sartre à Robbe-Grillet," *Revue des Lettres Modernes,* nos. 94–99 (1964), p. 110.

common between the picture and the point at which the narrator
begins to animate it:

> But the composition is so involved that . . . no specific thought can be
> discerned. It is merely a tired face, rather thin, and narrowed still further
> by several days' growth of beard. This thinness, these shadows which
> accentuate the features without, on the other hand, indicating the slightest
> individual characteristic, nevertheless emphasize the brilliance of the wide
> open eyes.
>   The military overcoat is buttoned up to the neck, where the regimental
> number is embroidered on a diamond-shaped tab of material. The cap is
> set straight on the head, covering the hair, which is cut extremely short,
> judging from its appearance at the temples. The man is sitting stiffly, his
> hands lying flat on the table which is covered with a red-and-white
> checked oilcloth. He has finished his drink some time ago. (TN 153)

In *Maison de rendez-vous*, the description of the blackmailer visiting
Manneret becomes linked to a discussion of that visit between the
narrator and Lady Ava, the glass broken by the blackmailer an analogue of the glass broken at Lady Ava's when the police make their
raid. The analogues can be natural—the crossroads interrelating in
The Erasers and *In the Labyrinth* or the figure eights of *The Voyeur*.
They can be based on artificial reproductions, such as photographs,
pictures, or statues, or they can be subjective repetition and variation
of the kind described by Barilli, in which the strongest psychological
analogues are found.[11] The flow they produce can almost be described as surreal, and the temptation to do so would be great were
the warning culled from the mistakes of Kafka's early readers not still
so clear. If the narrating consciousness of a single human being dominates everything that is reported, the reader's mind must become
caught up in the narrative for him to see the clear interrelation between things, situations, and events.

---

[11] See Gerard Genette, "Sur Robbe-Grillet," *Tel Quel*, no. 8 (Winter, 1962),
pp. 42–43. For lists of the repeated relations between events in *Maison de
rendez-vous*, see Alter, *La Vision du monde d'Alain Robbe-Grillet*, pp. 67–68.

Conclusion

Conclusion: A Third Way
in Modern Fiction

THE WORKS OF ROBBE-GRILLET display no specific formal organization, yet they are highly structured, more structured than even Beckett's works, which retain their consistent internal form. Robbe-Grillet's structure, however, cannot be generalized, for his point is precisely that each man lives the forms necessary to his own life. Kafka's and Beckett's protagonists live through the life cycle deemed essential by their creators; Robbe-Grillet's characters live by the necessity of their own lives, lives that Robbe-Grillet fashions for them but that remain unique to each creation. Therefore Robbe-Grillet must appear, ultimately, as an artisan rather than as a moralist; he describes a progression, he does not judge it. With Beckett and Kafka the form of the novel lends it its basic judgment, its basic humanity. Robbe-Grillet's novels achieve their humanity not by passing judgment on the nature of man, but rather by describing the appearances made by the functions and processes that make men individual. Robbe-Grillet's works point to a wholly untried area of fiction—to the exploration of single narrative consciousnesses, of consciousness verbalized. In one respect they are a withdrawal from the extreme dead end to which Beckett has pushed his experiments; Robbe-Grillet attempts to reintegrate his tradition into normal story-telling fiction.

Robbe-Grillet has twice written about Beckett's theater. In grasping the nature of Beckett's dramatic works, Robbe-Grillet allows further insight into his own art:

. . . the two tramps remain intact and unchanged. And so we are sure, this time, that they were not just puppets whose role is simply to mask the fact that there is no main character. It is not the Godot they are supposed to be waiting for *who has "to come into being,"* but they, Didi and Gogo. Suddenly, while we are watching them, we grasp this major function of theatrical representation: to show what the fact of *being there* consists of. For this is precisely what we had never before seen on a stage, or at any rate hadn't seen so clearly, with so few concessions and so much evidence. The standard theatrical character only *plays a part*, like all those people we meet who are running away from their own existence. In Beckett's play, on the other hand, everything that happens is as if the two tramps were on the stage *without having a part to play*. (TNN 126)

Not only does he deny the significations so many readers (and more audiences) have superimposed on Beckett's works, but he also again makes clear the importance of the viewer if the condition of being there—presence in the situation—is to be understood.[1] Gogo and Didi, for Robbe-Grillet, are the created correlatives for the opening statement of this article: "The condition of man, says Heidegger, is to be there. It is probably the theatre, more than any other representation of the real, that reproduces this situation the most naturally. The theatrical character is *on stage*—that is his primary quality: he is *there*" (TNN 119).

Robbe-Grillet sees Beckett's novels as an avoidance of presence, as a reduction in the possibilities one has of apprehending man. In 1953, when he wrote his essay on *Godot*, and still in 1957 when he appended to it his thoughts on *Endgame*, he neglected to mention that Beckett in his novels was concerned precisely with restricting

---

[1] Among the many examples in Robbe-Grillet's own works, probably the most prominent are the repeated *now* of *Jealousy* and the constant present of changing relationships of *Maison de rendez-vous*.

any picture of man to one hero whose point of view constantly de-
creases his field of vision, that Beckett's primary effort lay in saying
some few words about the man himself. Yet Robbe-Grillet sensed
Beckett's quest and, while not actually saying that he had brought
signification to his plays and novels, was sorry to note that these
works cause their readers to find "meaningful conclusions" that are
not really present.[2] At this point he shows how far beyond Beckett
his fiction has developed: he is correct that Beckett's works still contain the trappings of the nineteenth- and twentieth-century metaphysics, and seventeenth- and eighteenth-century also; Beckett mentions details by name. No such reference is made in the works of
Robbe-Grillet. He has returned to a literature of pure narrative. The
institutionalized philosophic categories that explain the fictions of
nineteenth-century writers—the dogmatic authorial reflection of
Hardy and of Proust, even of Camus—do not appear in Robbe-
Grillet's novels. Instead, things are alone, things and people are in
movement, situations appear, all without explanation. These are
objects within a labelless universe at which one looks every day, objects that retain their associations and their places in each person's
system of relevance and propriety. Whereas Beckett more and more
attempts to eliminate objects, Robbe-Grillet edits them, uses them to
explain the particular mind of the character viewing them. Beckett's
interests do not consider the individual mind; his quests are for the
common characteristics, however displayed, of a general mind, a
human mind. Robbe-Grillet is interested in individual perception
and chooses his heroes for what they are capable of seeing; the individual mind points a way, according to the nature of its perceptions,
to an explanation of one mind that can then be abstracted to fit a
general mind. Or perhaps this says too much for Robbe-Grillet's
conscious artistic aims; perhaps, for the moment, he wishes to do no
more than tell a valid tale that simultaneously can show its readers
some of the mechanics involved in seeing properly that which is in
the outside world, that which is in the memory, that which is in both

---

[2] Bruce Morrissette, "Les Idées de Robbe-Grillet sur Beckett," *Revue des
Lettres Modernes*, no. 100 (1964), p. 66.

the definite and possible future. Further, Robbe-Grillet understands that these visions are interrelated—the later novels begin to rely almost exclusively on such interrelationships.

Robbe-Grillet's comments about Kafka are far less specific. Asked if Kafka was much of an influence on his work, he replied, "Kafka was and remains for me the most important, without any doubt."[3] But this merely places Kafka at the top of a list of possible influences, among whom are other writers as disparate as Joë Bousquet and William Faulkner; whether or not the use of a narrative conscious- ness as the controlling point of view comes directly from Kafka is hardly relevant. *Towards a New Novel* says little about the work of Kafka until the end.

Now the one thing we find convincing, when we read him with an un- prejudiced eye, is the absolute reality of the things Kafka describes. The visible world of his novels is certainly, for him, the real world and what is behind it (if there is anything) seems to be valueless in comparison with the evidence of the objects, words, actions, etc. The hallucinatory effect comes from their extraordinary clarity, and not from any indecision or vagueness. There is no doubt that nothing is more fantastic than precision. Perhaps Kafka's staircases do lead somewhere else, but they are there, you look at them, stair by stair, and follow the details of the banisters. Perhaps his grey walls *are* hiding something, but one's memory stops short at them, at their cracked plaster and at their lizards. Even what the hero is search- ing for disappears before the obstinacy with which he pursues it, his journeying, and his movements, which are the only things Kafka makes us aware of, the only real things. Throughout the work, man's relation- ship with the world, far from symbolic, is always direct and immediate. (TNN 159)

It becomes immediately clear that Kafka's technique, not Kafka's world, interests Robbe-Grillet. And their worlds do differ strongly— the kinds of situation described, the details each considers important, the conversations and the interactions of characters. The constant differences should render foolish the obvious parallels reviewers un- relentingly discover between the worlds of these two writers. Robbe- Grillet notes: "For the last twenty years we have been able to judge how little remains of the Kafkan universe in the works of his self-

---

[3] Letter to the author, January 7, 1966.

styled descendants, who confined themselves to reproducing his metaphysical content and forgot about the master's realism" (TNN 159). Not the world but the point of view, the way in which that world is described, the techniques of linguistic juxtaposition—these make up Robbe-Grillet's debt to Kafka. It is no accident that Robbe-Grillet should, in praising Kafka, single out elements of description that he uses in his own fiction—the quick movements of the lizard's head in *Jealousy*, the staircase leading in the apartment of Eduard Manneret. But other writers have spoken of lizards and staircases; the point of view from which reality is described alone establishes Robbe-Grillet's relationship to Kafka, and to Beckett.

Appendixes, Bibliography, Index

APPENDIX 1: KAFKA IN FRANCE

The fate of Kafka's work in France parallels, in broad outlines, its reception throughout the Western world: slow discovery by a limited public, fascination on the part of those who read his works, misunderstanding by writers whose talents were committed to other styles, obscurity during the war, popular and critical rediscovery, consequent general misunderstanding (with one or two rare exceptions), and at last the beginning of insight into his works. All postwar French critics have noted the pattern described above (in their own idiom, of course, and with the natural exclusion of the last step); one of the most lucid, Mme Marthe Robert, Kafka's French editor and one of his principal translators, explains how "Kafka was adopted in France, virtually naturalized, like no other foreign writer ever was.[1]" Because of the great part she played in the French postwar discovery of Kafka, her several essays and her introduction to the collected works of Kafka form a useful description of that process.[2] She describes Kafka as totally foreign to France; when he finally arrived "the right of extraterritoriality was in the end an angelic privilege: coming from nowhere and appearing before all Kafka naturally seemed to have fallen out of the heavens, even for those writers and critics the least inclined to take heaven for their standard of literary judgment."[3]

Among those who first reacted to Kafka, the tendencies were either uncertainty as to the meaning of Kafka's works or meaning directed toward a definite and therefore limited understanding of Kafka. Gide, for example, reproached Groethuysen for having said so little about Kafka's personality. Mme Robert concedes that Gide was right to do so but notes

[1] Letter to the author, January 21, 1966.
[2] See the complete list of her scholarship in the bibliography.
[3] Marthe Robert, "Kafka in Frankreich," *Akzente* 13 (August, 1966): 310–320.

that in turn, when Gide brought *The Trial* to the stage, he allowed himself also to be satisfied with generalizations and ideas insufficiently thought through, resulting in the continued disorder of ideas about Kafka's work.

The limited conceptualization of Kafka's works, which to its adherents was at least self-contained, was that Kafka's work was pure surrealism: " 'The Metamorphosis,' in effect, had been published in 1928, that is to say at a time when surrealism, already vulgarised, was for the extended public the very idea of modernity. Immediately people held on to nothing about the story except the whole range of the most obvious 'fantastic' characteristics—black humor, onirism, cruelty—they included the story without hesitation in the surrealist spirit, itself also bizarre and deliberately provoking."[4] Though the surrealist label is now difficult to take seriously if applied to Kafka, says Mme Robert, nonetheless he suffered under it through the thirties. "The most superficial similarities are often the most striking" —to such an extent that in 1940 André Breton presented Kafka as restless dreamer occupied in brewing strange mixtures in an obscure room somewhere in a fantastic Prague. Mme Robert lays the blame for surrealist interpretation not only on André Breton, but also on the first French translators of Kafka. These, she claims, were poets and writers who themselves were either closely linked to the surrealist movement or, worse, directly under the influence of Breton himself.

The difficulty of properly translating ambiguity or forcing it into previously drawn contexts resulted in the use, in French,[5] of archaic or noble-sounding words, even if such implications were at best only partly intended by Kafka. Mme Robert remarks that ". . . the most badly treated in this respect was certainly *The Castle*, where the key words are terms that are thoroughly current, nevertheless having for German ears a noble or archaic ring; the French keeps no trace of this sense, except in those words which are simply outdated."[6] *Herren*, for example, could have been translated as *seigneurs* or as *messieurs*; Vialatte the translater chose the latter, although in this instance the former might have been the better choice. *Gehilfe* becomes *aide* rather than the more prosaic *commis* or *employé*; *Landvermesser* is translated as *arpenteur* rather than *geometre*, *Kerze* as *cierge* rather than *bougie*, and so on. The very title, in German, *Schloss*, loses the ambiguity between "castle" and "lock," in English as well as in French; in the latter it becomes *Chateau*.[7]

---

[4] *Ibid.*, p. 313.

[5] In conversation on February 1, 1966, Mme Robert called any attempt at a really good translation of Kafka into French an impossibility.

[6] Robert, "Kafka in Frankreich," p. 315.

[7] From my conversation with Mme Robert, February 1, 1966. She later incorporated this into the *Akzente* article, p. 316. It is missing in the original Berlin paper.

Since the only existing texts in French were translations of such poor quality, Mme Robert concludes that irrelevant interpretations could not have been avoided: when only theological or metaphysical translations are available, the interpretations will be of the same order. She has not found, however, a complete excuse for the myriad of offered interpretations of Kafka's works in France; the conclusions of French critics have been too close to those of critics in Germany, the United States, and elsewhere to imply that the fault lies with the translations rather than with the reader.

The second coming for French Kafka critics followed World War II; the new breed appeared in the guise of existentialists. They adopted Kafka much as the surrealists had. After the war, France was prepared for Kafka, far more than it had been in 1928. Mme Robert suggests that the Kafka vogue swept France because citizens had lived through events like those in the novels and in such stories as "In the Penal Colony": "Where had one seen before the sinister uniform described at the beginning of *The Trial*? The arbitrary arrests? The tranquil, and inhuman, functioning bureaucracy that crushes the individual under a mound of paper? Such anarchy in order? Victims torn to pieces in diabolic complicity with their executioners? Surely not in any book, but they had appeared in life, and simultaneously literature and life were forever changed."[8] That which could not be explained, from the war of the past and in the contemporary life, was termed, then as now, Kafkaesque; by naming the horror, each citizen found it easier to cope with the world he had lived in and was then still living in. A word rendered life easier to cope with and reinstated the average citizen in his comfortable, secure, and unchallenged place in society: "Before the absurdities of life, of the war and the post-war period, in face of the false mysteries of bureaucracies and politics, one found a kind of consolation in telling oneself, 'It's Kafkaesque'. . . . The name of Kafka thus entered popular speech and soon attained the weight of a slogan."[9]

With this kind of popularity, it is easy, as Mme Robert points out, to conclude that few could escape without being influenced by Kafka; yet she argues: ". . . in any case, it must be noted, Kafka could not have had, at the same time, all the disciples that are attributed to him."[10] Of course, she is correct—and yet she overstates her case. By citing in one breath Sartre, Robbe-Grillet, Michaux, Camus, and others as writers whom the popular press has classed together as examples of the Kafkaesque, she hopes to discredit any relationship they each may have to Kafka's form and stylistic point of view. It always seems necessary, in effect, to guard his reputation from comparison with later writers as if such comparison

[8] Marthe Robert, *Kafka et la loi de son oeuvre*, p. 43.
[9] *Ibid.*, p. 44.
[10] Letter to author, January 21, 1966.

could hurt Kafka.[11] Only his ideas, she claims, had any influence in France. Yet his ideas are the least original aspects of his writing. She contradicts herself when she concludes that Kafka cannot be classified as an existentialist; she forgets that his *ideas*, as implied by his narrative structures, parallel that philosophy more closely than they do any other line of thought (although of course he is not an existentialist theoretician).

Dealing to such a great extent with Kafka's ideas places a scholar very much in the mainstream of French thinking about Kafka. As Professor Reiss points out, "Kafka has had quite a vogue in France where, on the whole, he has been viewed as a thinker rather than as an artist."[12] In this part of Mme Robert's thought on Kafka,[13] she parallels closely the work of Maja Goth, whose exhaustive study compares Kafka with writers and movements in France from 1928 and 1955.[14] Overall, Maja Goth finds little of Kafka's influence: she sees instead a great deal of parallel thought and philosophy. Always the surrealist theme dominates. Kafka's work, she says, contains elements that are surrealist in nature: revolt, despair, irrational phenomena. It is dubious to consider these elements the property of the surrealists; at best they are parallel phenomena, available to any artist or writer working in the early twentieth century. But further, to claim that the work of Kafka is filled with revolt, despair, and irrational elements is to interpret that work according to a series of imposed philosophies, none more than momentarily valid. And in no way does Mme Goth demonstrate these elements to be present in Kafka's style. Only when speaking of Kafka's humor does she begin to discuss the concrete nature of Kafka's style; her value judgments evolve from this analysis but for her to claim that Kafka's phenomena are often irrational (and therefore quite like the phenomena of the surrealists) is to avoid comprehending Kafka's work. One might well turn her charge against the surrealist reading of Kafka against herself: "Without a doubt the surrealists helped bring Kafka into vogue. But it seems they either read him badly, or they refused what was essential in his contribution."[15] There is, Mme Goth concludes, no one in France influenced by Kafka, therein she agrees with Mme Robert. Perhaps a close affinity of ideas does exist. There has been virtually no mention of the relation between Kafka's narrational point of view and that of

[11] See also Marthe Robert, *L'Ancien et le Nouveau: De Don Quichotte à Franz Kafka*, in which she finds more "honorable" comparisons and analogies for Kafka—Quixote, Ulysses, King Arthur.

[12] H. S. Reiss, "Recent Kafka Criticism (1944–1955)—A Survey," in *Kafka: A Collection of Critical Essays*, ed. Ronald Gray, p. 166.

[13] There is the other part, too. When she discusses Kafka's ideas in *Quichotte*, she deals, despite herself, with his narrative structure.

[14] Maja Goth, *Franz Kafka et les lettres françaises: (1928–1955)*.

[15] *Ibid.*, pp. 62, 63.

the French writers. Beckett has been dismissed in the general classification of "one of these mentioned in the newspapers" by Mme Robert; Mme Goth devotes 2 out of 260 pages to him. The former mentions Robbe-Grillet with Beckett; the latter, although Robbe-Grillet had already published *The Erasers* (1953) and *The Voyeur* (1955) when her study appeared, does not mention him. Nor does she mention Nathalie Sarraute and Michel Butor.[16]

Maja Goth's conclusion, arrived at circuitously through an examination of Kafka's themes as displayed in the works of his literary progeny, is on the whole correct. It bears little relationship to the work she has gone through, but it is sufficiently general to embrace both her work and many another attempt to see the relationship between Kafka and those writers in France who had read his work. Of the surrealists, of Michaux, of Blanchot, Bataille, and Beckett, of Camus and Sartre, she says: "For them, the importance of their meeting with Kafka is considerable, but the contact itself should in no way place their originality, their primal contribution, in doubt."[17] The question that remains rises from her dismissal of so-called imitators of Kafka: is everyone who understands and uses the metaphysical implications of Kafka's structure and point of view necessarily attempting to imitate him, or, more correctly, is it not probable that Breton, Michaux, Bataille, Camus, Blanchot, and Sartre all would have written what and as they did had Kafka never existed? The proper subject here is not one of influence; the realm of ideas is the incorrect direction of inquiry. It is necessary to search in the style of French writers after Kafka in order to find his closest literary heirs.

Although Marthe Robert and Maja Goth are the only French critics to deal directly with the question of Kafka in France, they are not alone in the French discussion of Kafka. Mme Goth, in the bibliography to her volume, cites most of the works on Kafka in France to 1955; it is necessary here to discuss only a few of the important examples from that period, as well as several more recent studies.

The postwar rush of Kafka criticism is best represented by Maurice Blanchot, Robert Rochefort, André Nemeth, and Michel Carrouges.[18] Each work has its limitations. Blanchot asks the major question about Kafka, which he cannot answer: "How to represent to ourselves this world that

---

[16] Nathalie Sarraute, *Tropismes* (1939), *Portrait d'un inconnu* (1948), *Martereau* (1953). More understandable is her not having considered Michel Butor's *Passage de Milan* (1954)—she would have had only two years to read it.

[17] Goth, *Kafka et les lettres françaises*, p. 255.

[18] Maurice Blanchot, "La Lecture de Kafka," *L'Arche*, no. 11 (November, 1945), pp. 107–116, and *La Part de feu*, pp. 9–34; Robert Rochefort, *Kafka ou l'irréductible espoir*; André Nemeth, *Kafka ou le Mystère juif*; Michael Carrouges, *Franz Kafka*.

escapes us not because it is uncontrollable, but because there is too much to control?"[19] The trouble is that here he touches not on the secret of Kafka alone, but on the secret of all great writing—the ability of an author to take everything he sees from the world and to create not a world view, but merely a world as he sees it, a world existing wholly. When Kafka, therefore, writes of a protagonist, he does so by showing the world become too much for that protagonist, by letting the hero become overwhelmed by the world. But Blanchot, like so many of those he criticizes, chooses only the part with which he himself can cope, the "ideas" he recognizes; he leaves the *trop* he has noticed to someone else.

Additions were made to the Kafka shelf in the early sixties,[20] but neither the newer generation of critics together nor the postwar people making themselves heard once more contributed anything to an understanding of Kafka. With the two preliminary exceptions, a few French academic voices have been raised against the traditional interpretation of Kafka's works. Pierre de Boisdeffre can still explain in 1962: "Kafka's life becomes confused with the creation of a work which places him in a context without his yet knowing what form the work will take. And the Proustian complexes are aggravated to the point of taking on proportions of a veritable malady of the personality: expressed in Freudian terms, it is a question of an Oedipus complex which has never been liquidated because it has taken on, with time, religious significance." And even beyond such pseudometaphysics, Boisdeffre still draws the one-to-one equivalents as of old: "Kafka's father is the despotic God of the Old Testament who forbids his son to pick the fruit of the tree of life, weighs him down with a primary and permanent guilt and constrains him to live in exile on the earth."[21]

[19] Blanchot, *La Part de feu*, p. 12.
[20] Michel Dentan, *Humour et création littéraire dans l'oeuvre de Kafka*; Joël Jakubec, *Kafka contre l'absurde*; Michel Carrouges, *Kafka contre Kafka*; Maurice Blanchot, "Le Pont du bois," *Nouvelle Revue Française*, no. 133 (January, 1964), pp. 90–104.
[21] Pierre de Boisdeffre, *Où va le roman?* p. 48.

APPENDIX 2: KAFKA CRITICISM

Reasons cited for the acclaim given to Kafka's work vary almost as widely as do the extremes to which the work is interpreted. In search of a general heading to contain all praise for his so-called theological, psychological, surrealistic, sociological, aesthetic, historical, and existential understanding of his fellow man, one must laud Kafka at least as a great observer of things, situations, and events, and as a fine recorder of his observations.

Of course, Kafka did not describe situations he observed. No matter how great his biographical anxieties and madnesses, it can be safely assumed he did not actually see Gregor Samsa in bed, nor was he in the audience when the ape made its report to the academy. That he described events in such terms as these may be attributed to a variety of psychological, biographical, or other causes, but, in themselves, as descriptions, the narrations assume the validity of honest perception. As any artist would, Kafka blended observed realities into a valid fiction.

The question thus becomes one of what is observed, toward what does the observer direct his attention? The question of Kafka's direction has been debated since Max Brod sought to mold his friend in his own Judaic image.[1] Since that time, criticism and scorn have been heaped upon Brod both for making Kafka over into a prophet and for his continued religious overinterpretation of Kafka in the years that followed. Yet no matter how strongly and perhaps foolishly Brod misinterprets his friend's work, his precritical, human realization of genius within the written word led him to disobey Kafka's request; he would not burn his friend's papers posthumously. Brod's own incessant writings about Kafka erase by only an iota the great debt modern literature owes him.

Kafka, however, is more than the prophet narrowly circumscribed by

[1] Max Brod, "Nachwort zur ersten Ausgabe," in *Der Prozess*, pp. 526–538, and his notes to *Das Schloss*, pp. 277–284.

Brod. Kafka's English translator Edwin Muir, himself a distinguished poet, repeated but hardly reinforced Brod's pronouncements. Ronald Gray gives the warning: "Kafka is primarily a writer of novels and short stories; any fame or notoriety he has as a religious thinker or critic of religion is secondary. . . . So far as the bulk of his work is concerned, it stands or falls on literary grounds, and no amount of original thought in any field could in itself make of him a great novelist."[2]

Since Brod's first words on Kafka, many other critics have seen Kafka's works from their individual restrictions; by attempting to examine the works through those interpreting filters, their minds, they tend to give the reader insight into themselves rather than into the works they examine, providing samplers in what Heinz Politzer calls literary Rorschach tests.[3] Yet the importance of previous Kafka criticism must not be underestimated; with an occasional blatant exception, little of it is totally wrong; some of it gives valuable partial insight into Kafka's writings.

Kafka turns not into himself, nor into others about him; he turns to the world, to appearances. It would be difficult to understand Kafka's works without the hundreds of interpretative studies that have gone by, studies that have fragmented Kafka's world to see it from one external point of view at a time. Reading this vast collection of studies can provide one of two results: either any subsequent consideration of Kafka will have to cope with the many fragmentary studies (which is the procedure of many books: a chapter on psychological interpretation, one on biographical, one on existential, and so on), or such a consideration will have to realize that a new formula must be found, a key that can combine the vast variety of fragments into a whole as complete as Kafka's view of the world must have been. A body of work that provides as many possible interpretations as does the world itself must be a relatively close description of that world. Only in the last ten years has serious criticism begun its attempt to see the unities of his work. One can wonder with Dieter Hasselblatt:

A half century of Kafka. Misunderstandings that stirred up a fuss. . . . Supposition, ignorance, disqualification, partial overestimation. Compilations, translations, and editions.

A half century of Kafka: spoiled, bored, irritated with attempts to understand Kafka "best." Kaleidoscopes of meanings, usurpations, practical applications, proclaimed exploitations, wrangles over method and limping vindications. Does Kafka belong to the arts and sciences? And if so, which? Does he belong to the readers? And if so, which? Does he belong to the past? The future? Max Brod? The capitalistic decadent West? The bureaucratic totalitarian systems of the East, their prophet of anticipation? The

---

[2] Edwin Muir, "Franz Kafka," in *Kafka: A Collection of Critical Essays*, ed. Ronald Gray, pp. 33–45; Ronald Gray, introduction to *Kafka*, p. 1.

[3] Heinz Politzer, *Franz Kafka: Parable and Paradox*, p. 21.

Germans, in whose language he wrote his works? The Czechs, in whose land he lived, worked and lies buried? The Americans and the French, in whose literature the first reaction to him took place, not only in learned articles but also in literary/cultural development? Or does Kafka belong to those who, unprejudiced and unencumbered, still have him in front of them?[4]

Hasselblatt establishes the problem in several of its dimensions: the dangers of misunderstanding and subsequent misinterpretation are everywhere. They have been present from the very beginning, from the several beginnings. Friedrich Beissner describes what happened when *The Trial* was at last generally published in Germany in 1950:

. . . it lay as a Christmas present on many a table, and most of its expectant readers were wearing unsuitable spectacles. Bafflement seemed general. Hadn't we been told that this novel was a glorious satire on the corrupt officialdom of the Austro-Hungarian monarchy? But granted that a satirist exaggerates, and has to exaggerate for clarity's sake, this surely went beyond all bounds, this caricature must inevitably miss the mark. And then, said others, weren't we told to expect a great allegory of one of the two manifestations of the divinity as taught by the Cabala, namely "Judgment," and weren't we to find in *The Castle*, according to trustworthy reports, a complementary picture, in the same kind of cipher, of the other manifestation of the divinity, namely "Grace"? But this didn't add up: far too many details and quite a few more important characteristics would simply not fit into the allegory. Perhaps we should try some other way, some other symbolic explanation? And so on.[5]

The interpretations of one man did not—do not—satisfy the literary sensibilities of another, who in turn misexplains his reactions to a third. A partial cause is the lack of concepts to describe new phenomena. One is not prepared to accept words as words; one has been taught that all words, when placed in a literary context, have meanings beyond or behind the surface. But in Kafka's works, "meaning" is no longer the question. Words are their own meaning; the picture presented is real. Gray cites Austin Warren's phrase, "There is here no possibility of allegorical sterilization," and himself continues: "Much as one would like to explain away the transformation of Gregor Samsa into an insect, calling it an allegory of the sense of degradation such as St. Augustine employed when he wrote that his soul had become a spider, the story will not allow it. Gregor is not dreaming; his fantastic plight becomes convincing reality, and all efforts at reducing it to terms we can admit in the everyday world merely diminish

[4] Dieter Hasselblatt, *Zauber und Logik: Eine Kafka-Studie* (Cologne: Verlag Wissenschaft und Politik, 1964), p. 9. All quotation by permission of the publisher.

[5] Friedrich Beissner, "Kafka the Artist," in *Kafka*, ed. Gray, p. 17.

its force. So it is with nearly all Kafka's symbols."[6] Perhaps the strongest
warning emanates from Kafka himself; Hasselblatt points to it, and lets it
stand as the major introduction to his book. His quotation from Kafka—
"Do not expect any help from explanations of the fictions. At best you will
understand the explanations. . . . Sewn up in these explanations you will
look for what you already know, and that which is really there you will not
see. (H424f)"—is, as he admits with the "f." following his page citation,
culled from two or three pages of what Brod has called Kafka's "Para-
lipomena." But the quotation is not out of context, even though Kafka is
speaking only of the difficulty in understanding poetry in Yiddish jargon.
Hasselblatt continues: "Explanations and help—both are driven off by
forty years of unsurveyable rampant Kafka criticism" and strengthened by
a reading public so shocked and helpless as to accept any explanation that
seemed to make sense. Meanings could take any form, according to the
orientation of the reader: "classical, bellelettristic, naturalistic, marxist,
surrealist." What was "really there" remained unseen. Hasselblatt concludes, "From the moment that Brod paradigmatically proclaimed the
the religious meanings of *The Castle* and *The Trial* in the Afterwords of
the first editions, the difficulty of understanding Kafka has always been
reduced and simplified to preestablished systems of comprehension."[7]

Reading Hasselblatt's book is a cleansing experience after examining the
myriad interpretations of Kafka's work. But the problem with the study,
after the initial satisfactory and highly sympathetic dismissal of partial
analyses, is its repetitive debunking of everyone who has written about
Kafka. Hasselblatt strikes the proper note when he announces his inten-
tions: "The intention here is not to add to the many meanings of Kafka's
work yet one more."[8] Nor will he; but neither does he add to the reader's
knowledge of Kafka beyond noting the limitations of those who have
previously written about him.

As has been stated already, a general introduction to the work of Kafka
is not intended here.[9] Nevertheless, between 1955 and the present, three
major studies of Kafka did appear, each moving the reader closer to a
phenomenological understanding of Kafka's work. Still, a full understanding of this kind has not yet been achieved. An occasional paragraph in an
article and the emphasis of Heinz Politzer's book *Franz Kafka: Parable*

[6] Gray, introduction to *Kafka*, p. 2.
[7] Hasselblatt, *Zauber und Logik*, pp. 11–12.
[8] *Ibid.*, p. 10.
[9] For a quick introduction to the variety of thinking about Kafka, a curious
reader should examine such collections of essays as those in the special issues
cited in the bibliography; or Angel Flores, *The Kafka Problem*; or Ronald Gray,
Kafka: A Collection of Critical Essays. The final essay in Gray, "Recent Kafka
Criticism (1944–55)—A Survey," by H. S. Reiss, is an excellent and thorough
survey of Kafka scholarship and pseudoscholarship during that period.

and Paradox are the few guides to seeing Kafka in the light of "what is really there." Wilhelm Emrich's *Kafka* attempts what he calls an interpretation limited to the work alone ("werkimmanente Interpretation"), but the line separating the immediate work and its interpretation, though relatively wide, is easily crossed by one who views it as a link between work and interpretation rather than as the division between two distinct methods of literary analysis. He begins, however, with the right idea: "Mostly Kafka's stories and novels begin with a sudden and incomprehensible loss of all normal possibilities for orientation. In an unguarded condition, as of sleep or distraction, the several heroes are, on awaking, abruptly displaced into a world which they are no longer capable of ordering or clarifying . . ."[10] But he immediately begins talking about the situation of Modern Man, generalizing and interpreting from Kafka's work in a manner unlike his previous description. Although Emrich's work provides the first real step toward understanding of Kafka, it remains as a whole merely an intelligent reading of Kafka from a point of view still too staunchly dedicated to interpretation and generalizing. Emrich's work, according to Hasselblatt, "is not free of out-of-place aspects, perspectives, premises, and concepts."[11]

A reading of Walter Sokel's *Franz Kafka: Tragik und Ironie: Zur Struktur seiner Kunst* entails much the same problem: metaphysical interpretation begins long before any attempt at an examination of the structure of Kafka's art has been exhausted. Again, Sokel has the proper direction; he suspects correctly the problems that lie before him:

> The question we are asking does not read: What is the meaning of Kafka's forms and pictures? Rather it reads: What are these forms and pictures (and gestures, situations, thoughts, dialogues, etc.) doing in his work? What are they accomplishing? What fabulating functions do they possess? For us the meaning of Kafka should not lie in what his work points to, but in what his work says. The principle of literalness is bound up for us with the principle of structure. The question, what does Kafka mean, becomes for us the question, what is he saying, and how do his statements hold together, how are they related to each other?[12]

Sokel's attempt to discover what is there soon becomes a comparative, story-by-story, thematic analysis that itself turns into a metaphysical vision of contemporary man, Sokel's vision more than Kafka's. The shifted emphasis must take place, since from the beginning Sokel's title has committed him to a tragic and ironic reading of Kafka's works.

[10] Wilhelm Emrich, *Kafka*, p. 17.
[11] Hasselblatt, *Zauber und Logik*, p. 28.
[12] Walter H. Sokel, *Franz Kafka: Tragik und Ironie: Zur Struktur seiner Kunst*, p. 27.

Heinz Politzer comes closest to taking Kafka at his word. A superficial reading of his book might suggest that he does little more than retell Kafka's stories; yet only by remaining close to the text can he begin to explain it. And so Politzer succeeds where his predecessors have failed: he establishes the emphases necessary to let the works be viewed as they were written, for he examines the physical make-up of Kafka's style; he explains that its apparent facile nature makes the reader feel as though some sort of interpretation were necessary. "If we probe the sentence for its actual content, we shall see that the words have been chosen in such a way that the reader is forced to focus his attention on what remains hidden behind or below the realistic narrative," he says. In this sense, Kafka himself can be blamed for many of the critical misinterpretations of his work by others; but Politzer, having recognized the trap, avoids it. Kafka's story ("Give It Up" in this case) "reports nothing a realist could not have expressed in exactly the same terms."[13] But nineteenth-century realism was born of empiricism and experimental science; twentieth-century realism, in fiction, is action and situation viewed with an admittedly jaundiced eye and described through a filter of predilection, to become a realistic interpretation of its original. Kafka—quite rightly, according to Politzer— merely describes from the point of view of a man with a necessarily impaired vision; Kafka's heroes, both here and in the longer stories and novels, explain neither their action nor actions they have witnessed. "Kafka did not try to solve this dilemma of man's existence. He simply stated it with all the strength he could muster from the weakness of a man born late in the development of his civilization. His parables are as multi-layered as their Biblical models. But, unlike them, they are also multi-faced, ambiguous, and capable of so many interpretations that, in the final analysis, they defy any and all."[14]

With Politzer the direction is established. Confusion results from attempts to "transcend" literature with the metaphysics of previous centuries. Given the hardly impeachable postulate that Kafka is a writer of great talent and probably of great genius, the myriad interpretations of his work prove only one point: that there rests within this body of work sufficient material from which such interpretation can grow. There exists only one other collection of material about which as many interpretations may stem: this is the world itself. Abundant philosophies grown from limited views of the world are paralleled by the variety of scholarly and pseudo-scholarly essays on the works of Kafka. The reason for such a parallel could well be found in the close relationship between Kafka's ability to describe and the world he sees, fictionalizes, and records. Only a writer who records

[13] Politzer, *Franz Kafka: Parable and Paradox*, p. 3.
[14] *Ibid.*, p. 21.

with a minimum of intervening filters, of intervening philosophies, can reproduce a world to which one may attach interpretations grown from that world itself. Each man's personal philosophies are finite, yet the total of man's interpretations of the universe is as great as the number of living men. Therefore it would be impossible to assume that Kafka had endowed the world of his fiction with his maximum of philosophies, since it would be impossible for any one man to be conscious, preconscious, and unconscious of so varied a series of philosophies. Far more plausible is the original hypothesis, that Kafka described as he saw with his artist's mind's eye, with the consciousness of his narrators; it is the critics who have learned to analyze beyond the intention of the narrative. Gray notes that "Kafka was not a systematic philosopher or man of religion, he was an artist, a writer, and there is no one body of doctrine to which all his work can be referred."[15] One must grasp Kafka's universe *in itself*: as such, his view of the world can best be understood from as nonphilosophic a distance as possible.

Everything in Kafka's universe is always there. But Kafka's works need readers in order to go beyond the mere descriptions that they are. In nineteenth-century human terms, that which is only described remains incomplete and begs for such an interpreting reader. Nathalie Sarraute speaks of the "needs" of Kafka's heroes:

All they want is to become, "in the eyes of these people who regard them with such distrust . . . not their friend, perhaps, but in any case, their fellow citizen" . . . , to be able to appear and justify themselves before unknown, unapproachable accusers, or to seek to safeguard, despite all obstacles, some paltry semblance of a relationship with those closest to them.
This humble pursuit, by virtue of its desperate obstinacy, of the depths of human suffering, the distress and complete abandonment that it brings to light, extends well beyond the domain of psychology and lends itself to all kinds of metaphysical interpretations.[16]

Beyond psychology—the analytic psychology of an author—all can lie open to interpretation. Kafka's heroes no less than Mme Sarraute's are bound by analyzed meaning only when the reader's interpretation will allow nothing more.

The works of Kafka are the still largely unrecognized juncture between external description and internal but nonanalytic monologue; Kafka's narrators report as they see. His style, possibly recognized not even by him for what it is, declines to indulge in the act of explaining why. And although seemingly impossible things or events appear in ways once labeled "absurd" ("absurd" being no longer a valid judgment, for a lack of ex-

[15] Gray, introduction to *Kafka*, p. 6.
[16] Nathalie Sarraute, *The Age of Suspicion*, p. 77.

planation is nothing more than the manner in which an author experiments away from the methods of the nineteenth century), such things or events are perfectly acceptable when one follows the glance of the narrator (realizing that as reader one sees only what he, the narrator, sees), understanding him by recognizing his world.

APPENDIX 3: BECKETT CRITICISM

Some Attitudes Toward Beckett's Style

Martin Gerard says of Beckett's style, "It is a prose which denies itself all spurious ornament and adjectival embellishment, even, for the most part, the alluring joy of metaphor." Niklaus Gessner calls it "Telegrammstil," a term proper in the sense that Beckett is attempting to confer the most important information in as few words as possible, but misused here because Gessner likens it in its apparent clumsy hedging to the speech of children. For Germaine Brée the language is generalized and accessible; and for Christine Brooke-Rose, the style "is simple and unfigurative. . . . Beckett is colloquial without ever being slovenly or flat." It has become even less adorned than was Kafka's, although to agree with the anonymous reviewer in *L'Esprit* that it is eruditely negligent, sometimes alienating, sometimes persuasive, unadorned, and not nearly as elegant as that of Kafka, is to deny not only the turned puns of *Molloy* but also to forget that *Murphy* and *Watt* are rich in complicated language and intricate constructions.[1] In fact, Beckett's style has moved to a point undiscovered by Kafka: Beckett's artistic development from *Murphy* to *How It Is* has been a movement from the baroque to Miss Brooke-Rose's "colloquial." Simultaneous with the winnowing out of unnecessary verbiage has come the decreasing importance of words as signs of meaning, and the greater stress on words in combination. Turns of phrase are pretty at the moment but reveal little of a universe that in Beckett's work becomes ever more gene-

[1] Martin Gerard, "Molloy Becomes Unnamable," *X* 1, no. 4 (October, 1960): 316; Niklaus Gessner, *Die Unzulänglichkeit der Sprache*, p. 51; Germaine Brée, "L'Etrange Monde des grands articulés," *Configurations Critiques*, no. 8, p. 95; Christine Brooke-Rose, "Samuel Beckett and the Anti-Novel," *London Magazine* 5, no. 12 (December, 1959): 40; "Samuel Beckett: Molloy," *Esprit*, September, 1951, p. 425.

ralized, an ever more valid experience for greater numbers of readers. Pin-gaud, in his notes to the Editions 10/18 edition of *Molloy*, uses Flaubert's term when describing the novel as moving well into the fold of the *livre sur rien* and notes the danger of such usage of language if the author wishes merely to demonstrate nonsignification; but, on the other hand, limited language, properly used, can bring forth profound results.[2] Such cleansing demands more of the writer than eliminating adjectives, how-ever. The whole concept of lyrical writing, nineteenth-century style—even the cold hardness of the symbolists—must be eliminated. As Fletcher points out, a full cleansing job demands that even the appearance of print on the page must change from the accepted paragraphs, sentences, and quotation marks. Kafka has already experimented with commas to elim-inate as thoroughly as possible the reading mind's ability to follow causal-ity in the narrative. Beckett, by doing likewise, attempts to establish the lack of logic in colloquially spoken words. Although this lack of apparent logic is truer of *How It Is* and *The Unnamable* than of the earlier novels, in a more limited form it can be applied to *Molloy* and *Malone Dies* also, as can the idea that "Beckett puts the familiar machinery of pedagogical instruction into reverse, strips his language of its literary props and make-weights, and thereby catches the sounds the mind makes in actually grap-pling with words, or rather with the elemental lumps of basic speech."[3]

The concept of repetition within elemental lumps of speech is found as early as *Murphy*; *Watt* is replete with them. And the necessity of under-standing their function precedes any comprehension of Beckett's work, for things as seen and the nature of things chosen to be seen constitute an important clue to the nature of the perceiving mind. Jacobsen and Mueller explain:

It would be possible to say, accurately, that no one writing fiction has ever compiled such change-ringing lists of mutations, variations, alternatives. . . . they lie, vast and exasperating deserts, before the reader's sullen eye. Shifts in the position of furniture within a room, in alternatives to a given schedule, in the cries of frogs, in the order of sucking stones, rotate, alter, switch, in the meaningless, meticulous logic of a madman. And even in many passages in which Beckett is not dealing in strict tabulations, the reader who has not grasped the object of Beckett's technique can only char-acterize as obsessive his repetitions. An object intrinsically insignificant (a bicycle, a hat, a dog, a garbage can, a stick) reappears like some neme-sis, shifting commonplace and horrifying aspects.[4]

[2] Bernard Pingaud, "Beckett le précurseur," in Samuel Beckett, *Molloy* (Paris: Editions 10/18), p. 295.
[3] John Fletcher, *The Novels of Samuel Beckett*, pp. 218, 220.
[4] Josephine Jacobsen and William R. Mueller, *The Testament of Samuel Beckett*, pp. 6–7.

Some critics understand a verbalized expression of the need to find the proper word; most do not. Gessner assumes that "this search for the right word, and the impossibility of finding the right word, are further signposts of the downfall of verbal expression in Beckett's texts."[5] Gessner's short-sightedness does not discuss the decline of speech in a contemporary world; rather it demonstrates the always present difficulty and the oft-found impossibility of discovering speech sufficiently clean to describe an event, object, or situation without human intervention. For Beckett is admitting that interpreting intervention is essential; he controls his prose from this position alone.

So it is possible to say along with Pingaud that Beckett marks the French beginning, with *Molloy*, of a kind of literature in which French writers are now the major experimenters. He adds that it is important to note that Robbe-Grillet's first article was devoted to *Godot*, and that reading Beckett's work caused the author of *The Erasers* to take the manuscript to the publishers Editions de Minuit, of which Robbe-Grillet soon became the literary editor.[6]

General Criticism

Samuel Beckett is not a metaphysician. His place in future intellectual history will be determined by the extent of his innovations in the arts of fiction and theater. Yet metaphysics is precisely the realm in which he reigns for the vast majority of those who consider themselves expert on the subject of Beckett's work. Therefore from the beginning the reader should recall Beckett's own warning; as Martin Esslin notes, "Lucky's speech in *Waiting for Godot*, richly interlaced with references to the results of numerous authorities like Puncher and Wattman, Testew and Essy-in-Possy (whose 'unfinished labours were crowned by the Acacacacademy of Anthropopopometry') is, among other things, a salutary warning against, and savage parody of, the belief that the sum of human wisdom, of 'thinking,' can be increased by citing the results of established authorities."[7] Obvious pseudometaphysical criticism is easily recognized. It is more difficult to separate valid insight from soul-felt description of Beckett's relevance to "our human condition," on which baroque phraseology suddenly shifts into a statement meaningful beyond the realm of the critic's personal life. Claude Mauriac, for example, after claiming Beckett to be soul brother to Kafka, says that "one cannot in any case deny the extraordinary impression, I do not dare say enrichment since it is a question of the consciousness

[5] Gessner, *Die Unzulänglichkeit der Sprache*, p. 53.
[6] Pingaud, "Beckett le précurseur," in Beckett, *Molloy*, p. 292–293.
[7] Martin Esslin, introduction to *Samuel Beckett: A Collection of Critical Essays*, p. 8.

of an absolutely poverty that Samuel Beckett gives us when one discovers him. Poverty which is our only fortune. Inexhaustible, fascinating poverty." No terms are ever defined, and Mauriac continues in his private vein until, without developing the realization, he concludes that the heroes of Beckett's novels "are all one and the same person."[8] Mauriac, and many others, leave such important structural considerations hanging in the mid-air of impressionistic discovery; momentary critique together with much pseudometaphysics seem to become the stuff around which most authorities function. Although some intelligent examination has been attempted on the works of Beckett, the body of Rorschach material surrounding Beckett's work is only slightly smaller than that surrounding Kafka—and this primarily because Beckett's work has a shorter history.

The critic's problem with Beckett's fictions and plays is making sense of the apparently undifferentiated flow of words that issues from the mouths or pens of his several narrators. "Stream of consciousness" is not, however, in question here. As John Fletcher points out:

Only a superficial reading leads one to think that *Molloy* is a rambling monologue leading nowhere in particular; only such a reading can have given rise to the unhelpful but often proferred opinion that this is a stream-of-consciousness novel. (We blunt our terms by thus misusing them; *Molloy* is no more a stream-of-consciousness novel than is Mauriac's *Noeud de vipères*; in both cases we are confronted with a hard, clear, uncompromisingly honest self-description. A book needs more than a first person narrator talking to and for himself before it can be bracketed with the last episode of *Ulysses*.)[9]

As in the works of Kafka, the style is dominated by the narrative point of view, the narrative consciousness, which does not stream forward but depends for its order on the stimuli that set it in action. The stimuli themselves are the major cause for much critical misunderstanding—they are viewed, pounced upon, and held to be the truth about Samuel Beckett. Hugh Kenner, after long conversation with Beckett, tells of his felt conclusion:

We are not, in short, like dogs excited by the scent of invisible meat, to snap after some item of information which the author grasps very well and is holding just behind the curtain. So to proceed is to misapprehend the quality of the Beckett universe, which is permeated by mystery and bounded by a darkness; to assail these qualities because they embarrass the critic's professional knowingness is cheap, reductive, and perverse. Like primitive astronomers, we are free to note recurrences, cherish sym-

[8] Claude Mauriac, "Samuel Beckett," *Preuves*, no. 61 (March, 1956), pp. 73, 76. The question of the single character is discussed in chapter 3, above.
[9] Fletcher, *The Novels of Samuel Beckett*, p. 135.

metries, and seek if we can means of placating the hidden powers; more for our comfort than for theirs.[10]

Mr. Kenner allows himself a lyric moment, and he does make excuses before the fact for whatever limitations his study may possess. But together with Anthony Curtis ("To try to worry out a meaning, to break the code of Beckett's mind, is a trap into which all but the wiliest fall. 'Don't interpret,' to adopt a celebrated piece of advice to a younger reviewer, 'interpretation dates you.' "),[11] Mr. Kenner warns of the danger inherent in the literary Rorshach test. Nor is he alone in realizing the repeated patterns, the symmetries and recurrences in Beckett's works: the last words of Beckett's short narrative, "The Expelled," show how clearly Beckett knew all his stories were the same. Any story will do, since inevitably each story will resemble another; the words may differ but the pattern will remain the same. It is as Friedrich Beissner had said of Kafka, "that great writers have in fact only one theme, a 'permanent note' running through all the manifold realizations and variations of the theme." The permanent note is present: the unsuccessful quest provides much the same structure for Beckett's work as for Kafka's. In no way, however, should each similarity imply specific influence of Kafka on Beckett. The unsuccessful quest is one of the basic motifs in all post-Renaissance European literatures, from *Don Quixote* through Proust and Joyce; within the rubric great variation is possible. Beckett does share that general permanent note with Kafka, just as his work is governed by a point of view similar to Kafka's, but their respective idioms make each writer unique. Of Beckett, Christine Brooke-Rose says, "As in the best 18th century prose, his effects are carefully built up and depend not on adornment but on pattern, a pattern made up of rhythm, repetition, antithesis, and lucid but long intricate periods." Overall, much the same may be said of Kafka. Yet there is a twofold difference. Although his specific terminology is unsatisfactory, Walter Strauss points out that "Beckett represents a step beyond Kafka; Kafka is intent on affirming his self in relation to an unseen God: in Beckett the self is in the process of disintegration . . . Beckett was to become the poet of vegetation (and here too he is different from Kafka, who is the poet of frustration), and he was to chart the path of nondirectional progress."[12]

---

[10] Hugh Kenner, *Samuel Beckett: A Critical Study*, p. 10.

[11] Anthony Curtis, "Mood of the Month—IV," *London Magazine* 5, no. 5 (May, 1958): 62.

[12] Friedrich Beissner, "Kafka the Artist," in *Kafka: A Collection of Critical Essays*, ed. Ronald Gray, p. 19; Brooke-Rose, "Samuel Beckett and the Anti-Novel," p. 40; Walter A. Strauss, "Dante's Belacqua and Beckett's Tramps," *Comparative Literature* 11, no. 3 (Summer, 1959): 252.

The double difference is anchored in two aspects of the new fiction that have already been discussed: narrative consciousness as the point of view and the structural thrust that it dominates. Kafka as narrator was able to express the horror of his situation not by describing horrifying aspects of the external world, but by the technique, the process of his description. Beckett can be no more than highly dissatisfied with what he sees; his mind has learned to accept so-called horror; such horror is no longer novel. The world of his view is not horrible, it simply *is*. Beckett's narrators often are not certain exactly what about it *is*, but to imply that his narrating consciousnesses merely vegetate would be to deny any "path of nondirectional progress." Whereas Kafka's quest pushes toward some unseen authority, some unseen bit of knowledge that would supply the key to all riddles, Beckett's narrators have no such great aim. Their goals are arbitrary, but, because of the absolute nature of each arbitrarily decided goal, failure must necessarily result. The impossibility of success is inherent in the nature of the quest. Since the several renaissances, every such quest is, directly or not, a search for absolute knowledge, which, being one aspect of Godness, is by definition unavailable to man. Therefore all human quests for knowledge must in the end be doomed to failure, if not within their own limited spheres then certainly in any sphere beyond the limited knowledge of the questing personality. No matter what one achieves, there are always greater challenges beyond the goal; even if the goal satisfies one man, it is not the final goal and at least in this sense the quest must be unsuccessful. Such failure is a basic theme in all great fiction, if for no other reason than to remind both reader and author of man's consistent humanity.

Beckett, from his intimate view of Joyce's attempt to achieve the goal of absolutes, is aware of the impossibility of Joyce's essays and certainly of the constant impossibility of achieving human omniscience. Citing a conversation, Kenner explains Beckett's view that "whereas 'the more Joyce knew the more he could,' this tendency towards omniscience and omnipotence need not exhaust art. 'I'm working with impotence, ignorance. I don't think impotence has been exploited in the past.' "[13] To explore omniscience would imply the ability to achieve Godness; Beckett rejects this possibility and tries the other end of the spectrum. His genius rests in an ability to form a quest out of the exploration of impotence. Paradoxically, he must demonstrate that complete impotence, itself an absolute, cannot be achieved, and the search for it must also remain unsuccessful. Aware of the impossibility of achieving the goal, a serious artist must then shift his emphasis; if the intellectual ends cannot be attained, the artist must attempt to perfect his art. Thus art itself becomes a main motif in Beckett's

---

[13] Kenner, *Samuel Beckett: A Critical Study*, p. 33.

writing—the continual insistence on the form of the thing, the style, dominates. The outside world is necessary only as a tool; it molds the art. His words about Proust—"He makes no attempt to dissociate form from content. The one is a concretion of the other, the revelation of a world" (P 88)—and of Joyce—"Here form *is* content, content *is* form. . . . He is not writing about something; he is writing something"[14]—elucidate Beckett's own later point of view as much as they do the methods of his subjects. But just as Beckett realizes that the impossibility of achieving his quest demands the abandonment of the hope of finding an ultimate answer, so he must conclude also that the hope of perfecting one's art is merely another unattainable goal. Doubt, the bastard child of hope and physical impossibility, haunts the tone of Beckett's vision.[15] Ruby Cohn explains that, "with increasing insistence through the years, Beckett's ideal of commitment to art is undercut by his awareness of the absurdity of that ideal (as of others, earlier abandoned) and of the inevitability of its failure. Not only does he mock his artist-heroes, but he turns his incisive wit against his own art."[16] Beckett himself says, when talking of Bram Van Velde: "There are many ways in which the thing I am trying in vain to say may be tried in vain to be said. I have experimented both in public and in private, under duress, through faintness of heart, through weakness of mind, with two or three hundred" (P 123). As always, Beckett's irony is too deeply laced with truth for one to laugh at length. Art, the principle of constant process, alone succeeds; and yet its success is momentary because in the next instant it is replaced by a new thrust of creating energy. Thereupon, however, it uses and acts against that tool which forms it, the material universe. Esslin links consciousness to the artistic process when he explains that "in Beckett's work, this tension between the transient, unendingly decaying nature of the material universe and the immaterial aspect of consciousness which incessantly renews itself in ever-recurring self-perception plays an important part."[17]

From impotence Beckett draws his image of the clown, the being of "nondirectional progress"; the clown does his imitation of the impossible throughout Beckett's narratives. Kenner notes:

The clown exploits impotence . . . when he allows to bubble up into sustained mimetic coherence his own inability to walk a tightrope, missing his footing, misplacing but never dropping his bowler hat (which catches on a button behind his collar and, obeying immutable mechanical laws, is car-

[14] Samuel Beckett, "Dante . . . Bruno. Vico . . . Joyce," *transition* 16–17 (June, 1929): 248.
[15] Perhaps for Beckett there is more doubt in English than there is in French. See chapter 3, note 9.
[16] Ruby Cohn, *Samuel Beckett: The Comic Gamut*, p. 6.
[17] Esslin, introduction to *Samuel Beckett*, p. 7.

ried round out of reach as he turns to clutch at the space where it was),
collapsing in an arc which carries his hands exactly to a graspable stan-
chion, retarding his pace to zero for long reflection, crowding six desperate
acrobatic movements into a split second. He does not *imitate* the acrobat;
it is plain that he could not: he offers us, directly, his personal incapacity,
an intricate art form. The man who imitates is the acrobat himself (all
ropewalkers are alike), adding to what we have seen before in other cir-
cuses some new miniscule difficulty overcome, moving on felt-shod feet a
little further along on the dreary road of the possible.

But Beckett is not interested in the possible; anyone can cope with it. The
artist must try the impossible with the foreknowledge that every effort is
doomed to the usual failure; one can only try. Beckett claims Bram Van
Velde is "the first to admit that to be an artist is to fail, as no other dare fail,
that failure is his world and the shrink from it desertion, art and craft, good
housekeeping, living" (P 125). Within that pattern are the aesthetics of
Beckett's vision—the artist's duty is to the impossible, whether it be in
terms of his quest's goal or in terms of perfecting his art. "The antecedents
of his plays are not in literature . . . [but] in Emmett Kelly's solemn deter-
mination to sweep a circle of light into a dustpan: a haunted man whose
fidelity to an impossible task—quite as if someone he desires to oblige had
exacted it from him—illuminates the dynamics of a tragic sense of duty."[18]
    An understanding of Beckett's work lies in recognizing that the apparent
surface chaos of Beckett's narratives is in reality a controlled movement
in a predetermined direction, enabling the reader to look with the eyes of
Beckett's narrators both at the universe described and at himself in the
position of a protagonist bounded, through his consciousness, by that
universe.

[18] Kenner, *Samuel Beckett*, pp. 33–34, 13.

BIBLIOGRAPHY

Major Works of Kafka, Beckett, and Robbe-Grillet

NOTE: Letters in parentheses refer to abbreviations used in this study. Dates do not mean dates of original publication.

1. Franz Kafka
- (E) *Erzählungen und kleine Prosa*. New York: Schocken Books, 1946.
- (A) *Amerika*. New York: Schocken Books, 1946.
- (PP) *Parables and Paradoxes*. New York: Schocken Books, 1958.
- (C) *The Castle*. New York: Alfred A. Knopf, 1959.
- (T) *The Trial*. New York: Alfred A. Knopf, 1960.
- (PC) *The Penal Colony*. New York: Schocken Books, 1961.

2. Samuel Beckett
- (P) *Proust* [includes *Three Dialogues*]. London: Calder and Boyars, 1963.
- (Mu) *Murphy*. London: Calder and Boyars, 1938 and 1963.
- (W) *Watt*. London: Calder and Boyars, 1963.
- (H) *How It Is*. New York: Grove Press, 1964.
- (Tr) *Three Novels* [the *Trilogy: Molloy, Malone Dies,* and *The Unnamable*]. New York: Grove Press, 1965.
- (STN) *Stories and Texts for Nothing*. New York: Grove Press, 1967.
- (C) *Cascando and Other Short Dramatic Pieces*. New York: Grove Press, 1967.
- (K) *Krapp's Last Tape and Other Dramatic Pieces*. New York: Grove Press, 1960.

3. Alain Robbe-Grillet
- (E) *The Erasers*. New York: Grove Press, 1964.

(V) *The Voyeur*. London: Calder and Boyars, 1959.

(TN) *Two Novels [Jealousy and In the Labyrinth]*. New York: Grove Press, 1965.

(TNN) *Snapshots and Towards a New Novel*. London: Calder and Boyars, 1965.

(MR) *La Maison de Rendez-vous* [in English]. New York: Grove Press, 1966.

SPECIAL ISSUES OF PERIODICALS

"Cinéma et Roman." *Revue des Lettres Modernes*, nos. 36–38 (Summer, 1958), pp. 3–195.

"Franz Kafka." *Modern Fiction Studies* 8, no. 1 (Spring, 1962).

"Franz Kafka du 'Procès' au 'Chateau.'" *Cahiers de la Compagnie Madeleine Renaud–Jean Louis Barrault*. Paris, 1961.

"Franz Kafka Number." *Monatshefte* 4, no. 1 (January, 1963).

"Formes et techniques du roman français depuis 1940." *Cahiers de l'Association Internationale des Études Françaises*, no. 14 (March, 1963), pp. 113–207.

"Midnight Novelists and Others." *Yale French Studies*, no. 24 (Summer, 1959).

"Le 'Nouveau Roman.'" *Esprit* 26, nos. 263–264 (July–August, 1958): 1–118.

"Le 'Nouveau Roman.'" *Revue des Lettres Modernes* 1, nos. 94–99 (1964).

"Le Roman d'aujourd'hui." *Arguments* 1, no. 6 (February, 1958).

"Samuel Beckett." *Modern Drama* 9 (December, 1966).

"Samuel Beckett." *Revue des Lettres Modernes*, no. 100 (1964).

"Samuel Beckett Issue." *Perspective* 11, no. 3 (Autumn, 1959): 119–196.

BOOKS AND ARTICLES

Abel, Lionel. "Joyce the Father, Beckett the Son." *New Leader*, December 14, 1959, 26–27.

Albéres, R. M., and Pierre de Boisdeffre. *Kafka*. Paris: Editions Universitaires, 1961.

Albrecht, Erie A. "Einstellungsgeschichte von Kafkas Landarzt." *Monatshefte* 46, no. 4 (April–May, 1954): 207–212.

Altenhöner, Friedrich. *Der Traum und die Traumstruktur im Werk Franz Kafkas*. Inaugural dissertation, Münster, 1964.

Alter, Jean. "The Treatment of Time in Alain Robbe-Grillet's *La Jalousie*." *College Language Association Journal* 3 (September, 1959): 46–55.

———. *La Vision du monde d'Alain Robbe-Grillet*. Geneva: Droz, 1966.

"*Amerika*." *Living Age*, no. 359 (November, 1940), pp. 292–293.

"*Amerika*." *New Yorker*, October 19, 1940, p. 109.

Anders, Günther. *Franz Kafka*. New York: Hillary House Publishers, 1960.

———. "Kafka: Ritual without Religion." *Commentary* 8 (December, 1949): 560–569.

Anstett, J. J. "La Colonie pénitentaire." *Les Langues Modernes*, no. 5 (1952), pp. 350–351.

Arendt, Hannah. "Franz Kafka: A Revaluation." *Partisan Review* 11 (Fall, 1944): 412–422.

Asher, J. A. "Turning Points in Kafka's Stories." *Modern Language Review* 57, no. 1 (January, 1962): 47–52.

Audrey, Colette. "La Caméra d'Alain Robbe-Grillet." *Revue des Lettres Modernes* 5, nos. 36–38 (Summer, 1958): 259–269.

Baker, James R. "The Castle: A Problem in Structure." *Twentieth Century Literature* 3, no. 2 (July, 1958): 74–77.

Barilli, Renato. "De Sartre à Robbe-Grillet." *Revue des Lettres Modernes*, nos. 94–99 (1964), pp. 105–128.

Barnes, Hazel. "The Ins and Outs of Robbe-Grillet." *Chicago Review* 15, no. 3 (Winter, 1961–1962): 21–43.

Barr, Donald. "One Man's Universe." *New York Times*, June 21, 1959, sec. 7, p. 4.

Barthes, Roland. *Le Degré zéro de l'écriture*. Paris: Éditions du Seuil, 1965.

———. "Introduction à l'analyse structurale des récits." *Communications* 8 (1966): 1–28.

———. "Littérature littérale." *Critique* 12 (September–October, 1955): 820–826.

———. "Littérature objective." *Critique* 10 (July–August, 1954): 581–591.

Bataille, Georges. "Le Silence de Molloy." *Critique*, May 15, 1951, pp. 387–396.

Baumer, Franz. *Franz Kafka*. Berlin: Colloquium Verlag, 1960.

Baumgaertal, Gertrude. "Franz Kafka: Transformation for Clarity." *Revue des Langues Vivantes* 26, no. 4 (1960): 266–283.

Beebe, Maurice, and Naomi Beebe. "Criticism of Franz Kafka: A Selected Checklist." *Modern Fiction Studies* 8, no. 1 (Spring, 1962): 61–74.

Beissner, Friedrich. *Der Erzähler Franz Kafka*. Stuttgart: W. Kohlhammer, 1952.

———. *Kafka der Dichter*. Stuttgart: W. Kohlhammer, 1958.

———. *Der Schacht von Babel: Zu Kafkas Tagebüchern*. Stuttgart: W. Kohlhammer, 1963.

Bense, Max. *Die Theorie Kafkas*. Cologne and Berlin: Kiepenheuer and Witachle, 1952.

Berger, Yves. "Dans le labyrinthe." *Nouvelle Revue Française* 8 (January, 1960): 113.

Bernal, Olga. *Alain Robbe-Grillet: Le Roman de l'absence*. Paris: Gallimard, 1964.

Bezzel, Christoph. *Natur bei Kafka: Studien zur Ästhetik des poetischen Zeichens*. Nuremberg: Carl, 1964.

Billy, André. "Gérard Bauër, défenseur de nouveaux romanciers." *Le Figaro Littéraire*, September 6, 1958, p. 5.

Blanchot, Maurice. "La Lecture de Kafka." *L'Arche*, no. 11 (November, 1945), pp. 107–116.

———. *Le Livre à venir*, pp. 256–260. Paris: Gallimard, 1959.

———. "Notes sur un roman: *Le Voyeur*." *La Nouvelle Nouvelle Revue Française* 3, no. 31 (July, 1955): 105–112.

———. "Où maintenant? Qui maintenant?" *La Nouvelle Nouvelle Revue Française* 2, no. 10 (October, 1953): 678–686.

———. "Où va la littérature?" *La Nouvelle Nouvelle Revue Française* 1, no. 7 (July, 1953): 98–107, and no. 8 (August, 1953): 291–308.

———. *La Part du feu*. Paris: Gallimard, 1949.

———. "Le Point de bois." *La Nouvelle Revue Française*, no. 133 (January, 1964): 90–103.

———. "Le Roman, œuvre de mauvaise foi." *Les Temps Modernes* 2, no. 19 (April, 1947): 1304–17.

———. "La Solitude essentielle." *La Nouvelle Nouvelle Revue Française* 1, no. 1 (January, 1953): 75–90.

Blanzot, Jean. "Les Romans de Samuel Beckett." *Le Figaro Littéraire*, May 13, 1961, p. 4.

Boisdeffre, Pierre de. *Une Histoire vivante de la littérature d'aujourd'hui*, pp. 303–304, 682–684. Paris: Livre Contemporain, 1959.

———. *Où va le roman?* Paris: Del Duca, 1962.

Bollnow, O. F. "Samuel Beckett." *Antares* 4, no 2 (March, 1956), pp. 31–36, no 3 (April, 1956), pp. 36–38, and no. 4 (June, 1956), pp. 42–43.

Bonnefoi, Geneviève. "Textes pour rien?" *Les Lettres Nouvelles*, no. 36 (March, 1956), pp. 424–430.

Bonnet, Gerard. "*Le Procès* ou la métamorphose." *Les Temps Modernes*, no. 201 (1964), pp. 1513–23.

Borchardt, Alfred. *Kafkas zweites Gesicht der Unbekannte: Das grosse Theater von Oklahoma*. Nuremberg: Glock and Lutz, 1960.

Born, Jürgen; Ludwig Dietz; Malcolm Pasley; Paul Raabe; and Klaus Wagenbach. *Kafka-Symposion*. Berlin: K. Wagenbach, 1965.

Bosquet, Alain. "Roman d'avant-garde et anti-roman." *Preuves*, no. 79 (September, 1957), pp. 79–86.

Bourdet, Denise. "Le Cas de Robbe-Grillet." *La Revue de Paris* 67 (January, 1959): 130–135.

Bourin, André. "Techniciens du roman." *Les Nouvelles Littéraires*, January 22, 1955, p. 1.

Bourniquel, Camille. "Le 'Nouveau' Roman." *Esprit* 26, nos. 263–264. (July–August, 1958): 1–2.

Bowles, Patrick. "How Beckett Sees the Universe: *Molloy*." *Listener*, June 19, 1958, pp. 1011–22.

Brée, Germaine. "L'Etrange Monde des articulés." *Configurations Critiques*, no. 8, ed. Melvin J. Friedman, pp. 88–91. Paris: M. J. Minard, 1964.

———. "New Blinds or Old?" *Yale French Studies*, no. 24 (Summer, 1959), pp. 87–90.

———. "The 'New Novel' in France." *The American Society Legion of Honor Magazine* 31, no. 1 (1960): 33–43.

Bremond, Claude. "La Logique des possibles narratifs." *Communications* 8 (1966): 60–76.

Brick, Allen. "The Madman in His Cell: Joyce, Beckett, Nabokov and the Stereotypes." *Massachusetts Review* 1, no. 1 (October, 1959): 40–55.

Brod, Max. *Franz Kafka: A Biography*. New York: Schocken Books, 1947.

———. *Franz Kafka als wegweisende Gestalt*. St. Gallen: Tschudy-Verlag, 1953.

———. *Franz Kafkas Glauben und Lehre*. Munich: Mondial Verlag, 1950.

———. "Notes on Kafka." *Seven Acts*, no. 3 (1956), pp. 1–13.

———. *Verzweiflung und Erlösung im Werk Franz Kafkas*. Frankfurt: S. Fischer, 1959.

Brooke-Rose, Christine. "L'Imagination baroque de Robbe-Grillet." *Revue des Lettres Modernes*, nos. 94–99 (1964), pp. 129–152.

———. "Samuel Beckett and the Anti-novel." *London Magazine* 5, no. 12 (December, 1959): 38–46.

Burns, Wayne. " 'In the Penal Colony': Variations on a Theme by Octave Mirbeau." *Accent* 17, no. 1 (Winter, 1957): 45–51.

Butor, Michel. *Essais sur les modernes*. Paris: Gillimard, 1964.

———. *Répertoire*. Paris: Éditions de Minuit, 1960.

Carrouges, Michel. *Franz Kafka*. Paris: Librairie Éditions Labergerie, 1964.

———. *Kafka contre Kafka*. Paris: Librairie Plon, 1962.

Carta, J. "L'Humanisme commence au langage." *Esprit* 28, no. 285 (June, 1960): 1112–32.

Champigny, Robert, "In Search of the Pure Récit." *American Society Legion of Honor Magazine* 27 (Winter, 1956–1957): 331–334.

Chapsal, Madeleine. "Un Célèbre Inconnu." *L'Express*, February 8, 1957, pp. 26–27.

———. "Le Jeune Roman." *L'Express*, January 12, 1961, p. 53.

Church, Margaret. "Kafka and Proust: A Contrast in Time." *Bucknell Review* 7, no. 2 (December, 1957): 107–112.

———. "Time and Reality in Kafka's *The Trial* and *The Castle*." *Twentieth Century Literature* 2, no. 2 (July, 1956): 62–69.

Clurman, Harold. *Lies Like Truth*, pp. 220–222, 224–225. New York: MacMillan Co., 1958.

Cmarada, Geraldine. "Malone Dies: A Round of Consciousness." *Symposium* 14, no. 3 (Fall, 1960): 199–212.

Coe, Richard N. *Beckett*. Edinburgh and London: Oliver and Boyd, Ltd., 1964.

Cohn, Ruby. *Casebook on Waiting for Godot*. New York: Grove Press, 1967.

———. "The Comedy of Samuel Beckett: 'Something old, something new—.'" *Yale French Studies*, no. 23 (Summer, 1959), pp. 11–17.

———. "Comment c'est: de quoi rire." *French Review* 35, no. 6 (May, 1962): 563–569.

———. "A Note on Beckett, Dante, and Geulineaux." *Comparative Literature* 12, no. 1 (Winter, 1960): 93–94.

———. "Philosophical Fragments in the Works of Samuel Beckett." *Criticism* 6, no. 1 (Winter, 1964): 33–43.

———. "Preliminary Observations." *Perspective* 11, no. 3 (Autumn, 1959): 119–131.

———. *Samuel Beckett: The Comic Gamut*. New Brunswick: Rutgers University Press, 1962.

———. "Samuel Beckett, Self-translator." *PMLA* 76, no. 5 (December, 1961): 613–621.

———. "Still Novel." *Yale French Studies*, no. 24 (Fall, 1959), pp. 48–53.

———. "*Watt* in the Light of *The Castle*." *Comparative Literature* 13, no. 2 (Spring, 1961): 154–166.

Collins, H. Platzer. "Kafka's 'Double-figure' as a Literary Device." *Monatshefte* 55, no. 1 (January, 1963): 7–12.

"The Core of the Onion." *Times Literary Supplement*, December 21, 1962, p. 988.

Cruickshank, John, ed. *The Novelist as Philosopher: Studies in French Fiction, 1935–1960*. London: Oxford University Press, 1962.

Curtis, Anthony. "Mood of the Month—IV." *London Magazine* 5, no. 5 (May, 1958): 60–65.

Daniel-Rops, A. "A French Catholic Looks on Kafka." *Thought* 23, no. 90 (September, 1948): 401–404.

David, Claude. "Kafka aujourd'hui." *Etudes Germaniques* 16, no. 1 (January–March, 1961): 33–44.

Davie, Donald. "Kinds of Comedy: All That Fall." *Spectrum* 2, no. 1 (Winter, 1958): 23–31.

Davin, Dan. "Mr. Beckett's Everymen." *Irish Writing*, no. 34 (Spring, 1956), pp. 36–39.

Delye, Huguette. *Samuel Beckett, ou la philosophie de l'absurde*. Aix-en-Provence: Presse Universitaire, 1960.

Dentan, Michel. *Humour et création littéraire dans l'oeuvre de Kafka*. Lausanne: Droz, 1961.

Döblin, Alfred. "Franz Kafka." *Literarische Welt* 3, no. 9 (1927): 1–4.

Dort, Bernard. "Des 'romans blanc.'" *Cahiers du Sud*, no. 334 (April, 1956), pp. 347–348.

————. "Des romans 'innocent?'" *Esprit* 26, nos. 263–264 (July–August, 158): 100–110.

————. "Epreuves du roman: Le Blanc et le noir." *Cahiers du Sud*, no. 330 (August, 1955), pp. 301–306.

————. "Sur 'l'espace.'" *Esprit* 26, nos. 263–264 (July–August, 1958): 77–82.

————. "Sur les romans de Robbe-Grillet." *Les Temps Modernes* 12, no. 136 (June, 1957): 1989–99.

————. "Le Temps des choses." *Cahiers du Sud*, no. 321 (January, 1954), pp. 300–308.

————. "Tentative de description." *Cahiers du Sud*, no. 334 (April, 1956), pp. 355–364.

Dreyfus, Dina. "De l'ascétisme dans le roman." *Esprit* 26, nos. 263–264 (July–August, 1958): 60–66.

————. "Vrai et fausses énigmes." *Mercure de France* 331, no. 1130 (October, 1957): 268–285.

Driver, Tom F. "Beckett by the Madeleine." *Columbia University Forum* 4, no. 3 (Summer, 1961): 21–25.

Durand, Philippe. "Cinéma et roman." *Revue des Lettres Modernes*, nos. 36–38 (Summer, 1958), pp. 58–65.

Edie, James. Introduction to *What is Phenomenology? and Other Essays*, by Pierre Thévanèz. Chicago: Quadrangle Books, 1962.

Eisner, Pavel. "Franz Kafka and Prague." *Books Abroad* 21 (Summer, 1947): 264–270.

————. *Franz Kafka and Prague*. New York: Arts, Inc., 1950.

Eloesser, Arthur. "Franz Kafka." In *Modern German Literature*, pp. 405–406. New York, 1944.

Emrich, Wilhelm. "Die Bilderwelt Franz Kafkas." *Akzente* 7, no. 2 (April, 1960): 172–191.

————. "Franz Kafka." *Akzente* 10, no. 5 (October, 1953): 516–526.

————. "Franz Kafka." *Deutsche Literatur im 20. Jahrhundert* 34, no. 2 (1964): 190–208.

————. *Kafka.* Frankfurt am Main and Bonn: Athenäum Verlag, 1964.

Erval, François. "Les Années 50." *L'Express,* December 31, 1959, p. 47.

————. "Romans—*Dans le labryinthe* par Alain Robbe-Grillet." *L'Express,* October 1, 1959, pp. 32–33.

Esslin, Martin. "Samuel Beckett." In *The Novelist as Philospher,* ed. John Cruickshank, pp. 128–146. London, Oxford University Press, 1962.

————. "The Theater of the Absurd." *Tulane Drama Review* 4, no. 4 (May, 1960): 3–15.

————, ed. *Samuel Beckett.* Englewood Cliffs, N.J.: Prentice-Hall, 1965.

Estang, Luc. "Lettre à un jeune romancier." *Esprit* 26. nos. 263–264 (July–August, 1958): 111–120.

Federman, Raymond. "Comment c'est." *French Review* 34, no. 6 (May, 1961): 594–595.

————. "Beckett and the Fiction of Mud." In *On Contemporary Literature,* ed. Richard Kostelanetz, pp. 255–261. New York: Avon Books, 1964.

————. *Journey to Chaos: Samuel Beckett's Early Fiction.* Berkeley and Los Angeles: University of California Press, 1965.

Fiedler, Leslie. "Search for Peace in a World Lost." *New York Times,* April 14, 1957, sec. 7, p. 27.

Fletcher, John. "Beckett et Proust." *Annales publiées par la Faculté des Lettres de Toulouse, Caliban I* (January, 1964).

————. "Beckett's Verse: Influences and Parallels." *French Review* 37, no. 3 (January, 1964): 320–331.

————. "Comment c'est." *Lettres Nouvelles,* no. 13 (April, 1961), pp. 167–171.

————. *The Novels of Samuel Beckett.* London: Chatto and Windus, 1964.

————. "Samuel Beckett et Jonathan Swift: Vers une étude comparée." *Annales publiées par la Faculté des Lettres de Toulouse, Litteratures X,* anno. 11, fasc. 1 (1962), pp. 81–117.

Flores, Angel. "Kafka's Prayer." *New York Herald Tribune Books,* August 10, 1947, p. 4.

————, ed. *The Kafka Problem.* New York: New Directions, 1963.

Flores, Angel, and Homer Swander, eds. *Franz Kafka Today.* Madison: University of Wisconsin Press, 1958.

Freiberg, Selma. "Kafka and the Dream." *Partisan Review* 23, no. 1 (Winter, 1956): 47–69.

Frey, Gesine. *Der Raum und die Figuren in Franz Kafkas Roman "Der Prozess."* Marburg: Elwert, 1965.

Friedman, Melvin J. "The Achievement of Samuel Beckett." *Books Abroad* 33, no. 3 (Summer, 1959): 278–280.

――――. "Book Reviews." *Wisconsin Studies in Contemporary Literature* 3, no. 3 (Fall, 1962): 100–106.

――――. "The Novels of Samuel Beckett." *Comparative Literature* 13, no. 1 (Winter, 1960): 47–58.

――――. "Samuel Beckett and the Nouveau Roman." *Wisconsin Studies in Contemporary Literature* 1, no. 2 (Spring–Summer, 1960): 22–36.

Frye, Northrop. "The Nightmare Life in Death." *Hudson Review* 12, no. 3 (Autumn, 1960): 442–449.

Frynta, Emanuel. *Kafka and Prague.* London: Batchworth Press, 1960.

Fürst, Norbert. *Die offenen Geheimtüren Franz Kafkas.* Heidelberg: W. Rothe, 1956.

Genette, Gérard. "Sur Robbe-Grillet." *Tel Quel,* no. 8 (Winter, 1962), pp. 34–44.

Gerard, Martin. "Molloy Becomes Unnamable." *X: A Quarterly Review* 1, no. 4 (October, 1960): 314–319.

Gessner, Niklaus. "Die Unzulänglichkeit der Sprache." Inaugural dissertation. Zürich, 1957.

Gibian, G. "Dichtung und Wahrheit: Three Versions of Reality in Franz Kafka." *German Quarterly* 30, no. 1 (January, 1957): 20–31.

Gilman, Richard. "Total Revolution in the Novel." *Horizon* 4, no. 3 (January, 1962): 96–101.

Girard, René. "Pride and Passion in the Contemporary Novel." *Yale French Studies,* no. 24 (Summer, 1959), pp. 3–11.

Giraud, Raymond. "Unrevolt among the Unwriters in France Today." *Yale French Studies,* no. 24 (Summer, 1959), pp. 11–17.

Glaser, F. B. "The Case of Franz Kafka." *Psychoanalytic Review* 51 (1964): 99–121.

Gold, Herbert. "Beckett: Style and Desire." *Nation,* November 10, 1956, pp. 397–399.

Goldmann, Lucien. "Les Deux Avant-gardes." *Médiations,* no. 4 (Winter, 1961–62), pp. 63–83.

――――. *Pour une sociologie du roman.* Paris: Gallimard, 1964.

――――. "The Theatre of Genet: A Sociological Study." *The Drama Review* 38 (Winter, 1968): 51–61.

Goodman, Paul. *Kafka's Prayer.* New York: Vanguard Press, 1947.

Gordon, Caroline. "Notes on Hemingway and Kafka." *Sewanee Review* 57, no. 2 (1949): 215–226.

Goth, Maja. *Franz Kafka et les lettres françaises.* Paris: Librairie S. Corti, 1956.

Gray, Ronald. "Review of Uyttersprot, *Eine neue Ordnung.* . . ." *German Life and Letters* 12 (1958–1959): 234–235.

————. "The Structure of Kafka's Works: A Reply to Professor Uyttersprot." *German Life and Letters* 13 (1959): 1–17.

————, ed. *Kafka: A Collection of Critical Essays.* Englewood Cliffs, N.J.: Prentice-Hall, 1962.

Greenberg, Martin. *The Terror of Art: Kafka and Modern Literature.* New York: Basic Books, 1968.

Gregory, Horace. "Beckett's Dying Gladiators." *Commonweal*, October 26, 1956, pp. 88–92. Reprinted in *The Dying Gladiators and Other Essays*, pp. 165–176. New York: Grove Press, 1961.

————. "Prose and Poetry in Samuel Beckett." *Commonweal*, October 30, 1959, pp. 162–163.

Grenier, Cynthia. "Alain Resnais of France—Explorations in the Unconscious." *Saturday Review*, December 23, 1961, pp. 37–38.

Gresset, Michel. "Le 'parce que' chez Faulkner et le 'donc' chez Beckett." *Les Lettres Nouvelles* 9, no. 19 (November, 1961): 124–138.

Guers, Yvonne. "La Technique romanesque chez Alain Robbe-Grillet." *The French Review* 35 (May, 1962): 570–577.

Guggenheim, Peggy. *Out of This Century.* New York: The Dial Press, 1946.

Gundvaldsen, Kaare. "The Plot of Kafka's Trial." *Monatshefte* 57, no. 1 (January, 1964): 1–14.

Haas, Vilem. "Prague in 1912." *Virginia Quarterly Review* 24 (Summer, 1948): 409–417.

Hahn, Bruno. "Plan du labyrinthe." *Les Temps Modernes* 16 (July, 1960): 164.

Hall, Calvin S., and Richard E. Lind. *Dreams, Life, and Literature: A Study of Franz Kafka.* Chapel Hill: University of North Carolina Press, 1970.

Hamilton, Carol. "Portrait in Old Age: The Image of Man in Beckett's Trilogy." *Western Humanities Review* 16, no. 2 (Spring, 1962): 157–165.

Hamilton, Kenneth. "Boon or Thorn? Cary and Beckett on Human Life." *Dalhousie Review* 38, no. 4 (Winter, 1959): 433–442.

Hartley, Anthony. "Samuel Beckett." *Spectator*, October 23, 1953, pp. 458–459.

Harvey, Lawrence E. "Art and the Existential in *En Attendant Godot*." *PMLA* 75, no. 1 (March, 1960): 137–146.

Hasselblatt, Dieter. *Zauber und Logik: Eine Kafka-Studie.* Cologne: Verlag Wissenschaft und Politik, 1964.

Hayes, Richard. "Nothing." *Commonweal*, May 25, 1956, p. 203.

Heller, Erich. "World of Franz Kafka." In *The Disinherited Mind*, pp. 175–202. Cambridge, Eng.: Bowes and Bowes, 1952.

Hermsdorf, Klaus. *Kafka: Weltbild und Roman*. Berlin: Rütten and Loening, 1961.

Hesla, David H. "The Shape of Chaos: A Reading of Beckett's *Watt*." *Critique* 6, no. 1 (Spring, 1963): 85–105.

Heselhaus, Clemens. "Kafkas Erzählformen." *Deutsche Vierteljahrschrift* 26 (1952): 376–383.

Hesse, Eva. "Die Welt des Samuel Beckett." *Akzente* 8, no. 3 (June, 1961): 270–277.

Hillmann, Heinz. *Franz Kafka: Dichtungstheorie und Dichtungsgestalt*. Bonn: H. Bouvier, 1964.

Hoefer, Jacqueline. "*Watt*." *Perspective* 11, no. 3 (Autumn, 1959): 166–182.

Hoffman, Frederick J. "Kafka's *The Trial*: The Assailant as Landscape." *Bucknell Review* 9 (May, 1966): 89–105.

————. *Samuel Beckett: The Language of Self*. Carbondale: Southern Illinois University Press, 1952.

Horst, Karl August. *Das Spektrum des modernen Romans*. Munich: C. H. Beck, 1960.

Howlett, Jacques. "Notes sur l'objet dans le roman." *Esprit* 26, nos. 263–264 (July–August, 1958): 87–90.

————. "Thèmes et tendances d'avant garde dans le roman aujourd'hui." *Les Lettres Nouvelles*, February 20, 1963, pp. 139–148.

————. "Les Tropismes de Nathalie Sarraute." *Esprit* 26, nos. 263–264 (July–August, 1958): 72.

Hubert, Renée R. "The Couple and the Performance in Samuel Beckett's Plays." *L'Esprit Créateur* 2, no. 4 (Winter, 1962): 175–180.

Hubler, William. *Four Prophets of Our Destiny: Kierkegaard, Dostoevsky, Nietzsche, Kafka*. New York: Macmillan Co., 1952.

Jaccotet, Philippe. "Remarques sur une nouvelle forme romanesque." *La Gazette de Lausanne*, May 25, 1957, p. 17.

Jacobsen, Josephine, and William R. Mueller. *The Testament of Samuel Beckett*. New York: Hill and Wang, 1964.

Jaffe, Adrian. *The Process of Kafka's Trial*. Ann Arbor: University of Michigan Press, 1967.

Jahn, Wolfgang. "Kafka und die Anfänge des Kinos." *Jahrbuch der Deutschen Schiller-Gesellschaft* 6, no. 3 (1962): 353–368.

Jakubec, Joël. *Kafka contre l'absurde*. Lausanne: Droz, 1962.

Janouch, Gustav. *Gespräche mit Kafka*. Berlin: S. Fischer, 1951.

Janvier, Ludovic. *Une Parole exigeante*. Paris: Éditions de Minuit, 1964.

Järv, Harry. *Die Kafka-Literatur*. Malmö: Cavefors, 1961.

"Kafka dans les estampes de Chancel." *Le Figaro Littéraire*, April 27, 1957, p. 4.

Kahler, Erich. "The Transformation of Modern Fiction." *Comparative Literature* 7, no. 2 (1955): 121–128.

Kanters, Robert. "Situation présente du 'nouveau roman.'" *Le Figaro Littéraire*, March 26, 1959, p. 3.

Karl, Frederick R. "Waiting for Beckett." *Irish Writing*, no. 34 (Spring, 1956), pp. 23–27.

Kauf, Robert. "Once Again: Kafka's 'A Report to an Academy.'" *Modern Language Quarterly* 15, no. 4 (December, 1954): 359–365.

Kelly, John. "Franz Kafka's *Trial* and the Theology of Crisis." *Southern Review* 5 (Spring, 1940): 748–766.

Kenner, Hugh. "The Absurdity of Fiction." *Griffin* 8, no. 10 (November, 1959): 13–16.

———. "The Beckett Landscape." *Spectrum* 2, no. 1 (Winter, 1958): 8–24.

———. "The Cartesian Centaur." *Perspective* 11, no. 3 (Autumn, 1959): 132–141.

———. *Flaubert, Joyce and Beckett: The Stoic Comedians.* Boston: Beacon Press, 1963.

———. *Samuel Beckett: A Critical Study.* New York: J. Calder, 1961.

———. "Samuel Beckett: The Rational Domain." *Forum* 3, no. 4 (Summer, 1960): 39–47.

———. "Samuel Beckett vs. Fiction." *National Review*, October 11, 1958, pp. 248–249.

———. "Voices in the Night." *Spectrum* 5, no. 1 (Spring, 1961): 3–20.

Kermode, Frank. "Beckett, Snow and Pure Poverty." *Encounter* 15, no. 1 (July, 1960): 73–77.

Kern, Edith. "Beckett's Knight of Infinite Resignation." *Yale French Studies*, no. 29 (Spring–Summer, 1962), pp. 49–56.

———. "Drama Stripped for Inaction: Beckett's *Godot.*" *Yale French Studies*, no. 14 (1954–1955), pp. 41–47.

———. "Moran-Molloy: The Hero as Author." *Perspective* 11, no. 3 (Autumn, 1959): 183–193.

Kostelanetz, Richard, ed. *On Contemporary Literature*, pp. 244–285, 511–519. New York: Avon Books, 1964.

Kraus, Wolfgang. "Der heutige Roman: Seine Autoren, seine Kritiker, seine Leser." *St. Galler Tageblatt*, January 6, 1961, p. 13.

Kunitz, Stanley. "Franz Kafka." In *Authors Today and Yesterday*, p. 366. New York: H. W. Wilson Co. 1933.

Kwant, Remy C. *Phenomenology of Language.* Pittsburgh, Pa.: Duquesne University Press, 1965.

Lalou, René. "*Malone meurt.*" *Les Nouvelles Littéraires*, November 8, 1951, p. 6.

Landsberg, Paul L. "Kafka and *The Metamorphosis.*" *Quarterly Review of Literature* 2 (Spring, 1945): 228–236.

Lange, Victor. "Franz Kafka." In *Modern German Literature, 1870–1940.* Ithaca, N. Y.: Cornell University Press, 1945.

Lawson, Richard H. "Der Landarzt." *Monatshefte* 49, no. 4 (October, 1957): 265–271.

Lee, Warren. "The Bitter Pill of Samuel Beckett." *Chicago Review* 10, no. 4 (Winter, 1957): 77–87.

Lefebve, N.-J. "*La Jalousie.*" *La Nouvelle Nouvelle Revue Française* 5, no. 55 (July, 1957): 146–149.

Leopold Keith. "Breaks in Perspective in Franz Kafka's *Der Prozess.*" *German Quarterly* 36, no. 1 (January, 1963): 31–38.

———. "Kafka's Stories in the First Person." *AUMLA, Journal of the Australasian Universities Language and Literature Association,* no. 11 (November, 1959), pp. 56–62.

Lerner, Max. "Franz Kafka and the Human Voyage." *Saturday Review of Literature,* June 7, 1941, p. 3.

LeSage, Laurent. *The French New Novel.* University Park, Pa.: Pennsylvania State University Press, 1962.

Lesser, Simon O. "The Source of Guilt and the Sense of Guilt: Kafka's *The Trial.*" *Modern Fiction Studies* 8, no. 1 (Spring, 1962): 44–60.

"Life in the Mud." *Times Literary Supplement,* April 7, 1961, p. 213.

Littlejohn, David. "The Anti-Realists." *Daedalus* 92, no. 2 (Spring, 1963): 250–264.

Lop, Edouard, and André Sauvage. "Essai sur le nouveau roman." *La Nouvelle Critique,* no. 124 (March, 1961), pp. 117–134, no. 125 (April, 1961), pp. 68–87, and no. 127 (June, 1961), pp. 83–107.

Loy, Robert J. " 'Things' in Recent French Literature." *PMLA* 71 (March, 1956): 27–41.

Lukács, Georg. *Franz Kafka oder Thomas Mann.* Hamburg: Hermann Lutcherhand Verlag, 1958.

———. *La Signification presente du réalisme critique.* Paris: Gallimard, 1960.

Madden, William A. "Myth of Mediation." *Thought* 26, no. 101 (Summer, 1951): 246–266.

Magny, Claude-Edmonde. "The Objective Description of Absurdity." *Quarterly Review of Literature* 2 (Spring, 1945): 211–227.

Magny, Olivier de. "Ecriture de l'impossible." *Les Lettres Nouvelles,* no. 11 (February, 1963), pp. 125–138.

———. "Panorama d'une nouvelle littérature romanesque." *Esprit* 26, nos. 263–264 (July–August, 1958): 3–17.

————. "Samuel Beckett ou Job abandonné." *Monde Nouveau-Paru* 11, no. 97 (February, 1956): 92–99.

Mailer, Norman. "A Public Notice on *Waiting for Godot*." In *Advertisements for Myself*, pp. 320–325. New York: G. P. Putnam's Sons, 1959.

Marissel, André. *Beckett*. Paris: Editions Universitaires, 1963.

————. "L'Univers de Samuel Beckett: Un Noeud de complexe." *Esprit* no. 320 (September, 1963), pp. 240–255.

Marsche, Maurice. "La Metaphore dans l'oeuvre de Kafka." *Etudes Germaniques* 19, no. 1 (January–March, 1964): 23–41.

Martini, Fritz. *Das Wagnis der Sprache*. Stuttgart: E. Klott, 1954.

Mauriac, Claude. "Alain Robbe-Grillet et le roman futur." *Preuves*, no. 68 (October, 1956), pp. 92–96.

————. "The 'New Novel' in France." *New York Times Book Review*, June 19, 1960, p. 5.

————. "Samuel Beckett." *Le Figaro Littéraire*, August 11, 1956, p. 2.

————. "Samuel Beckett." In *The New Literature*, trans. Samuel I. Stone, pp. 75–90. New York: George Braziller, 1959. Original French title, *L'Allittérature contemporaine*. Paris: A. Michel, 1959.

————. "Samuel Beckett." *Preuves*, no. 61 (March, 1956), pp. 71–76.

Mauroc, Daniel. "*Watt*." *Table Ronde*, no. 70 (October, 1953), pp. 155–156.

Mayoux, Jean-Jaques. "Samuel Beckett: *Comment c'est*." *Mercure de France*, no. 1174 (June, 1961), pp. 293–297.

————. "Samuel Beckett et l'univers parodique." In *Vivants Piliers*, pp. 271–291. Paris: Julliard, 1960.

————. "Le Théatre de Samuel Beckett." *Etudes Anglaises* 10, no. 4 (October–November, 1957): 350–366.

Mercier, Vivian. "Beckett and the Search for Self." *New Republic*, September 19, 1955, pp. 20–21.

————. "Mathematical Limit." *Nation*, February 14, 1959, pp. 144–145.

————. "Savage Humor." *Commonweal*, May 17, 1957, p. 188.

————. "Samuel Beckett and the Sheela-Na-Gig." *Kenyon Review* 23, no. 2 (Spring, 1961): 299–328.

Merleau-Ponty, Maurice. *Phénoménologie de la perception*. Paris: Gallimard, 1945.

————. *The Primacy of Perception*, ed. James M. Edie, trans. Arleen B. Dallery. Chicago: Northwestern University Press, 1964.

————. *Sens et non-sens*. Paris: Nagel, 1948.

————. *Signes*. Paris: Gallimard, 1960.

Micha, René. "Une Nouvelle Littérature allégorique." *La Nouvelle Nouvelle Revue Française* 3, no. 16 (April, 1954): 696–706.

Middleton, Christopher. "Randnotizen zu Romanen von Samuel Beckett." *Akzente* 4, no. 5 (October, 1957): 407–412.

Miesch, Jean. *Robbe-Grillet.* Paris: Editions Universitaires, 1965.

Miller, Karl. "Beckett's Voices." *Encounter* 13, no. 3 (September, 1959): 59–61.

Mintz, Samuel I. "Beckett's *Murphy*: A 'Cartesian' Novel." *Perspective* 11, no. 3 (Autumn, 1959): 156–165.

Montgomery, Niall. "No Symbols Where None Intended." In *New World Writing*, no. 5 (1954), pp. 324–337.

Moore, John R. "Farewell to Something." *Tulane Drama Review* 5, no. 1 (September, 1960): 49–60.

Morrissette, Bruce. *Alain Robbe-Grillet.* New York and London: Columbia University Press, 1965.

———. "Clefs pour *Les Gommes.*" Afterword to *Alain Robbe-Grillet, Les Gommes,* pp. 269–314. Paris: Editions 10/18, 1962.

———. "En relisant Robbe-Grillet." *Critique* 15, no. 146 (July, 1959): 570–608.

———. "The New Novel in France." *Chicago Review* 15, no. 3 (Winter-Spring, 1961–1962): 1–19.

———. "New Structures in the Novel: *Jealousy* by Robbe-Grillet." *Evergreen Review* 3, no. 10 (October, 1959): 164–190.

———. "Oedipus and Existentialism: *Les Gommes* of Robbe-Grillet." *Wisconsin Studies in Contemporary Literature* 1, no. 3 (Fall, 1960): 43–73.

———. *Les Romans de Robbe-Grillet.* Paris: Éditions de Minuit, 1963.

———. "De Stendhal à Robbe-Grillet: Modalités du 'point de vue.'" *Cahiers de l'Association Internationale des Études Françaises,* no. 14 (March, 1962), pp. 143–163.

———. "Surfaces et structures dans les romans de Robbe-Grillet." *The French Review* 31 (April, 1958): 364–369.

Morse, Mitchell. "Beckett and the Contemplative Life." *Hudson Review* 15, no. 4 (Winter, 1962–1963): 512–524.

Muir, Edwin. *Transition: Essays on Literature and Society.* Reprint edition. Folcroft, Pa.: Folcroft Press, 1959.

Muller, André. "Techniques de l'avant-garde." *Théatre Populaire,* no. 18 (May, 1956), pp. 21–29.

Murray, David. "A Review of *Murphy* and *Malone Dies.*" *Dalhousie Review* 37, no. 1 (Spring, 1957): 104, 106.

Nadeau, Maurice. "Beckett: La Tragédie transposée en farce." *L'Avant-scène,* no. 156 (1957), pp. 4–6.

———. "Le Jeune Roman." *Les Lettres Nouvelles,* March 25, 1959, pp. 1–2.

———. *Littérature présente,* pp. 274–279. Paris: Corrêa, 1952.

———. "Nouvelles Formules pour le roman." *Critique* 13, nos. 123–124 (August–September, 1957): 707–722.

――――. *Le Roman français depuis la guerre*, pp. 155–159. Paris: Gallimard, 1963.

――――. "Samuel Beckett, l'humour et le néant." *Mercure de France* 312, no. 1056 (August, 1951): 693–697.

――――. "Samuel Beckett ou le droit au silence." *Les Temps Modernes* 7, no. 75 (January, 1952): 1273–82.

Neider, Charles. *Kafka: His Mind and Art*. London: Routledge and K. Paul, 1949.

――――. "Review of 'Dearest Father.'" *Saturday Review of Literature*, September 18, 1954, pp. 27–28.

Nemeth, André. *Kafka ou le Mystère juif*. Paris: Vigneau, 1947.

Neumeyer, Peter F., ed. *Twentieth Century Interpretations of "The Castle."* Englewood Cliffs, N. J.: Prentice-Hall, 1969.

Neuse, Werner. "Franz Kafka." *Books Abroad* 9 (Summer, 1935): 266–268.

Noon, W. T. "Modern Literature and the Sense of Time." *Thought* 33, no. 131 (Winter, 1958–1959): 571–604.

Norès, Dominique. "La Condition humaine selon Beckett." *Théatre d'Aujourd'hui*, no. 3 (1957), pp. 9–12.

Olles, Helmut. "Samuel Beckett." *Welt und Wort* 15, no. 6 (June, 1960): 173–174.

"Paradise of Indignity." *Times Literary Supplement*, March 28, 1958, p. 168.

Paris, Jean. "The New French Generation." *The American Society Legion of Honor Magazine* 31, no. 1 (1960): 45–51.

Paulding, Gouverneur. "Samuel Beckett's New Tale." *New York Herald Tribune Book Review*, September 16, 1956, sec. 5, p. 2.

Paulsen, Wolfgang. "Franz Kafka." *Monatshefte für Deutschen Unterricht* 39 (December, 1937): 373–388.

Peyre, Henri. "Trends in the Contemporary French Novel." In *New French Writing*, ed. Georges Borchardt, pp. 73–88. New York: Criterion Books, 1961.

Piatier, Jacqueline. "*Comment c'est.*" *Le Monde*, February 11, 1961, p. 9.

Picon, Gaëten. *Panorama de la nouvelle littérature française*. Paris: Gallimard, 1960.

――――. "Le Probleme du *Voyeur*." *Mercure de France* 325, no. 1106 (October, 1955): 303–309.

――――. "Du roman expérimental." *Mercure de France* 330, no. 1126 (June, 1957): 300–304.

Pingaud, Bernard. "Dans le labyrinthe." *Les Lettres Nouvelles* 7, no. 24 (October 7, 1959): 18–20.

――――. "L'Ecole du refus." *Esprit* 26, nos. 263–264 (July–August, 1958): 55–59.

————. "Je, Vous, Il." *Esprit* 26, nos. 263–264 (July–August, 1958): 91–99.

————. "Lecture de *La Jalousie*." *Les Lettres Nouvelles* 7, no. 50 (June, 1957), 901–906.

————. "Molloy." *Esprit* 19, no. 9 (September, 1951): 423–425.

————. "*Molloy*, douze ans après." *Les Temps Modernes* 18, no. 200 (January, 1963): 1283–1300.

————. "L'Oeuvre et l'analyse." *Les Temps Modernes* 21, no. 233 (October, 1965): 638–646.

————. "The School of Refusal." *Yale French Studies*, no. 24 (Summer, 1959), pp. 18–22.

————. "La Technique de la description dans le jeune roman d'aujourd'hui." *Cahiers de l'Association Internationale des Etudes Françaises*, no. 14 (June, 1962), pp. 165–177.

————. "Y a-t-il quelqu'un?" *Esprit* 26, nos. 263–264 (July–August, 1958): 83–85.

————, ed. *Ecrivains d'aujourd'hui*. Paris: B. Grasset, 1960.

Politzer, Heinz. "The Egghead Waits for Godot." *Christian Scholar* 42, (March, 1959): 46–50.

————. "Franz Kafka, Metaphysical Anarchist." *Renascence* 6, no. 2 (Spring, 1954): 106–111.

————. *Franz Kafka: Parable and Paradox*. Ithaca, N.Y.: Cornell University Press, 1961.

————. "From Mendelssohn to Kafka: The Jewish Man of Letters in Germany." *Commentary* 3 (April, 1947): 344–351.

————. "Prague and Rilke, Kafka, and Werfel." *Modern Language Quarterly* 16, no. 1 (March, 1955): 49–62.

————. "Probleme der Kafka Forschung." *Monatshefte* 42, no. 6 (October, 1950): 273–280.

————. "Recent Trends in Kafka Criticism." *Books Abroad* 27, no. 2 (Spring, 1953): 143–144.

Pongs, Hermann. *Franz Kafka: Dichter des Labyrinths*. Heidelberg: Wolfgang Rothe Verlag, 1960.

Pouillon, Jean. "Molloy." *Les Temps Modernes* 7, no. 69 (July, 1951): 184–186.

Poulet, Robert. "Alain Robbe-Grillet et le roman futur." *Rivarol*, no. 8 (1956), pp. 17–18.

————. *La Lanterne magique*, pp. 236–242. Paris: Debresse, 1956.

Pritchett, V. S. "Irish Oblomov." *New Statesman*, April 2, 1960. p. 489.

Radke, Judith. "The Theatre of Samuel Beckett: 'Une Durée à animer.'" *Yale French Studies*, no. 29 (Spring–Summer, 1962), pp. 57–64.

Rahv, Philip. "*Amerika*." *Nation*, October 26, 1940. p. 396.

————. *Image and Idea*, pp. 111–127. Norfolk, Conn.: J. Laughlin, 1949.

————. Introduction to *Selected Stories of Franz Kafka*. New York: The Modern Library, 1952.

Rainoird, Manuel. "*Les Gommes* d'Alain Robbe-Grillet." *La Nouvelle Revue Française* 1, no. 6 (June, 1953): 1108–09.

Reed, Eugene. "Moral Polarity in Kafka's *Prozess* and *Schloss*." *Monatshefte* 46, no. 7 (November ,1954): 317–324.

Reiss, H. S. *Franz Kafka: Eine Betrachtung seines Werkes*. Heidelberg: L. Schneider, 1952.

Rexroth, Kenneth. "Point Is Irrelevance." *Nation*, April 14, 1956, pp. 325–328.

Rhein, Phillip H. *The Urge to Live: A Comparative Study of Kafka's "Der Prozess" and Camus' "L'Etranger."* Chapel Hill: University of North Carolina Press, 1964.

Ricarou, Jean. "Aspects de la description créatrice." *Médiations* 1, no. 3 (Autumn, 1961): 13–32.

————. "Description et infraconscience chez Alain Robbe-Grillet." *La Nouvelle Revue Française* 8 (November, 1960): 890–900.

Rickets, Milton. "Existentialist Themes in Beckett's *Unnamable*." *Criticism* 4, no. 2 (Spring, 1962): 134–147.

Ricoeur, Paul. "Sur la phenomenologie." *Esprit* 21, no. 209 (1953): 821–839.

Robert, Marthe. "Amérique." *L'Arche* 25 (March, 1947): 152–156.

————. *L'Ancien et le nouveau: De Don Quichotte à Franz Kafka*. Paris: B. Grasset, 1964.

————. "Une Figure de Whitechapel, notes inédites de Dora Dymant sur Kafka." *Evidences*, no. 28 (November, 1952), pp. 38–42.

————. "L'Humour de Franz Kafka." *Revue de la Pensée Juive* 4 (June, 1951): 61–72.

————. *Introduction à la lecture de Kafka*. Paris: Editions du Sagittaire, 1946.

————. "Introduction pour Franz Kafka: *Lettre au Père*." *La Nouvelle Nouvelle Revue Français* 1, no. 4 (April, 1953): 577–578.

————. "Introduction pour méditation de Kafka." *Les Temps Modernes* 4, no. 36 (October, 1948): 684–695.

————. "Kafka en France." *Mercure de France*, no. 1174 (1964), pp. 241–255.

————. *Kafka et la loi de son oeuvre*. Paris: Gallimard, 1960.

————. "Kafka in Frankreich." Paper presented at the Kafka Colloquium, University of Berlin, February 17, 1966. German translation with additions in *Akzente* 13, no. 4 (August, 1966): 310–320.

————. "La Lecture de Kafka (avec des extraits de lettres). *Les Temps Modernes* 8, no. 83 (October–November, 1952): 646–660

————. *Presentation de Kafka*. Paris: B. Grasset, 1953.

————. *Presentation du journal de Kafka*. Paris: B. Grasset, 1954.

————. "Les *Tagebücher* de Franz Kafka." *Les Temps Modernes* 6, no. 74 (December, 1951): 1145–47.

Rochefort, Robert. *Kafka, ou l'irréductible espoir*. Paris. Julliard, 1947.

Roudiez, Leon A. "The Embattled Myths." In *Hereditas*, ed. Frederic Will. Austin, Texas: University of Texas Press, 1964.

Rougemont, Denis de. *Les Personnes du drame*. New York: Gallimard, 1945.

Rousseaux, André. "L'Homme désintégré de Samuel Beckett." In *Littérature du vingtième siècle*, pp. 105–113. Cinquième Série. Paris: A. Michel, 1955.

Royer, Jean Michel. "Le Voyeur accélére." *Les Lettres Nouvelles* 3, no. 29 (July–August, 1955): 144–148.

Rubinstein, William C. "Franz Kafka's 'Hunger Artist.'" *Monatshefte* 44, no. 1 (January, 1952): 13–19.

————. "Franz Kafka's 'Report to an Academy.'" *Modern Language Quarterly* 13 (December, 1952): 322–376.

Ruhleder, Karl H. "Franz Kafka's 'Das Urteil': An Interpretation." *Monatshefte* 55, no. 1 (January, 1963): 13–22.

Salinger, Herman. "Franz Kafka Parallels." *Monatshefte für Deutschen Unterrichte* 39 (October, 1947): 415–416.

Saporta, Marc. "Pro-romans et pré-textes." *Preuves*, no. 128 (October, 1961), pp. 32–34.

Sarraute, Claude. "La Subjectivité est la caractéristique du roman contemporain." *Le Monde*, May 11, 1961, p. 7.

Sarraute, Nathalie. *Tropisms and The Age of Suspicion*, trans. Maria Jolas. London: Calder and Boyars, 1963.

Savacool, John. "Paris Puzzler." *New York Times*, November 2, 1951, sec. 2, p. 3.

Schneider, Alan. "Waiting for Beckett." *Chelsea Review* 1, no. 2 (Autumn, 1958): 3–20.

Scholes, Robert. "George is My Name." *New York Times Book Review*, August 7, 1966, p. 1.

Schulz-Behrend, G. "Kafka's 'Ein Bericht für eine Akademie.'" *Monatshefte* 55, no. 1 (January, 1963): 1–6.

Scott, Nathan A., Jr. *Rehearsals of Discomposure*. New York: King's Crown Press, 1952.

————. *Samuel Beckett*. London: Bowes and Bowes, 1965.

Seaver, Richard. "Samuel Beckett: An Introduction." *Merlin* 1, no. 2 (Autumn, 1952): 73–79.

Seidlin, Oskar. "Franz Kafka-Lackland." *Books Abroad* 21 (Summer, 1948): 244–246.

Selz, Jean. "L'Homme finissant de Samuel Beckett." *Les Lettres Nouvelles* 5, no. 51 (July–August, 1957): 120–123.

Shenker, Israel. "Moody Man of Letters." *New York Times,* May 6, 1956, sec. 2, p. 1.

Shroder, Maurice Z. "The Nouveau Roman and the Tradition of the Novel." *Romanic Review* 17, no. 3 (October, 1966): 200–214.

Simon, Alfred. "Le Degré zéro du tragique." *Esprit* 31, no. 323 (December, 1963): 905–909.

———. "Samuel Beckett de les rendez-vous manqués." *Esprit* 21, no. 4 (April, 1953): 595–598.

Simon, Pierre-Henri. "Sur le sense de l'antiroman." *Preuves,* no. 123 (May, 1961), pp. 52–55.

Slochower, Harry. *No Voice Is Wholly Lost.* . . . , pp. 103–125. New York: Creative Age Press, 1945.

Sokel, Walter H. *Franz Kafka: Tragik und Ironie: Zur Struktur seiner Kunst.* Munich: A. Langen, G. Müller. 1964.

———. "Kafka's Metamorphosis: Rebellion and Punishment." *Monatshefte* 48, no. 4 (April–May, 1956): 203–214.

Sollers, Philippe. "Sept Propositions sur Alain Robbe-Grillet." *Tel Quel,* no. 3 (Summer, 1960), pp. 49–53.

Sontag, Susan. *Against Interpretation.* New York: Farrar, Strauss, and Giroux, 1966.

Spahr, Blake Lee. "Kafka's 'Auf der Galerie': A Stylistic Analysis." *German Quarterly* 33, no. 3 (May, 1960): 211–215.

Spann, Meno. "Die Beiden Zettel Kafkas." *Monatshefte* 47, no. 7 (November, 1955): 321–328.

Spector, Robert Donald. "Kafka's 'The Stoker' as Short Story." *Modern Fiction Studies* 2, no. 2 (May, 1956): 80–81.

Spender, Stephen. "Lifelong Suffocation." *New York Times Book Review,* October 12, 1958, p. 5.

———. "Upward Kafka and Vanderpost." In *The Destructive Element,* pp. 243–245. London: Jonathan Cape, Ltd., 1935.

Spiegelberg, Herbert. *The Phenomenological Movement: A Historical Introduction.* The Hague: Nijhoff, 1965.

———. "Phenomenology." *Encyclopedia Brittanica* (New York, 1965), 17: 810–812.

Spilka, Mark. *Dickens and Kafka.* Bloomington: Indiana University Press, 1963.

Stallman, Robert W. "Analysis of 'The Hunger Artist.'" In *Franz Kafka Today,* ed. Angel Flores and Homer Swander, pp. 61–70. Madison: University of Wisconsin Press, 1958.

———. "Kafka's Cage." *Accent* 8, no. 7 (Winter, 1948): 117–124.

Steinberg, Erwin R. "The Judgment in Kafka's *The Judgment.*" *Modern Fiction Studies* 8, no. 1 (Spring, 1962): 23–30.

Stoltzfus, Ben. *Alain Robbe-Grillet and the New French Novel.* Carbondale: Southern Illinois University Press, 1964.

————."Camus et Robbe-Grillet: La Connivence tragique de *L'Etranger* et du *Voyeur.*" *Revue des Lettres Modernes*, nos. 94–100 (1964), pp. 153–166.

————. "*Le Voyeur* by Alain Robbe-Grillet." *PMLA* 77, no. 4 (September, 1962): 499–507.

Strauss, Walter A. "Dante's Belacqua and Beckett's Tramps." *Comparative Literature* 11, no. 3 (Summer, 1959): 250–261.

Tauber, Herbert. *Franz Kafka: Eine Deutung seiner Werke.* Zürich and New York: Verlag Oprecht, 1941.

"Tentation au village." *Les Lettres Nouvelles* 1, no. 4 (June, 1953): 493–494.

Thévenàz, Pierre. *What is Phenomenology?* ed. James Edie. Chicago: Quadrangle Books, 1962.

Thibaudeau, Jean. "*Comment c'est.*" *Les Temps Modernes* 16, no. 180 (April, 1961): 1384–92.

Thiébaut, Marcel. "Le 'Nouveau Roman.'" *Le Revue de Paris* 65, no. 10 (October, 1958): 140–148.

Tindall, William York. "Beckett's Bums." *Critique* 2, no. 1 (Spring–Summer, 1958): 3–15.

————. *Samuel Beckett.* New York: Columbia University Press, 1964.

Torrance, Robert M. "Modes of Being and Time in the World of *Godot.*" *Modern Language Quarterly* 28, no. 1 (March, 1967): 77–95.

Trahan, Elizabeth. "'A Common Confusion': A Basic Approach to Franz Kafka's World." *German Quarterly* 36, no. 3 (May, 1963): 269–278.

"Trente Ans après, l'Allemagne découvre à Paris l'écrivain qui prophétisa le nazisme, Kafka." *Paris-Match*, August 7, 1954, p. 57.

Tyler, Parker. "Kafka and the Surrealists." *Accent* 5 (Autumn, 1945): 23–27.

————. "Kafka's and Chaplin's America." *Sewanee Review* 48, no. 2 (Spring, 1950): 299–311.

Unterdecker, John. "Samuel Beckett's No-Man's Land." *New Leader*, May 18, 1959, pp. 24–25.

Uyttersprot, Hermann. *Eine neue Ordnung der Werke Kafkas? Zur Struktur von "Der Prozess" und "Amerika."* Antwerp: De Vries-Brouwers, 1957.

————. "*The Trial:* Its Structure." In *Franz Kafka Today*, ed. Angel Flores, pp. 127–144. Madison: University of Wisconsin Press, 1958.

————. *Zur Struktur von Kafkas "Der Prozess". Versuch einer Neuordnung. Langues Vivantes*, no. 42. Brussels: Didier, 1953.

————. "Zur Struktur von Kafkas Romanen." *Revue des Langues Vivantes* 20 (1954): 5.

Vigée, Claude. "Les Artistes de la faim." *Comparative Literature* 9, no. 2 (Spring, 1957): 97–117.

Vivas, Eliseo. "Kafka's Distorted Mask." In *Creation and Discovery*, pp. 29–46. New York: Noonday Press, 1955.

————. "Kafka's Distorted Mind." *Kenyon Review* 10 (Winter, 1948): 51–68.

Wagenbach, Klaus. *Franz Kafka: Eine Biographie seiner Jugend. 1883–1912.* Berlin: Francke, 1958.

Walker, Roy. "Love, Chess and Death: Samuel Beckett's Double Bill." *Twentieth Century* 164 (December, 1958): 533–544.

Walser, Martin. *Beschreibung einer Form.* Munich: C. Hanser, 1961.

Warhaft, Sidney. "Threne and Theme in *Watt*." *Wisconsin Studies in Contemporary Literature* 4, no. 3 (Autumn, 1963): 261–278.

Warshaw, Robert. "Kafka's Failure." *Partisan Review* 16, no. 4 (April, 1949): 428–431.

Webster, Peter Dow. "American Individualism, or the Problem of Joseph K. and Hamlet." *American Imago* 5 (November, 1948): 4–23.

————. "A Critical Fantasy or Fugue." *American Imago* 6, no. 4 (December, 1949): 297–309.

————. "Dies Irae in the Unconscious." *College English* 12 (October, 1950): 9–15.

————. "Franz Kafka's 'In the Penal Colony.'" *American Imago* 13, no. 4 (Winter, 1956): 339–407.

Weightman, J. G. *The Novelist as Philosopher.* New York: Oxford University Press, 1962.

Weinberg, Kurt. *Kafkas Dichtungen: Die Travestien des Mythos.* Bern: Francke, 1963.

Weiner, Seymour S. "A Look at Techniques and Meaning in Robbe-Grillet's *Le Voyeur*." *Modern Language Quarterly* 23, no. 3 (September, 1962): 217–225.

Wellershoff, Dieter. *Versuche über Hemingway, Camus, Benn und Beckett.* Cologne: Kiepenheuer and Wisch, 1963.

Wellwarth, G. E. "Life in the Void." *University of Kansas City Review* 28, no. 2 (October, 1961): 25–33.

Weltsch, Felix. *Religion und Humor im Leben und Werk Franz Kafka.* Berlin: F. A. Herbig, 1957.

West, Rebecca. "The Twentieth-Century Civil Servant." In *The Court and The Castle*, pp. 221–241. New York: Macmillan Co., 1957.

Wiese, Benno von. *Die deutsche Novelle von Goethe bis Kafka.* Düsseldorf: A. Bagel, 1962.

Wilden, Anthony. "Ecosystems." *General Systems Yearbook*, 1972. Washington, D.C. (in press).

Wilson, Edmund. "A Dissenting Opinion on Kafka." *New Yorker*, July 26, 1947, pp. 58–64.

Worsley, T. C. "Cactus Land." *New Statesman*, August 13, 1955, pp. 184–185.

Zeltner-Neukomm, Gerda. *Das Wagnis des französischen Gegenwartromans*. Reinbek bei Hamburg: Rohwolt, 1960.

INDEX

A. SEE *Jealousy*

All That Fall: 103

Amerika: life cycle in, 31–32, 33

anthropomorphization: of nature, 3, 49, 50; in nineteenth century, 126, 127; in Robbe-Grillet, 132, 133

atmosphere: in Robbe-Grillet, 140–141, 147–148, 150–151

Balzac, Honoré de: and Robbe-Grillet, 127, 128, 130; mentioned, 150

Barthes, Roland: on Robbe-Grillet, 124–125; and *chosisme*, 126; effect of, on Robbe-Grillet, 128th.; mentioned, 131

Beckett, Samuel: and Kafka, 7, 78, 81, 104, 106, 107, 109, 112, 113, 171, 181, 185, 186; and Joyce, 7, 95, 186, 187; and Proust, 7, 106, 112, 187; and Robbe-Grillet, 7, 109, 119–132 *passim*, 136–137, 149, 152, 159–161, 163; quest pattern in, 9, 74–75, 76–77, 78, 80, 85–90 *passim*, 90–92, 115, 185–186; form in work of, 10; and phenomenology, 12; and realism, 71–72, 72–73 n.; and ritual structure, 74; critical response to, 181–188; mentioned, 8, 9, 182, 183. SEE ALSO titles of works

Beissner, Friedrich: on Kafka, 18, 42–43, 45 n., 175, 185

Bendemann, Georg. SEE *The Judgment*

Bousquet, Joë: 162

Breton, André: 168

Brod, Max: and Kafka, 173, 174, 176

Butor, Michel: 171

'Le Calmant": skepticism of, 114

Camus, Albert: and Robbe-Grillet, 127, 132, 141, 145, 161; mentioned, 169, 171

Cascando: 103

The Castle: life cycles in, 23, 28–35 *passim*; unity of narration in, 44–45 n.; point of view in, 48; mentioned, 81, 168, 176

chosisme: in Robbe-Grillet, 127, 129, 131. SEE ALSO Barthes, Roland

ciné-roman: 142

Cohn, Ruby: on Beckett, 76, 77, 105, 109, 111 n., 112, 114, 187; on Kafka and Beckett, 81, 113

'The Cell": 25

"The Coming of the Messiah": 39–40

Conrad, Joseph: 87

The Counterfeiters. SEE André Gide

"The Country Doctor": point of view in, 50–52; mentioned, 6

Didi. See *Waiting for Godot*
"A Dream": 23
duration. See atmosphere
Durrell, Lawrence: 150

"Echo's Bones": 78
Eh Joe: 103
Endgame: 103
The Erasers: Barth on, 124; sub-
    jectivity in, 129; objectivity in, 130;
    and phenomenological theory, 132;
    change in, 139; discussion of time
    in, 153; mentioned, 134, 135, 143,
    146, 156, 183
erlebte Rede: 49
exoticism: in Robbe-Grillet, 144–145,
    154
"The Expelled": 185

Faulkner, William: and Robbe-Grillet,
    152; mentioned, 5, 162
Federman, Raymond: on Beckett, 78–
    79, 82, 85, 95, 112 n.
film techniques: in Robbe-Grillet, 142
Flaubert, Gustave: literary experi-
    ments of, 4–5, 136; mentioned, 182
Fletcher, John: on Beckett and ritual,
    74; on Beckett, 85, 86, 91, 93, 94,
    115; mentioned, 182, 184
Ford, Ford Madox: 46
Frieda. See *The Castle*
Friedman, Melvin: on Beckett, 77 n.

Genêt, Jean: and Robbe-Grillet, 141
Gide, André: 139, 167–168
"Give It Up": 45, 178
Gogo. See *Waiting for Godot*

Happy Days: 72
Hardy, Thomas: 161
Heidegger, Martin: 108, 112, 160
How It Is: 72, 85, 94, 96, 105, 115,
    181, 182
humanism: in Robbe-Grillet, 127, 128,
    131, 133

The Hunger Artist: 29, 39
Husserl, Edmund: 10, 13. See also
    phenomenology

The Immortal: 142
industrialization: and literature, 3–4
instantanées: 142
"In the Caravansery": life cycles in,
    25; point of view in, 48
"In the Labyrinth": time in, 154; point
    of view in, 155–156; mentioned,
    136, 140
"In the Penal Colony": 29, 39

James, Henry: effect of Flaubert on, 5;
    mentioned, 150
Jealousy: link with phenomenological
    theory, 131; analysis of, 134, 137–
    138, 145–146, 146–147, 151; unity
    of narration, 140; point of view in,
    142–144; time in, 154, 155; men-
    tioned, 160 n., 163
"Josephine the Singer, or the Mouse
    Folk": 29–30
Joseph K. See *The Trial*
Joyce, James: and Beckett, 7, 95, 186,
    187; and Robbe-Grillet, 7, 123, 152;
    mentioned, 5
The Judgment: life cycle in, 24, 27,
    35, 37, 38–39; point of view in, 47,
    52–68; mentioned, 6

K. See *The Castle*
K. See "A Dream"
Kafka, Franz: technique of, 5; first and
    third person narration of, 6, 46–50,
    50–68 *passim*; and Beckett, 7, 78,
    81, 104–113 *passim*, 171, 181, 185,
    186; and Robbe-Grillet, 7, 127, 132,
    133, 149, 159, 162–163; quest pat-
    tern in works of, 9, 74–75, 78, 185,
    186; form in works of, 10; and phe-
    nomenology, 12; critical response to,
    17–19, 42–46, 173–180; life cycle in
    works of, 18–40; unity of narration
    in, 42–43; and Thomas Mann, 43;

critical response to, in France, 167–172; and surrealism, 168, 170, 171; and Max Brod, 173, 174; mentioned, 7, 8, 9, 156, 182, 183. SEE ALSO titles of works

Kafkaesque: 27, 40, 41, 49, 169

Keller, Gottfried: mentioned, 87

Kenner, Hugh: on Beckett, 73 n., 74, 105, 108–109, 184–188 passim

Klamm. SEE The Castle

Krapp. SEE Krapp's Last Tape

Krapp's Last Tape: 96–103

Last Year at Marienbad: 142, 155

"Leopards in the Temple": 40

life cycle: in Kafka, 19–40 passim, 68; defined, 20–22; in Beckett, 74–77. SEE ALSO quest pattern; titles of works

MacMann. SEE Malone Dies

Maison de rendez-vous: narration in, 135–136; imagination and juxtaposition in, 139, 140–141; time in, 154; mentioned, 151, 156, 160 n.

Malone. SEE Malone Dies

Malone Dies: quest pattern in, 75, 90–92; and skepticism, 114–115; mentioned, 7, 72, 76, 111, 115, 182

Mann, Thomas: and Kafka, 43; mentioned, 150

Mathias. SEE The Voyeur

Maupassant, Guy de: and Robbe-Grillet, 7

McLuhan, Marshall: 110–111

media: and perception, 110–111

Mercier et Camier: quest pattern in, 77; mentioned, 85

Merleau-Ponty, Maurice: and phenomenology, 10, 11, 12, 131; and idea of perception, 125. SEE ALSO phenomenology

The Metamorphosis: life cycle in, 20, 23, 25–26, 29, 31, 35, 37, 38–39; unity of narration in, 44; point of view in, 47, 49; mentioned, 168, 175

Molloy: quest pattern in, 75, 76, 77, 115; structure of, 85–90; point of view in, 106; relation of, to objective world, 116–120; style in, 181, 182, 183; mentioned, 7, 111, 113, 114

mood. SEE atmosphere

Moran. SEE Molloy

Morrissette, Bruce: on The Voyeur, 134; on unity of narration, 140; on Jealousy, 151; on time, 155; mentioned, 5 n., 131, 132, 135 n., 149

Murphy: quest pattern in, 77, 78–81; mentioned, 94, 113, 115, 181, 182

narrator. SEE Kafka; Robbe-Grillet

"Nature, Humanism and Tragedy": 126, 127–128

Nausea. SEE Sartre, J. P.

"On Parables": 40

Our Lady of the Flowers: 141

phenomenological novel: Beckett's contribution to, 107; Robbe-Grillet's contribution to, 127; mentioned 12

phenomenology: 10–13, 106–107, 131. SEE ALSO Husserl, Edmund; Merleau-Ponty, Maurice; Sartre, J. P.

Poèmes: 78

point of view. SEE titles of works

Proust, Marcel: and Beckett, 7, 106, 112, 187; and Robbe-Grillet, 7, 123, 152, 161; mentioned, 5, 150

quest pattern: in Kafka, 9; in Beckett, 9, 76–90 passim, 90–92, 93–96, 115; in Robbe-Grillet, 10, 149–150; in Beckett and Kafka, compared, 74–75, 78, 81, 185–186. SEE ALSO titles of works

"The Question of Our Laws": 26-27

realism: of Zola, 4; and point of view, 43; in Beckett, 71–72, 72–73 n.; theater of, 99; in Robbe-Grillet, 125, 127; psychological, in Robbe-Grillet, 138–139; nineteenth-century, 178; twentieth-century, 178

"A Report to an Academy": life cycle in, 23, 27–28, 32, 36–37; mentioned, 6

ritual. SEE life cycle

Robbe-Grillet, Alain: literary progenitors of, 7, 123, 124; quest pattern of, 10, 149–150; and phenomenology, 12; and Beckett, 109, 119–127 *passim*, 132, 136–137, 149, 152, 159–161, 163; and theory of the novel, 123–133 *passim;* critical response to, 123–133 *passim,* 149–150 n.; and Joyce, 123, 152; and Proust, 123, 152, 161; realism of, 125, 127; and Balzac, 127, 128; humanism of, 127, 128, 131; and *chosisme,* 127, 129, 131; and Kafka, 127, 132, 133, 149, 159, 171; and Camus, 127, 132, 141, 161; subjectivity and form, 129–130, 133, 147; and Sartre, 132; narration, first and third person, 135–136, 137; psychological realism of, 138–139; atmosphere in, 140–141, 147–148, 150–151; and Genêt, 141; and film techniques, 142; exoticism of, 144–145, 154; psychological time in, 151–154, 155; and Faulkner, 152; point of view as structure in, 153, 155–156; on Beckett's theater, 160; on Kafka's work, 162–163; mentioned, 8, 9, 169, 171. SEE ALSO titles of works

Robert, Marthe: on Kafka, 160–170 *passim*

Rossmann, Karl. SEE *Amerika*

Samsa, Gregor. SEE *The Metamorphosis*

Sapo. SEE *Malone Dies*

Sarraute, Nathalie: on Kafka, 179; mentioned, 5, 171

Sartre, J. P.: influence of, on Robbe-Grillet, 132; mentioned, 10, 12, 112,

169, 171. SEE ALSO phenomenology

"The Sirens": 30

skepticism: 114

Snapshots: 142

The Stranger. SEE Camus, Albert

subjectivity: 129–130, 133, 147

surrealism: 168

symbolism: and aesthetic mode, 4; mentioned, 182

Textes pour rien: 78

Tolstoy, Leo: 150

Towards a New Novel: 123, 124, 129, 162

The Trial: life cycle in, 20–39 *passim*; point of view in, 47, 49–50; in France, 168, 169; mentioned, 6, 9, 176

Trilogy. SEE separate titles

unity: of narration, 42, 115, 134–135, 140; of meaning, 43; in point of view, 43–44

The Unnamable: quest pattern in, 77, 92–96; point of view in, 106; mentioned, 7, 72, 76, 87, 112, 115, 182

The Voyeur: time in, 153–154; mentioned, 124, 134, 143 *passim*, 151, 156

"The Vulture": 37–38

Waiting for Godot: 85, 95, 96–97, 103, 183

Wallas. SEE *The Erasers*

Watt. SEE *Watt*

Watt: quest pattern in, 77, 81–85 *passim*, 94, 105, 113–114, 181, 182; protagonist described, 82–83; chronology in, 82, 84–85; and *Molloy*, 87

"Whoroscope": 112 n.

Winnie. SEE *Happy Days*

Zola, Emile: 4